Journey
to the
Sacred

Mending a Fractured Soul

JANE A. SIMINGTON,
RN, BSN, BA (Psych), MN, PhD

Taking Flight

Journey to the Sacred: Mending a Fractured Soul
by Jane A. Simington, RN, BSN, BA (Psych), MN, PhD

First Printing – January 2003

Copyright© 2002
Taking Flight Books
17823 – 93 Street
Edmonton, Alberta
Canada   T5Z 2H8

Taking *Flight*

Web site: www.takingflightbooks.com

Canadian Cataloguing in Publication Data
Simington, Jane
   Journey to the sacred : mending a fractured soul / Jane A. Simington.

   Includes bibliographical references and index.
   ISBN 1-894022-82-3

1. Spiritual healing.   I.   Title.
BT732.5.S545 2003   291.4'42   C2002-911459-4

Cover and page design by
Brian Danchuk, Brian Danchuk Design

Author Photograph by
McMaster Photographers, Edmonton

Designed, Printed and Produced in Canada by
Centax Books, a Division of PW Group
Publishing Director – Margo Embury
1150 Eighth Avenue, Regina, Saskatchewan, Canada S4R 1C9
(306) 525-2304   Fax: (306) 757-2439
centax@printwest.com   www.centaxbooks.com

Journey to the Sacred:
  Mending a Fractured Soul

Introduction

A t some point in life, each of us struggles in our attempt to make sense of the circumstances surrounding a difficult life experience. The catastrophic event may be situational, such as the loss of a job, the loss of a loved one to death, the loss of a body part, or the loss of the sense of self so deeply felt following victimization. The event may be developmental, such as is experienced as the nest empties, or with the recognition of changes to the physical body associated with aging. These turning points – times after which life will never be the same, force us to leave behind what we have previously treasured. We grieve for what we no longer have. But moving forward in life requires that we not only survive but that we grow from the lessons learned as we wrestle the physical, emotional and spiritual responses of our grief.

While other authors describe the physical and emotional responses to loss, and prescribe strategies for managing these effects, few address the spiritual torment experienced as we attempt to find meaning in what has happened and new purpose for the rest of our life. Yet soul pain is agony of the greatest intensity, for soul's nagging questions will not be silenced until we find answers which fit into our view of the world – a view which may have been drastically altered by the experience.

Others have written personal stories of the movement into soul following a traumatic life experience, and there exists literature describing healing methods used around the world. Some authors compare the concepts contained within the religions of the East and West and others address human spirituality outside a framework of religion. Yet no previous work has combined all of the above. No previous author has paralleled the lived experiences of soul's struggle in the dark night, the archetypical stories of dream and symbol, the stories of myth and folklore, the stories of faith traditions and the stories of ancient and indigenous beliefs and practices of spirituality and healing. No previous work presents a framework from which modern day soul therapy, either self induced or prescribed by a professional, can suspend. No previous work provides a language for soul work. No previous work draws on the ancient and the modern, on science and on folklore, on religion and on spirituality, as well as on theory, practice and research, to provide definitions and descriptions for concepts of the spirit which can fit into the health and healing practices used by those of us who personally heal and professionally practice within the modern Western world. No previous work demonstrates the effectiveness of these practices in healing soul pain and in achieving self transformation. Nor does any previous work describe how these methods can be used to assist a wounded other in their healing journey.

In the past five years over three hundred articles, addressing the lack of attention to the spiritual concerns of people, have appeared in the scholarly journals of psychology, social work, nursing, physiotherapy, and occupational therapy. These professions assist during times when life seems overwhelming. The authors are reminding us that the spiritual dimension of our humanness has a pervasive influence on thought, behavior, and general health and well-being. And while care of the human spirit is primary to healing in virtually all other cultures, past and present, Western society's models of helping and practices of religion, have paid little attention to the needs of the fractured human soul. The resurgence of interest is based upon a growing recognition of this void, of the need for soul healing, and of the differences between spirituality and religion.

The content within this book flows from my own need to survive, until sunrise, the dark night of grief. During my time in the oubliette –

the French dungeon without door or window, I searched for answers to appease the nagging questions which oozed steadily from the ever widening fissures at the core of my being. Unable to find soul healing in the methods prescribed by the systems of the Western world or in the religion of my upbringing, I turned to education. In graduate school, I researched the ancient roots of healing. I immersed in a parallel process of discovering ancient and more wholistic methods, along- side the modern theories of psychology, sociology, anthropology, gerontology, nursing and more. I recognized that only in the cultures influenced by Western thought (in an effort for scientific purism) is there a lack of spirituality as the core of healing practice.

Determined to understand spirituality in its distinction from religion, and desperate to still the turbulence within my own soul, I thrust every ounce of available energy into doctoral education. I dissected each belief, each dogma, each creed, which I had, for so long, given lip service to. I needed to make sense of my Christian upbringing, but discovered the teachings of Jesus had, over the centuries, been altered numerous times for political and financial gain. I studied folklore and mythology, the goddess stories, and astrology. I studied Shamanism and the religions of the East. I examined the research on near- death experience, and on past life regression. I pondered at sacred sites in Europe, in Asia, in Peru, Venezuela and Mexico. I marveled at the natural order, and I listened to the sacredness of the life stories being shared by those I journeyed beside. My bleeding wounds were bathed and bandaged in the ways of the indigenous peoples of North and South America, by the Kahuna Healers of Hawaii, and by the Chi and the Ki energy of China and Japan. I discovered in these methods a sacredness often lacking in the health and helping methods of the Western world.

I now work with those who are attempting to thrive beyond difficult life experiences. I work with those who are grieving the many losses in life. I work with women who have been abused. I work with survivors of torture. I work with women in a federal penitentiary. I listen for soul pain. I prescribe strategies for soul healing.

The content within this book teach us how to move from survival to transformation. It provides a new paradigm. For in addressing soul pain we must be able to view life beyond physical and emotional boundaries, beyond the boundaries of religion and culture, beyond the boundaries of our limiting filtering system.

Acknowledgments

I would like to express deep appreciation to the many unnamed people whose stories are interwoven into my own. It is my sincerest hope that the dignity of each is maintained as your messages of integrity and courage are shared.

I am grateful to my parents. You planted deeply, seeds which others have watered. Thank you to each sister and brother, each friend and colleague, who walked so gently beside me during those intensely dark days. In your own unique way, you each helped to lighten the load.

But most especially, I am thankful for the encouragement of my husband, Bill, and daughters Elana and Jodi. May you each reap a millionfold the joy you have brought to my life.

And while I would give anything to have learned, in any other way, the lessons shared in this book, I am aware that my son, Billy, has been my greatest teacher. I am tremendously grateful, Billy, for the love and the vibrant short life you shared with us.

Table of Contents

Ancestors, powerful spirits,
Who live amongst us:
Your tombs are the mountains,
Your waterfalls are the clouds: the
plants are your jewels.
Sumatran Incantation

In Search of Spirit

Have you wondered why a first toy given an infant, is a rattle? Why are we, even as children fascinated by rocks and sea shells? What is it about the campfire that mesmerizes? What is it about the flute that charms? What is it, about the beat of the drum and the repetition of the mantra that lures our attention? What is stirred within? What primal memories are awakened? To what ancestral connections are we drawn? What dormant seeds are watered as we capture glimpses of animal shapes in the clouds that float overhead?

When we are ten years old and pitch our tent in the backyard, or at the lakeshore, are we remembering happier times, more communal times, more sacred times? Are the times in our modern tepee a recount of the events of other camps and of other fires?

Welcome on this journey to the sacred. Close your eyes for a moment as we begin the travel. Allow your soul to be fed by the lore of the Medicine Stories. Feel your connection to the Earth Mother. Reclaim the pride of your tribal role. Know that willingness to journey is the key to unlocking the shackles which bind the spirit. Break open the fetters. Let spirit soar. Let soul healing happen.

Spirit belongs to the Air Chief's Clan. Spirit rides the wind, and comes on the wind, taking the form of a cloud when there is a need to send a message to someone on the Good Red Road of physical life.

Recall the sacred stones. Remember their use in sacred ceremonies and for healing purposes. Remember their whispered messages. Know that, like their shell relatives of the seas, they gladly share the history they hold with those who are versed in the sacred "language of the stones."[1]

Remember the mantra, and the chant, and the rhythm of the dance. Recall the steady beat of the drum as it guides our journey to the world of spirit where we will receive guidance for healing. Its relentless rhythm will provide a constant reminder of the regular heartbeat of the Earth Mother and will reinforce the profound and unremitting connection between the Earth, ourselves, and all of creation.

Allow the memories to rekindle. Permit every cell to resonate in joy as they refill with the beat of the drum, the call to reconnect in Oneness with the energy of the Great Spirit.

Soul remembers. Soul longs to re-experience the wholeness of Sacred Union. We instinctively know that our feelings of brokenness result from being apart from this Oneness. We comprehend that the unending search to fill the desperate void is because we are unsure of how to reconnect with our spiritual essence. We have come to recognize, "that the amber glow of the age of progress is not casting enough light on the path ahead."[2] Yet we spend years involved in activities designed to drown out the sounds and blind ourselves to the sights, effectively obliterating markers placed along our path to guide our journey inward.

For many, the catalyst creating the willingness to respond to the soul's nagging comes only following the traumatic aftermath of a personal crisis. The painful sting of loss frequently initiates the need to reframe the view we hold of the world and of our place within it.

During such times, so deep are we in the depths of despair that we can barely grope along. We crave to feel the sun shining on our faces, and to experience the warmth of its glow, but we are unable to imagine how that could ever happen again, since we can barely remember what it once felt like.

We know the journey raises concerns related to our spiritual growth and development. Unsure of the path and fearing the terrain, often obscured by a veil of religious dogma and shrouded in a mask of cultural taboo, we struggle in our attempt to make the journey.

We need only examine past civilizations to comprehend that many road maps to guide our travels have been provided to humankind throughout history. Exploring ancient and sacred places, such as Machu Picchu and Stonehenge, can remind us that these have been created by those who have already discovered what Robert Frost termed, "the secret that sits in the center and knows."[3] In their wisdom these ancestors have left monumental markers for those who would follow behind.

One such ancient artifact is housed in a small unassuming monastery in Bangkok, Thailand. This powerful reminder of our own ability to unearth the sacred within came to light in 1957 when a small band of monks was asked to relocate in order that a freeway might be constructed through their property.

Their monastery housed a gigantic clay Buddha. As the crane lifted the huge structure, the clay began to crack. Fearing for the ancient treasure, the head monk ordered the equipment removed and the placement of a tarp-covering over the Buddha. Before retiring, he ventured into the rainy night to check the condition of the beloved treasure. To his amazement a gleam was reflected from the clay mound back to the light of his torch.

Beneath eight inches of chiseled-away cast-clay, the monks discovered a solid gold Buddha! The impressive creation stands eight and one-half feet tall, weighs two and one-half tons, and is said to be valued at over $196 million.

Historians believe that, four centuries earlier, keepers of the Golden Buddha cast it with clay in an effort to prevent their treasure from being carried off by the invading Burmese. It would appear the monks were all killed for their secret remained intact until that rainy night a few decades ago.

Gazing in awe at the Golden Buddha one can not help but reflect on the symbolism so aptly described by Jack Canfield. [4] We are all like this clay Buddha, covered in a hard shell created out of fear and hurt.

For some, the clay has been forming even before birth. As we move through life our layers thicken and harden, shielding us, we believe, from further hurt but, in actuality separating and isolating us from our connections to others and the world. And yet, deeply buried underneath these many layers of hardened clay is our own "Golden Buddha", "Golden Christ", "Golden Essence", which is our real self.[5] Much like the monk with the hammer and chisel, our task now is to discover, once again, the brightness within.

In my doctoral study, and during the years of research and clinical practice that followed, I hungered to determine what constitutes spiritual well-being. While somewhat satisfied with the general findings, not until I marveled at the symbolism of the Buddha's clay covering, did I piece together a definition of spirituality which fit into the world view that had been shaped by the knowing of my lived experience. For the first time I was able to define spirituality in a way that corresponded to this knowing. The Golden Buddha symbolized what I could now more fully comprehend.

Spirituality is often referred to as a journey. I knew my painful experience had forced me to retrace the steps of life numerous times and trudge new and unfamiliar terrain. It had been a long and arduous journey – one of searching and of longing – one that had taken me deep within the caverns of my soul. I knew Job. I had shared his lament. "If I cry out 'Injustice!' I am not heard. I cry for help but there is no redress. He has barred my way and I cannot pass; he has veiled my path in darkness; he has stripped me of my glory, and taken the diadem from my brow. He breaks me down on every side, and I am gone; my hope he has uprooted like a tree." [6]

My pain constantly reminded that I was not in charge and that I had placed my faith and trust in the wrong places and in the wrong things. Jesus, though far away for most of the journey, in his complete solidarity with me as a human being was not spared my suffering. In the pit of despair I learned as the Jesuit poet Gerard Manley Hopkins had, "In a flash, at a trumpet crash, I am all at once what Christ is, since he was what I am."[7] And I choose to add "and 'is' what I am."

Eventually, like Jonah,[8] I was spit back into life by the great fish. Although, like Arthur Frank in *At the Will of the Body*,[9] I was "three days late, covered with slime and smelling like a fish," I had found in the movement upward hope to live with integrity. I had learned the peace of solitary stillness. That is one-quarter of the lesson. The second quarter of the lesson was to be with others. I learned to witness life's suffering and to reach out. From the Talmud,[10] the Jewish book of wisdom, I learned that every blade of grass has an angel bending over it, whispering "grow." Finally, from the Chinese holy book, the *Tao Te Ching*,[11] I learned to:

See the world as myself.
Have faith in the way things are.
Love the world as myself; for only then can I care for all things.

My journey to find healing enticed me to re-enter the halls of formal learning. I immersed myself in the numerous theories from various "ologies." The theories of psychology and sociology, anthropology, gerontology, thanatology and nursing gave me a language for my experience and helped immensely in the cognitive understanding of my grief. Unfortunately, and as everyone who has ever experienced a traumatic life event knows, there are affective as well as cognitive responses to grief. My head and heart refused to work together. For my broken heart I found no reprieve from the literature. I experienced immense vacillation. Just as my head felt comfortable with a solution I had obtained from one or another theory, my broken heart would cry out "and what about . . .?"

Most frightening was my awareness that the "ologies" were void of any solutions for the tempest raging within my soul. For the most part, the theories neglected to address the realness of the soul concerns which follow in the wake of trauma and result from the experience of loss.

While recognizing the immense cognitive and practical value of what I received in my university education, the acknowledgment that the superficial content was unable to feed my ravenous soul drove me to hungrily research the root of each introduced notion and concept. Without conscious awareness the investigation plunged me into a parallel process of seeking answers in the literature and practices of more ancient times. I was surprised, a number of years later, to discovered that people referred to these ancient beginnings as "New Age" beliefs.

There is nothing new about New Age thought. What is referred to as New Age is far from new; it is ancient; it is primal. It is the knowing of the sacred and of the relationship between the sacred and healing, which was part of the lived experience of all before the Age of Scientism.

I left the schools holding four degrees; none in theology (which is often described as the study of God). I have built instead a personal theology from an accumulation of one-quarter formal learning mingled with three-quarters lived experience. My theology pours forth from a discourse with God in which I dissected and debated every theory, every experience, every theological word and notion I had ever heard of or believed in. Now, after three days in the slime and stink, I choose to continue to view the vastness of the oceans, the skies and the land. I choose to continue to see the changing face of God. I do not want any longer to view the world through the eyes of modern-day "ologies." In their efforts to become scientific and researchable, each has designed parameters which dictate to those who follow what is meaningful to observe, to measure and to describe. Observations that do not fit the measuring criteria are, therefore, easily rejected as being unreal. This has created a predetermined filtering system which places blinders over the eyes and muffs over the ears of those who belong. Placing parameters around knowledge attainment blocks the very process of knowing. Knowing is expanding. To know is to grow in an evolutionary way. Just as a river never stops flowing until it reaches the ocean, so the evolutionary process in one's own life, and in the life of the collective, is a never-ending journey to know the ultimate – God.

During my time in the whale's belly I opened the Pandora's box of my belief system. The ghosts and the witches, the snakes and the bats stored within sprang to the surface for release. It took twelve years to gather the scatterings. I choose to no longer lid the container. I would rather let the dreads and fears flow through freely than to ever again force them down and seal them under. It is easier to trust when I can see first-hand what is coming and what is going, than to believe I must hide away what is not nice to see, or hear or believe.

Our modern-day "ologies" have made us "hide," and hiding makes us fearful. When we fear, we must control. We must control ourselves, others and the world around us. We must make very sure to shove down and cover over anything which does not fall within the "normal" range as determined by our acceptable measuring instruments. But with each tucking our need to control increases, for we dread what might escape should the lid be forced off.

I no longer choose fear. I choose to explore, to discover, and to know every possible path that can lead to the sacred. I want to see the face of God in more and more shapes, in more and more places and in more and more practices.

My study of spirituality rose from a deep personal need to prevail until sunrise through the dark night of grief. I have wrestled with God. Oh, how I wrestled! I know the longing to receive the blessing dream as Jacob did.[12] I share with you the struggle, and I share with you the blessing.

My desperate need guided the focus of my graduate and doctoral work. The search to know healing took me far beyond the literature. It led to an understanding of practices developed in more ancient, perhaps more sacred, times. My bleeding wounds were bathed and bandaged in the ways of the indigenous peoples of North and South America, by the Kahuna healers of Hawaii, by the Chi and the Ki energy of China and Japan. I discovered in these methods an awareness of the sacred often lacking in Western methods of health delivery. I studied at sacred sites in Europe, in Asia, Peru, Venezuela and Mexico. I pondered the natural order, and I listened to the sacredness of the life story being shared by those I journeyed beside.

My mind filled, my hands became skilled, my soul exploded.

The definitions and descriptions of spirit and soul, of spirituality and religion which follow incorporate the knowledge I gained through these experiences, through course work, through the books I have read, the places I have visited, the people I have met, and the practices I have learned. Information is incorporated which has been gathered from Shamanism and from the religions of the East, which aided in discerning the truth concealed beneath the dogmas of Christianity, as well as from numerous sources developed for connecting with Divine Guidance, including Mythology and Astrology. A knowing of energy fields and energy healing, and a belief in Hildegard of Bingen's[13] vision is included. In her visions, Bingen saw that consciousness is not contained within us, but that we reside within consciousness. Most importantly, my definition of spirituality includes a knowing of the Sacred Fire within.

I believe that spirituality can be defined as a triune journey to discover the three R's of life: remembering, relating and reconnecting.

The first journey is the journey of remembering. Spirituality is a journey of remembering who we really are. It is a journey of rediscovering and reclaiming our Golden Essence, our True Essence, our Divine Essence. It is remembering that the Spirit, the Life Energy that created all things also created us, continues to flow through us, is part of us. Our spirit, our life energy, is part of the Creative Energy, the Creative Force. The Fire of Creation burns deep within us. Our spirit, our Life Energy, is a part of the same life energy that penetrates all living things, even the burning core deep within the earth. We are a part of the Life Force of the Creator, and of all that has been created.

The symbol of the Golden Buddha reminds us that like the clay used to protect the true essence within, our heavy casting obstructs our radiance from shining forth, hindering others from seeing our Creative Fire. It likewise hinders us from detecting the gleam being reflected to us from those around us. Happily, it takes only a few chinks before a gleam can be picked up by the torch of another, who might be trying desperately to find some light in the darkness.

Spirituality, then, is also a journey of relating. It is a journey deep within the cavern of clay, to discover there the Eternal Flame.

The journey within becomes the catalyst for the journey without. Once the flame is fanned the energy from the ever-increasing brilliance penetrates and erodes the clay envelope. We become a beacon. We detect the gleam reflected from the luminescence of others. In our willingness to share the energy vibrations from our ever-increasing fire, we come to be surrounded by those who are able to resonate in synchrony with us. Our ever-increasing vibrations draw to us the ever increasing vibrations of the splendor that surrounds us.

Spirituality, then, is also a journey of reconnecting. It is the ever-increasing awareness of the wonder and expanse of the universe, an ever-increasing attentiveness to the "awfulness" of the Sacred Fire in all of creation. Spirituality is realizing our place within the universe and our connection to the splendor, the might, the Godness in All, to know and honor that we are a part of the All.

Spirituality is a process. It is not a final product. Spirituality is an ever-increasing awareness of the Sacred Presence within, within others, within all that has been created. It is the development of an ever-escalating and deepening love relationship, an intimate bond with the Divine Energy that is within, and surrounding, and connecting All.

Spirituality is a journey that takes us deeper and deeper into our hearts and into our minds. It is an infinite and circular process of expanding love and expanding consciousness. With each new lesson comes an increased capability for love. With each expression of love comes an increased capacity for learning and understanding. The mastery of each lesson is the impetus for propelling us deeper into further possibilities for love and knowing love.

But like the clay covering on the Golden Buddha, our fear blanket can shroud us in darkness and block our process of knowing. Like moles, we can choose to trust the darkness of our encasement, and remain blind to the glow surrounding us. We can continue to hide in the darkness of our clay womb, devising strategies to convince our soul that the journey to light is not for us. We rationalize: "I have studied; I have learned; I have passed the exams; I have the answers. The experience does not fit my model, my image.

We have free will. The choice is always ours.

But, if we are not ready to smash the idols we have created, we risk the possibility of retarding soul growth. Soul growth demands the creation of new images which can support the acceptance of new knowledge as the journey unfolds

The Power that gives life to all things
and gives us of Itself that we may know It,
must not be taken for granted.
Fill my darkness, Light of Power,
Knowledge of the Unknowable.
I will worship You Light of Light
though I only see
one Glowing Spark
in the darkness of my soul.

Margaret Joy Borle

The Power That Gives and Maintains Life

"The Glowing Spark," "Light of Power," "Fire Within" – each are metaphors to teach that we are not separate from the Eternal Flame, but are a part of the source. These metaphors are to remind us that what we call "our spirit" is a continuation of "The Light of Light," "God," the "Great Mystery."

The energy which maintains us, and every other piece and part of creation, from rock to humankind, is maintained by the force of the Great Mystery. This energy, referred to as "Universal Energy," "Holy Spirit," "Great Spirit," and which is often depicted as the wind, the breath of life, holds us together like glue, binding us to All.

With every breath we take into our being, the Wind – the energy of the Great Spirit, the energy which feeds and sustains spirit energy within All, feeds and sustains us.

The life spark within every cell is the energy of the Great Spirit. Any cell cut from the flow, cannot maintain itself. Soul atoms reside in every gene, there to hold and house Divine Energy. Yet the soul is also a part of, and in continual communication with, the consciousness surrounding us. Our soul energy, composed of the degree of Divine Energy we have amassed, streams continually from our core, extending beyond and into our consciousness. Our consciousness penetrates and intermingles with the consciousness of every other human being and with the consciousness of the entire collective.

Everything in creation has consciousness, its own energy field. Human beings have consciousness. Animals have consciousness. Trees and rocks have consciousness. Each is an energy field. Each energy field intermingles with every other energy field. Every energy field is a part of the collective soul, the All.

Through our consciousness to consciousness connection with All, we each have the potential to tap knowledge and wisdom which can be used to expand our capabilities beyond what is generally considered the normal range. Most human beings never reach their potential, or function to the maximum of their capabilities, because their belief system restrains movement beyond their predetermined view of self. Much about our beliefs informs and reinforces a limited view of our potential. Limited beliefs seal us in and block us from seeing how far our light can really extend.

Yet, there are times when we ponder the faded memories of a deeper knowing. Each of us has experiences when we capture a glimpse of ourself outside the parameters of the carton into which our world view has boxed us. Our consciousness to consciousness connection is why someone telephones right after we think of them. It is also why we can sense when someone in a car in the next lane is watching us. It is why we can walk into a room where a husband and wife are speaking very politely to each other, yet we "know" there is tension. We sense the "atmosphere of artificiality" which permeates the room.

Through this same connection we can communicate, from a distance, whenever there is a need to make contact. Putting the belief of our consciousness-to-consciousness connection to All into practice can change lives and relationships in numerous ways.

A number of years ago my husband fled our home carrying a wound inflicted by a hurtful comment I had made. No sooner had the door closed when I regretted my words. Recognizing the intensity of the pain he must be feeling, I wanted to quickly apply "ointment" to repair the damage. I decided to practice a healing strategy I was just learning, based upon a belief in consciousness-to-consciousness connection. After doing a breathing exercise to still my thoughts and connect me to my place of center, I began to consciously send love directly from my heart out into the universe. I asked that the love move in my husband's direction and surround him. I sent as much love energy as I was capable of. I asked that the energy cloak him in love and compassion, and that it work for his greater good. Very shortly, I was able to visualize him. I saw him standing by the boards in the hockey rink, a place he used to frequent during happier times. I began to visualize myself next to him. In a few seconds I was beside him. We were each surrounded by our own golden radiance, yet melded together in a common glow. In the visualization, I asked for forgiveness. I asked that he come home. Very shortly, he arrived.

As I expressed my regret, my amazed husband shared how he had sensed my presence and heard my call. This moving incident, in which I found myself capable of sending love to heal a fractured relationship, was a beginning step in solidifying my knowing of the powerful abilities we each have, because we are not separate from but are, through our consciousness-to-consciousness connection, a part of the All.

This same connection allows us to not only communicate at a distance with loved ones who are physically alive, but also permits us to communicate with those who have dropped the robe of physical life (died). I had spent the last days of my father's life at his bedside. Because of this, and the time spent with my mother before and following the funeral, I had been absent from my usual responsibilities as the choir director. I had limited opportunity for rehearsal prior to the Easter service. Our choir had become known in our small community for the inspiration and joy which flowed from it. I knew many congregants, as well as visitors, would attend the celebration in the hope that once again the music would draw them closer to the sacred.

I spoke to my dad about this dilemma. I reminded him it was not my fault the choir had not had their usual preparation. I asked that he somehow provide assistance to amplify our accomplishments. That Easter morning, as I walked into the church I felt surrounded by my father's presence. He had not been a musician, yet my pleading for assistance with this musical endeavor had been heard and my request was granted. The choir's performance was outstanding, excelling in caliber, I believe, any performance prior and perhaps since.

It is through our consciousness-to-consciousness connection that prayer is heard. And it is through our consciousness-to-consciousness connection that we too can perform what might be considered miracles. This is how Jesus calmed the seas, and the winds. This is why the rain dance works. This same connection is why a healer can channel useable energy for healing purposes.

We too can communicate with the trees and the rocks, the clouds and the lightning bolts. Because of this connection, we too have the ability to communicate, as did St. Francis of Assisi with the birds and the animals.

Since ancient times, people have individually and collectively connected with the power available to them from the natural world and the animal kingdom. Even today, the sky nation and animal guides offer their characteristics, wisdom, insight and protection to those who honor these sacred relationships. In our culture it often takes the silence of the "forced-to-a-standstill," which follows crisis, for us to discover the sacredness of the natural world and the sacredness of our connection to that world.

As a palliative care nurse I learned much about the preciousness and the value of this connection. One woman, who had for many years worked as a Christian missionary in Africa, shared her gratitude in learning the belief of drawing on the Divine within All during times when we need help and solace. In later life she had conceived a long-desired child, but the intense joy quickly turned to overwhelming sadness as the couple bore the news that their child would face extreme mental and physical challenges. In her grief she penned numerous poems describing both the sorrow she felt and the strategies she used to sooth the anguish within. She wrote of finding God in each interaction with the natural world and the animal kingdom. After she died, her husband bequeathed to me a book of her poems, asking that I share them with any who might benefit. In The Robin's Song[1] she depicts one of the many ways in which our flame can be rekindled by connecting to the Divine Spark which burns brightly in all of God's creatures, even a tiny feathered being:

The skies were dark, the clouds were gray,
The day was fraught with pain;
When, high above the street, I heard him, singing . . . in the rain.

Upon a bough the robin perched, his throat was swelled in song;
While underneath, the people passed'
A busy, hurrying throng.

He sang to me of God's great love, this tiny, feathered bird.
I listened, 'twas a message sweet;
My heart was deeply stirred.

And though the day was gloomy
He didn't wear a frown.
Serene and calm, he warbled, in his brown and orange gown.

His twitters echoed in my heart, far deep into the night.
Because his sonnet I had heard,
Once more my way was bright.

I doubt he'd dreamed, or planned,
The lessons I would gain;
Or that he'd helped me learn the art of singing in the rain.

The author reminds us that humans are not the only beings capable of giving and receiving love. Those of us who care for dogs or horses are well aware of their capacity. Numerous studies have shown the positive effects of pet therapy.[2] People who own pets leave hospital, following surgery or illness, sooner than those who have no pets awaiting them. Pets in nursing homes and palliative care units provide a way in which the lonely and abandoned can have their touch needs met. Caring, loving touch has been shown to be necessary for physical survival, for emotional stability, for intellectual and cognitive balance, and for spiritual well-being.[3] Animals do not care if we are no longer beautiful in the eyes of the world. They give love unconditionally, even therapeutically. For decades dogs have guided the visually impaired, and are now also showing their ability to alert epileptics of an oncoming seizure. Horses too are proving their abilities to enhance life and promote healing. People with multiple sclerosis have reported an overwhelming sense of peace and calm, an increased level of energy, and even reversal in neurological symptoms following frequent contact with horses and horseback riding.[4]

Like the ancients, and indigenous peoples of today, we too can learn to connect to the healing powers available to us in the animal kingdom and the natural world. Every "green-thumbed" gardener already knows the results of sending positive, loving thoughts and words to their plants. Dorothy Gurney said that she felt closer to God in her garden than anywhere else on earth,[5] while others find the same closeness in the meadow, by the sea, in the mountains or the dessert.

There is evidence that the reason we feel so much better in nature is because the grass, the forests and the oceans are able to pull positive ions from us and neutralize them in the negative ions created by these environments. Positive ions in our bodies and in our energy fields are harmful to our health. Places that are polluted or closed off from fresh air are heavily infiltrated with positive ions. Practitioners who work with the human energy field, and use universal energy for healing purposes, believe maleficent forces such as envy, hatred, jealousy, fear, anger and anxiety harbor within the energy carried on the positive ion.[6] Negative ions are beneficial to our health. This is why the air feels invigorating following an electrical storm. Lightning frees millions of negative ions into the atmosphere. We, and all the life sustained by the Earth Mother, grow in an abundance of negative ions.

Spiritual leaders around the world have shown by example that human beings need contact with power places in the natural world. During difficult times they each made a retreat to a place where they could not only maintain but could strengthen their own sacredness. To receive solace and sacred wisdom The Buddha sought the Bodhi tree; the Herican Baba of India went to a mountain cave; Jesus retreated to the dessert. When Jesus needed reprieve he often went to the sea. During his agony, when abandoned by man, he sought the comfort of the garden.

During my graduate education I was employed as a nursing director in a long-term care facility. I love to sing and used to sing to the residents. Nearly every morning someone would request the time-honored "I Walk in the Garden Alone."[7] "He walks with me and he talks with me and he tells me that I am his own . . . The joy we share as we tarry there . . . none other has ever known." The song inevitably brought tears. Later I would revisit, with the teary-eyed individual, the memory rekindled by the lyrics. Each story revealed moments of joy when the person had felt deeply connected to God, or moments of sadness when they had felt deeply disconnected from God. Each story revealed a keen understanding of the Divine Presence available to them in the natural world.

Many in this nursing home, and many in our urban culture, have lost their contact with the heartbeat of the Earth Mother. Many no longer know how to connect to the healing powers available to them in the natural and animal kingdoms. Most of us no longer know how to grow our own food, or how to use plants and minerals for healing purposes.

When we lose our ability to be in synchrony with the natural world, we also become disconnected from our own personal rhythm. We feel out of sync with our selves and with everything around us. We feel tense and anxious and are easily blown off course by the least whiff of difficulty. To begin to re-establish, to maintain, and to strengthen our connection, we need only close our eyes as we firmly plant our feet and breathe in, feeling the joy of the pulse coming into our bodies from the Earth Mother's molten heart.

We enter the consciousness of animals, plants, rocks, even rainbows, just as we enter the consciousness of other human beings. We give and we receive. All are separate, yet exist as one in the universal consciousness.

This consciousness, of which we are a part, is not limited by parameters of time and space. Time and space are ideas of human creation. They are relative concepts. This means they exist only and because we have given them meaning. And the meanings we ascribe are very dependent on culture and circumstance.

Recall an afternoon when you were submerged in a favorite activity. How quickly did the time go? Someday soon, watch a pot of water boil. Does the time move as quickly as when doing a favorite activity? It generally takes less than three minutes to bring water to a boil yet, as we wait, it can seem like twenty.

Ask an older person, spending life's remaining years in a long-term care facility, about how circumstances have altered their sense of time. Ask when the last visitor left; then ask the nurse. There will be no consistency in the two answers. Truly, time can fly or stand still. It really is a matter of perception. When we are busily involved in tasks we enjoy there are rarely enough hours in a day to accomplish all we intend. But when we no longer have meaningful activity, time seems endless.

People from cultures less driven by the "face on the clock," hold perceptions of time quite different from our own, but from which we can learn much. A number of years ago I was drawn into conversation with a middle-aged Cree woman. We spoke of her peoples' view of being "on time" for appointments. Believing I would offer insight on the importance of keeping commitments, I instead found myself retreating, feeling deep personal and social concern. I was alarmed as she identified ways in which we have become more focused on time than on personal growth and relationships.

In examining her notions I recognized that, in many ways, we have not mastered machines. They have mastered us. Tools, such as the clock, the cell-phone, the computer and e-mail, designed to assist in saving us time, now enslave many. These technologies can easily tie us to continuous labor, stripping us of precious moments of personal peace, and of opportunity for developing and strengthening family bonds. Time robbed can not be reclaimed.

The definitions which we hold of time and space dictate not only how we live our lives, they also define us to the world and the world to us. If we stop at our skin we have limits. If the world is separate from us, we cannot tap into the energies around us. Our present will not influence the future. Prayer will be useless.

But we do not stop at our skin. We are not limited. We are limitless. We extend into the consciousness of the All. The consciousness of the All, including every aspect of our consciousness, exists in the relative now. The present moment, the now, contains past, present and future. This is why we have déjà vu. This is why we have fleeting glimpses of former lives. This is why mystics can describe future events.

Because time and space are now, nothing is static. The future, even though foreseen by the most clairvoyant human being, or foretold in a dream, can be changed. That is why some prophesies do not manifest. The prediction will only come true if the energy being invested continues to flow in exactly the same way. By changing the energy, we change the outcome. There are many possible outcomes. In many ways the effect depends on us.

An incident a number of years ago convinced me we need not be like flags flapping in the direction determined by the winds of prophecy. The night before my youngest daughter and a friend were driving back to college, I had an intensely disturbing dream in which I saw them involved in a tragic vehicle accident. While I tried to dissuade them from leaving, I did not trust the dream message enough to alarm them, or make them stay. Yet moments after they drove off I was overwhelmed by a pervasive dread. My day became a continuous prayer of beseeching for their protection. I begged the mighty Archangel Michael to put his armor around them and shield them from danger.

Toward evening the telephone rang. I knew instantly it was news of their accident. The call was from the police cruiser in which my daughter and her friend were now safe. Their car had been destroyed. An out-of-control vehicle had bolted into their lane, side-swiping and propelling their vehicle into the guard rails of an overpass. A severed light standard had collapsed over my daughter's car.

Shamans and healers from many cultures believe that the Creator bequeathed to human beings the ability to direct the elements. Our thoughts influence the path of the energy lines that feed the earth. Our thoughts can change the course of the energy lines. I knew my prayers had been heard and answered. I knew prayer had saved my daughter's life. I knew prayer had changed the course of the outcome foretold in the dream. The energy of prayer had altered the results of the accident. The future was changed in the now.

And like the future, the past is also a part of the relative now. The energy of the past can also be altered. Many who struggle with past offenses believe nothing can be done to change what has previously taken place. One of the most difficult things to resolve in grief is unfinished business. When a loved one has died, and because they are usually no longer visible, we often believe they are no longer available to us.

We harbor guilt over wrongs done, and suffer regret over the good undone. We long to resolve past hurts and make up for the times when we did not love as we should have. If we believe we are limited to what our nervous system registers, we can spend years or even the rest of our lives drowning in these raging emotions. But if we begin, even slowly, to acknowledge our spiritual energies and to know that spiritual energies extend beyond us to all eternity, we will be able to comprehend that we can be present in the past and the future. We can be in the consciousness of our loved ones, living or dead. Every past event can be brought into the now. We can send love and receive love. We can send forgiveness and receive forgiveness. We can resolve the pain of the past. We can heal the effects of past wounds which, if unhealed, continue to have an impact on the future.

We need only expand our consciousness to tap the tremendous powers to which we are already connected. It is the strengthening of the Fire Within, the increased flow of Divine Energy into our beings and the radiating of this increased flow from our beings to the All that increases the connection.

The journey to the sacred, the journey within to the place of stillness, and the journey without, to the connection with All, begins by saying "yes" to the possibilities of greeting ever expanding images of the sacred. It is a willingness to allow this knowing, the opening of awareness, that expands consciousness.

It is said that to know is to love. As we come to know, awe moves us forward.

The journey is a circular track, ever expanding, ever evolving. The catalyst for the travel is desire – a desire to know. Our invitation is freely accepted. The Divine is love. Love is Divine. The flow of love to us increases. With the increased flow, our image of the Divine changes, grows, expands. Each image is more loving. We grow in knowing love. We desire more, more knowing, more loving.

We discover; we understand; we experience; we know; we love. And we begin again. With each beginning, each revolution, each personal evolution, we pour into the collective an increased measure of the Divine Love that is ever increasing and radiating from our very core. As we move forward we move the entire collective forward. As we personally evolve, the entire collective evolves.

As we fill with Divine Love, we become more and more ourselves Divine. Our knowing expands and our ability to connect in synchrony with higher and finer vibrations – vibrations we could once not resonate with – increases.

We have been given incredible potential. We can choose to be empowered or disempowered. As we take even the tiniest steps to remove the blanket of hurt and fear that is smothering us, we move ourselves and the All on a profound journey. Our willingness to travel the sacred path of healing thrusts us, and therefore the entire collective, into an ever-increasing Oneness with the Divine.

The journey to the sacred is a journey of evolution. We have not only been gifted, but charged with the responsibility to be co-creators of an evolving universe.

Hidden deep within each of us
is something special waiting to surface
something waiting to grow into a great work,
when discovered – so too will be greatness.
                    Jane A. Simington

Soul Growth

When we are wounded, when the cloak of darkness entwines so tightly that we can scarcely draw our next breath, when we feel so inadequate, so small, it is difficult to envision that we could be more. From this place of terror, it is frightening to dare imagine such grandeur as being a glowing ember of Divine Energy.

In our suffering we have learned to stay with the familiar. While we have moments when we long for more, we have learned the safety of being with what we know.

Yet the first step, the beginning effort, must be ours. We have been given the choice, light or darkness, joy or sorrow. We recognize the voice, even though it has become dim, distant and timid. We must heed the prodding.

If we but sneak a peak, lift for just a second the corner of our covering, unmistakable evidence of a greater reality beckons. We are more. We belong. We are not separate. We are a part. We are a part of a much greater plan.

The energy that cements us, that connects us to the All is visible everywhere. Make a cup of tea; watch the steam rise. Take a walk; observe the heat waves lifting from the parched soil. Pay attention to the outer glow of your shadow. As Einstein informed us, all is energy.[1]

The energy received through our organs of sight, sound and touch is interpreted by our nervous system. Each organism's nervous system has a different capacity for receiving and interpreting energy frequencies. When people sustain hearing loss they loose the ability to interpret sound outside their decibel range. Yet this same sound is easily audible to others. When a person becomes visually impaired they are unable to behold many sights once available to them. Nerve damage to the eyes, ears and other sensory organs interferes with the ability to see, hear, taste, smell and feel sensations which are readily perceptible to others. Each sensation results as a transfer of energy vibration. Yet even though some nervous systems can no longer interpret certain sights, sounds and smells, the energy vibrations being sent from the environment to the sensory organs are no less real.

Each morning as I jog, I delight in watching the enthusiastic commitment with which my dog trails his nose along the pathway. He is intent on investigating every scent, sometimes even pausing to note the differences in the fragrances of wild blossoms. I do not doubt the realness of what he smells. Nor do I doubt there are sounds and sights that my dog and the deer along the trail see and hear which most humans cannot. Even though I have never seen electrical or sound waves, my daily use of electricity, the radio, television and the telephone confirm my belief in these energies.

Signs of this invisible reality are everywhere, even within us. The human body is a grand, yet delicate, energy system. Energy transfer continually takes place within and between every cell of our bodies. Our major systems function when energy is transferred. The electrical discharge can be measured to determine brain, heart and muscle strength; the frequency and regularity of these vibrations increase or decrease in response to health and illness. The energy of which we are made, and on which we function, is not only contained within, but radiates from us.

Everything has an aura, an energy field, surrounding it. A number of years ago I was astonished to discover that I could see the aura with naked eyes. Stopping one afternoon to gaze from my balcony at a particularly grand fir tree, I was awed that the tree did not end at the tip of its needles. The beautiful fir was surrounded by a light which appeared much like the glow surrounding a candle flame. As I watched, I noticed that the white light moved back and forth as if the tree was breathing. As I watched I realized the light surrounding the tree blended into a similar light surrounding the next tree, and the next, and the next. The glow surrounding each tree, yet connecting them one to the others, ebbed and subsided as if the trees were breathing in harmony, or perhaps communicating.

Soon after the initial experience with the trees, I found I too was surrounded by light. Spending longer than usual one evening in front of the mirror, I found myself staring at a shadowy glow bathing my head and upper body. (As if to convince me of its reality, an intermittent soft-blue electric-like light began to flicker off and on as it pulsated down my neck and arms, first one side, then the other.)

Not long after I began to see similar light surrounding others. It was several years before I recognized that the light surrounding and connecting myself to others contained colors other than white and faint blue. One afternoon, while listening intently to a conference speaker, I was drawn in wonderment to the vibrant purple-magenta streaks that flashed from his head and upper body. He was passionately sharing beliefs about the need to return concepts of the sacred to education. His belief in the spiritual realities were being expressed, not only in words, but were also being projected into his energy field.

Our energy fields contain the energy which pours forth from us. Our energy fields contain aspects of our spiritual, emotional and physical realities. These dimensions of our humanness are not separate but are interdependent upon each other, and are in a continual process of exchanging energy, one with the other, and with all in creation.

We cannot, therefore, be physically well when we are bleeding emotionally or wounded spiritually. Body, mind and spirit are inseparable. What affects one aspect affects the others, and the whole. When, for example, our soul longs for forgiveness, we express emotions of guilt and regret and we bear the pain in our physical bodies, often as a backache, to remind us of the weight of the burden we carry.

Our culture does not recognize soul pain. We have lost the knowledge to diagnosis the symptoms of soul distress, and the skill to provide soul healing. This lack of acknowledgment has driven any expression of soul pain "underground," forcing those struggling with soul wounds to disguise their suffering in more socially acceptable ways. But the physical ache reveals the crack in the foundation.

A while ago a young man arrived seeking help for depression. He repeatedly stated the depression began after he broke his leg. As I directed the focus from the depression (emotional symptom) to the broken leg (physical symptom) he told me that his limb had been fractured doing a job he very much disliked. He felt he was wasting his time, his talents and his abilities. When I asked what he would really like to do (spiritual need), he disclosed a desire to be an artist, but his parents had convinced him that an artist's wages could not provide him a decent living. He had gone to college and obtained a degree in a field with plenty of available positions.

This man shared a story of soul pain. He was off course. The purpose for his life could not be accomplished under the circumstances in which he felt forced to live. He was thwarted in his ability to develop and share the unique talents and abilities he had been given. His soul's anguish revealed itself emotionally in symptoms of depression. His physical body responded with a broken leg to keep him from working at a job that was interfering with his soul's purpose.

While I clearly heard a story of soul pain, his culture and education had conditioned him to believe the "problem" needing to be resolved was depression. He hoped that "talk-therapy," and perhaps a referral for some mood-elevating drugs could relieve the symptoms. He was amazed, but instantly recognized the truth, as I guided the discussion away from emotional symptoms toward the direction of soul and the meaning and purpose of his life. He continues to work as a social worker, but now incorporates his art as an art therapist. His purpose in life is being accomplished. His soul now knows joy, and he is no longer plagued by feelings of pervasive sadness and overwhelming dread.

Reports from those who practice the science of psychoneuroimmunology indicate that as high as 80 to 90% of physical symptoms have their roots in psychological or spiritual concerns. Since psychology really means the study of the soul, I believe there are very few, if any, physical and emotional symptoms that do not stem from rot at the spiritual root. Our world is filled with suffering requiring soul mending, yet soul pain is rarely discussed, assessed, or diagnosed.

While modern medicine, in the Western world, has made fantastic headway in eradicating acute and catastrophic illness, the escalation in cancer, chronic and autoimmune diseases, in social problems, in alcoholism, in drug abuse and family violence indicates something very significant and deep-seated is lacking in our individual and collective lives. When the cry from a tormented soul is not heard, the physical and emotional body demonstrates the "woundedness' at the core. When treatment is aimed only at removing physical pain and decreasing emotional suffering, but does not address the soul's torment, efforts are futile or at best short-lived.

The energy vibrations surrounding the physical body of someone in physical, emotional or spiritual distress are not warm, smooth and balanced as they are in wellness, but are instead excessively hot, cold, erratic or irregular. Assessment of a person's energy field is a beginning step in any one of the energy-transfer healing methods being reintroduced. These methods are quickly accepted by those who witness the results, and by those who have experienced the failure of the health-care system to meet the deeper needs of people.

Ancient healing practices are based upon an in-depth understanding of the human energy field, and of the connection between each human energy field and the All. These techniques flow from knowing that human beings are spiritual beings, and that the body is a "mortal coil"[2] inhabited by a spirit, in order to fulfill a unique purpose for the individual's greater good, as well as for the greater good of All. These practices are methods of healing. While a cure may also be sought and attained, the primary goal is not curing the physical body, but healing the soul. It is clearly recognized that for maximum physical and emotional life the spirit must by fully alive. Fundamental to healing is an understanding that physical and emotional suffering is rooted in the soul concerns of people.

Recall the numerous biblical references of Jesus telling us that soul illness is displayed in the human body. His words are clear in response to those who challenge his ability to forgive sins. "Which is less trouble to say, 'Your sins are forgiven' or 'Stand up and walk'?"[3]

In their closeness to the Creative Force in All, ancient people knew, as Jesus did, that the energy in the universe, the Breath of the Divine, was available to strengthen and support the Creative Force within human beings. The healing arts draw from the Creative Force. While all of the methods which use energy transfer are developed based upon this knowing, Reiki, the method of energy transfer for healing purposes which originated in Japan, clearly describes the source of the energy, Rei (Divine) and Ki (Energy). Life stories of great healers from around the world, regardless of religious background, tell of the healers' understanding of the source of this energy and of the abilities of human beings to draw upon this energy for healing purposes. Recall the hemorrhaging woman who thought if she but touched the cloak of Jesus she would be healed. Remember, as Jesus turned to her he asked, "Who touched me?" And while Peter tried to disway Jesus saying, "Lord the crowds are thick and pressing around you!" Jesus insisted, "Someone touched me I know that power has gone forth from me."[4]

Yet we hold many prejudices against healing. We believe that it takes a saint to heal. We do not feel gifted enough, so we feel both embarrassed and challenged by the notion that we too can transmit healing energy.[5] Biblical references remind the ordinary person to be responsive to their healing mission. "And these are the signs that will be associated with believers; in my name they will cast out devils; they will have the gift of tongues; they will pick up snakes in their hands, and be unharmed if they drink deadly poisons; they will lay hands on the sick, who will recover."[6] Jesus did not say saint. He said ordinary "believers." And again, "Even though I am a nobody, there is not a thing these arch-disciples have that I do not have as well. You have seen done among you all the signs that mark the true apostle, unfailingly produced: the signs, the marvels, the miracles."[7] False humility – fear of unworthiness, not only interferes with the development of potential, it keeps us from reaching out to another.

Healing, which draws on Divine Energy, strengthens the soul of the healer, the soul of the person receiving, and the soul-to-soul connection. I frequently hear people who have attended workshops to learn one of the several laying-on-of-hands healing techniques tell of the soul healing that has occurred for themselves personally as they draw Divine Energy through them for the healing of another. They begin to feel an increased sense of peace and tranquility, of joy and happiness, and almost all feel an increase in personal energy. Their awareness expands and they notice beauty in things and in places where they had not previously seen it. Those who draw universal energies to assist others also render accounts of the positive changes that transpire in their relationships. A woman whose primary goal for learning the techniques was to relieve her partner's distressed breathing, told with delight of the parallel strengthening occurring in their tenuous marriage, along with the improvement in her husband's quality of life after only a few weeks of treatment.

During the practice of any one of the healing arts, Divine Energy, often referred to as universal energy, since it is the energy of the All, is drawn into the heart center of the person acting in the healing role. Here, the energy drawn from the universe blends with compassion (for the person requesting healing) held in the heart of the helper, and flows from the heart center down through the healer's palms. The healer then directs the energy to the recipient with the intention to promote healing of the highest order.

Compassion and intention appear to be the qualities which strengthen the ability to channel useable universal energies for healing purposes. Compassion is often described as "love without hooks,"[8] a love that is given to another without any attachment to the results. Desiring to be in control of the final outcome actually interferes with the healer's capabilities. To let go of any attachment or personal need to obtain specific results, a healer guides the process with the intention to help and to heal in the best way possible. When energies are directed for the greatest good results may differ from those anticipated, but they are often much beyond what is thought humanly possible.

Healing is soul work. Healing allows soul energy to break through. Increased soul energy increases the frequencies of the vibrations being emitted from us.

I love to remember the grade-six science experiment that introduced me to the concept of energy. The teacher placed a tuning fork on each of our desks. As he struck his, each of ours rang in the same tone, at the same frequency, as the one that was struck. I recalled this experiment years later as Wayne Dyer, in Real Magic,[9] reminded us that we are like tuning forks. We resonate with the vibrations surrounding us.

As we chip away at the clay, as we allow light to shine on our wounds, and as we respond to the invitation to open our consciousness, our minds and hearts, we begin to resonate with the higher and higher frequencies that come to surround us. We attract different people, people who resonate inkind with our newer and higher vibrations. Old acquaintances no longer come around. We no longer "have anything in common." Their slower vibrations no longer resonate with our finer, thinner more rapid vibrations. They no longer feel in sync with us.

Our finer vibrations draw to us the lessons of higher vibrations, lessons we can now comprehend, lessons we need in order to continue our circular- evolutionary growth process. We begin to recognize the truth in the Zen proverb, "When the student is ready the teacher will appear." The teacher comes in many forms. The teacher may be a memory, a dream, a poem, a song, the story of another, a myth, a workshop, a movie, a stream, a tree, a rainbow, a rock. As the old saying goes – like attracts like.

The vibrations of increased soul energy pouring forth from us into the universal consciousness have a potential impact on the consciousness of every other human being, as well as on the consciousness of the entire collective. Our tremendous co-creative powers mark each of us with an enormous responsibility to be the best companion, for others on the journey,[10] we can possibly be, and to advance peace and Godness in our world. Because we are energy vibrations, and because vibrations resonate in synchrony with like vibrations, it is imperative that we are continually mindful about what radiates from us. What we send out in thought, word and deed has a powerful boomerang effect. As the proverb states, "As a man thinketh in his heart so is he." And, "If a man returns evil for good, from his house evil will not depart." As well as "A joyful heart is the health of the body, but a depressed spirit dries up the bones."[11] remind us that our thoughts and deeds do "come home to roost." What we want to bring into our lives, we must send out from us in thought and in deed. We can not have peace-filled and harmonious relationships if we focus on our faults and those of others. If we want love we must send love from us. If we want joy we must send joy from us.

When I was a child I loved to spend time with my father. I was the youngest girl in a large family. In order to have his undivided attention I learned early in life it was up to me to be with him when he was normally alone. On early summer mornings my dad would walk to the far pasture to bring the cattle to the barn for milking. I liked to wake up early and go with him to share special moments.

My playmate and favorite brother was a year younger than I was. We spent many hours exploring the world together. He taught me to raft and make forts and showed me the places where the wild ducks nested. We also, however, frequently engaged in struggles to determine dominance in the pecking order of our family.

One morning, after a preceding day that was particularly filled with arguments, I went on an early morning adventure with my dad. As we walked we discussed the previous day. I was surprised to learn his view on the conflict with my brother. When we arrived at the base of the hill, Daddy called to the cattle as he usually did. The cows, upon hearing his voice, began their obedient jaunt from the pasture up the lane to the barn. As we waited by the pond, my father asked me to pick a stone and throw it into the water. As I did, he invited me to notice how the splash created a ripple effect across the entire pond. My young mind was amazed by the reaction. Realizing my ability to grasp the lesson, Daddy told me to pretend I was the rock and the lake was our family. I recall remaining very silent, but I recognized the deep importance of what he was sharing. In that moment I realized the splash I was making, that was being sent out from me was not only affecting me and my brother but, in a rippling manner, it was affecting my entire family.

My father's instruction peaked my desire to know. I frequented our outdoor classroom, eager to learn. The stones became my teachers. Through their tutelage I garnered valuable life lessons. From their ripples I learned about influence. I saw the intermingling of three and four and five circles made by the splashes of the rocks, and I saw the impact of these circles on the ripples of the first. During those hot summer days of childhood I became aware, not only of the influence we have on others, but also of the influence others have on us. I noticed how deeply all the ripples from one rock penetrated the ripples of the others. While I valued the positive effects, I pondered if this was always a good thing. Did others always send me what was helpful, right, just, true? Was there a way I could keep this from happening? Was there a way to protect myself from the hateful thoughts of others?

I remembered having feelings of fear and hurt when the teacher projected anger at someone else. Were the teacher's angry ripples, and the ripples from my wounded brother and other classmates, bumping into mine?

I disliked the teacher. She was an unhappy woman, and cruelly projected her bitterness on her small charges. As I watched the rippling circles move slowly back from the shore to the area where the rock had first fallen, I learned that what we send out comes back in like manner.

That summer, with the stones, I felt smug in realizing that while the teacher miserably influenced my life and the life of all in that one-room school, the ripples of her influence would eventually return to her. But now, in adulthood, and after being broken myself on the proverbial wheel of life, I have a different perception of her bitterness. While as a child it was difficult to endure, and painful to see my brother receive the brunt of her malice, I am able to comprehend the reasons for her actions and the rationalization she must have used to condone her behavior. Knowing now that she herself was a victimized human being, desperate for love, I feel more need to convey empathy than hatred, to send thoughts of compassion and prayer rather than project more anger her way, in hope that these messages can somehow dissolve the ripples from the past.

Years after I had left the one-room school I was reminded of the stones and the ripples. In an emergency situation, the triage nurse is the first contact most patients and family members have with hospital staff. The nurse in this position has a powerful influence on whether an atmosphere of calm and confidence or one of chaos prevails. To a great extent, either situation depends very much upon what emotions are being projected to the family, and to other staff during this initial assessment.

Later in my career, as a clinical supervisor in gerontology, the power of our influence upon another was once again reinforced. I noted that within minutes of one agitated older person beginning to pace, a second, and then a third, and a fourth, and even a fifth, would join the first as they moved in a circle around the nursing unit.

Harnessing the interest of the nursing students was essential to test my assumptions. If the restless "vibes" from the first were being projected into the environment, and being "picked up" by those who followed, why could more positive influences not be picked up as well? Could the more positive vibes being purposefully sent to another change the outcome of the behavior? The students agreed to the test. Each was assigned an agitated older person from the nursing unit roster. They were to read the chart, make a pre-visit, then write a "before" description of any thoughts and feeling that arose about the assigned person. They were to keep this description in a sealed envelop until completion of the assignment.

Each morning upon awakening, and each evening before retiring, the student nurse was to consciously think of, and mentally send, three positive thoughts conveying love and caring to the older person. When on the unit, the student was to again send the same positive thoughts before entering the person's room and prior to providing any care. In their verbal and written reports on the older person, students were to be exact in what had been observed, heard, smelled, touched. They were encouraged not to subjectively elaborate in any way.

Results, even after one week, were impressive. As the nursing students shared summaries of the previous week's documentation of "their" older person's behavior, and their post description of their own thoughts and impressions of the person, they recognized the significance of what had taken place.

In every case, students felt a warming of the relationship with the older person. In the post description they viewed each person in a different, more positive light. The restless behavior, as measured by the pacing episodes, of all of the older individuals had decreased with the receipt of caring, loving energy being projected their way. While striking-out at staff was a familiar behavior for all of these individuals, in not one case had a student been struck at.

How could eager and caring nursing students have a positive impact on the lives of five agitated older people? Were the older people feeling the positive effects of the loving, caring thoughts being purpose-fully projected their way? How could loving, caring thoughts decrease restless, agitated behavior?

In the preface to Elizabeth O'Conner's book, *Search for Silence*,[12] N. Gordon Cosby wrote: "The only journey that ultimately matters is the journey into the place of stillness deep within one's self. To reach that place is to be at home; to fail to reach it is forever restless."

"To fail to reach it is forever restless." In my grief I knew restlessness. I knew longing. I knew searching. I knew the anxiety of searching for answers that seemed to evade, answers needed to heal a broken heart, an anguished soul.

In our restlessness, in our attempt to find the stillness, can we be assisted by another? Does the love and compassion we covey to others assist their soul journeys? Were the loving, caring thoughts projected to the older agitated adults by the nursing students able to calm the wake of past ripples in traumatized souls?

In *Ageless Body, Timeless Mind*[13] Deepak Chopra emphasizes that every cell in our body is constantly eavesdropping on our thoughts. I have come to know the truth of this. I have seen numerous examples of the power of thinking to create success or failure, health or illness.

I believe this is so because thought is the voice of the soul. The soul lives within every cell. It is the soul that knows our thoughts and is affected by them. Every cell in our body holds a memory of our every experience of soul joy, as well as every experience of soul pain. Soul heal-ing requires the release of soul pain from each cell, and the infusion of soul joy into the space made available by the release. Soul healing begins by changing our thinking, our soul talk. Soul healing begins by sending messages of love inward. Love is the seed that will grow into joy to fill the spaces left by the release of soul pain.

While the soul knows our thoughts, and holds the memory of our experiences, because of our consciousness-to-consciousness connection with all others, the soul also knows and is affected by the thoughts of others. You do not have to tell someone you like or dislike them. The soul-to-soul communication has occurred long before your mental abili-ties have figured it out well enough to put words to your emotions.

I hear many stories in my professional and personal life of fractured relationships. Each time, I return to the wisdom gained from Daddy's lessons and from the teachings of the ripples and the stones.

I have learned the power of my thoughts to influence for worse, and then for better, numerous events in my life. I encourage others to recognize that our thoughts are not contained within us, but that they radiate beyond us, like the ripples in the pond, becoming part of the larger pond, the collective "soup." I have them ponder the lessons I gleaned from the ripples and the stones, from the emergency room, and from the ability of student nurses to decrease restlessness for five agitated older people because of their willingness to consciously and purposefully send thoughts of love and care. I ask those who come for counsel to recall the change in the image of the older person held by the students after the week of sending love and care. I ask them to ponder any change that might be necessary in their thinking about their own relationships. I remind them that the soul knows their thoughts, and that the soul of their partner, friend, son or daughter also knows their thoughts.

The first step in changing any relationship is to create new thoughts about our selves, the other, and the relationship. I teach about the power of love. "Someday, when we have mastered the winds, the waves, the tides and gravity, we shall harness for God the energies of love. Then, for the second time in the history of the world, man will have discovered fire."[1]

Angels of God my guardians dear.
Because of God's love,
you have been assigned to me here.
Every moment of this day be at my side.
Enlighten me. Guard me. Rule me.
Guide me.

Traditional Prayer to the Guardian Angel

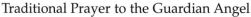

Soul Armor

A human being is an "open system." This means that, when unprotected, we are open to the influences surrounding us. We can be invaded by bacteria and viruses set adrift from someone ill. In the same way, we can "pick up" and are influenced by the thoughts, words and actions of others. Their thoughts, words and deeds can literally penetrate our being. This is why it is difficult for someone in a chaotic environment to remain in emotional balance. In the previous chapter, the family members coming into the emergency department and the agitated older people were "affected" by the "free-floating" anxiety emitted by the anxious triage nurse and by the other restless residents.

We all know people who radiate peace and calm. We love to be near them. We leave their presence feeling "filled," energized. We know we have somehow garnered some of their hope, their peace and their positiveness. Yet we also recognize there are others whose presence we dread. They "drain" us, "suck us dry." When we leave their company we feel "low," "fearful," "drained," "empty." We are also aware that there are some who do not have our best intentions at heart. They think negative, perhaps even hateful or evil thoughts about us; and they may project misfortune on us. We all recognize, at least at some level, the impact of the positive as well as of the negative influences others can have on us. Those who fully comprehend the possible effects of being a system open to environmental influences seek ways to protect themselves from the negative impact.

Our ancestors had a much clearer understanding, than do we today, of the forces of good and evil. They developed shielding practices to protect themselves from harmful influences. Smudging, which is a practice of surrounding oneself with the smoke from the sacred fire burning within a ritual pot, is a common shielding method. Smudging is used in many religions and in many parts of the world. North American Aboriginal peoples cleanse and protect themselves and their surrounding space with the smoke of burning sweet grass or sage. Peoples from the Eastern world burn incense of various fragrances depending on the reason for the cleansing.

The intent of shielding is to purify the energy field of the person and the surrounding environment of anything that may be harmful, and to provide a protective shield to keep evil from penetrating. The practice of using incense in religious worship, in many Christian churches, is rooted in the practice of shielding.

Smoke rising from the incense burners, and from the smoke of the pipe used by Indigenous peoples during sacred ceremonies, also symbolizes prayer sent from human beings to the Creator. In smoking the pipe, every pinch of tobacco is burned to fine ash to honor each sacred part of creation which has contributed to the tobacco's growth. This reminds us that spirit is in all things, and is required for all things. Each tobacco flake embodies the spirit essence of All. As the smoke ascends toward the heavens it carries with it prayers of gratitude and prayers of petitions for guidance, for nurturing, for healing and for protection.

I work with people who convey life stories filled with intensely painful emotions. People who seek healing know their "woundedness" is interfering with their ability to achieve fullness of life. Their pain is often intensified by the frequent invasion of hurtful memories. Because of their inability to define their own boundaries many are an easy target for re-victimization by those who choose to prey on their vulnerability.

When we have been traumatized, especially if the trauma has occurred early in life, we have a confused sense of personal space. Personal space is a psychological term for the invisible bubble that surrounds us. It is our energy field, our aura, our consciousness. When our personal space has been frequently invaded we lose a sense of our own boundaries. The abuser has stolen our sacredness so frequently that our aura is fractured and continually leaks precious energy. We see that others are stronger, more solid, grounded, contained. They appear more powerful, more knowledgeable, more worthy than we. It seems that they have all the answers and we have none. We want what they have. We are aware of our brokenness, of our emptiness, and we desperately want to be intact, full, whole and complete. We long to believe that what they have and what they promise can fill our void. This makes us vulnerable, and when we are vulnerable we can easily be manipulated, for we so urgently want to believe that what they tell us is the truth.

As a first step in the healing process, I teach those carrying such a heavy burden to "shield." Shielding helps to cleanse and seal the energy field, defining the boundaries and preventing further leakage of sacred energies. Shielding also provides a protective armor to ward off further victimization. But shielding is not only important for the person requiring healing assistance; it is also essential for anyone attending another in his or her recovery.

When we give words to our experience, the pain lodged deep within each cell, stored there since the incident, is released into our energy field. The energy containing the pain of the experience moves beyond us, permeating the energy fields of those around us and trickling into the larger environment.

When I began "walking-beside" others who were living through difficult life circumstances, I quickly recognized the critical importance of shielding myself from the negative influences that surrounded this work. As I listened to stories of pain, and often of horror, I could sense the impact on my own energy field, and could feel the thickness of the fear and dread that permeated my being and my office space.

When people tell stories of being victimized by others, the energy released into their fields, and subsequently into the larger environment, contains not only their own pain, fear and anger, but also bears the influence of hate and other harmful emotions projected unto them by their perpetrators. Counselors and other helpers who are oblivious to the harm that can come to their unprotected energy fields can become physically and emotionally unbalanced, even after a short time in practice.

I have learned to smudge using sage burned in a seashell container. I cleanse and protect myself and my office each morning, and repeat the ritual following a visit from a person who conveys the overwhelming pain of deep woundedness. While the most common method for guarding against the effects of negative influences is smudging, a shield can also be visualized during meditation. Each morning during mediation, I visualize a soft silk-like sacred pink veil or crystal-like cocoon surrounding me. I ask that this shield allow only good things to move from me to others, and that only good things are permitted to enter my sacred space. I like this visualization for I can quickly reinforce the shield when the need arises. I apply a similar sacred wrap to others at the end of an energy healing treatment. The wrap surrounds them, seals in the healing energies, and protects them from physical, emotional and spiritual harm. I also teach a shielding exercise in which the gift of the golden light of healing and love is visualized descending from the Spirit of the Creator into the crown of the head and moving downward throughout the body, filling it to overflowing, and wrapping the body in a shield of protective crystal light.

Many religious practices, which have all but lost their traditional meanings, sprang from primal ritual based on an awareness of good and evil forces in the world and the need to guard against harmful infiltration. Practices such as the sprinkling of oneself and one's surroundings with blessed water, placing blessed palms at the home's entrance, dusting sacred salt at the doorway, anointing the body with blessed oils, and the burning of candles, all rise from the core-need for protection from spiritual intrusion. I encourage the resurgence of these practices for the purposes they were first intended. Whether or not we have been deeply wounded, or work with others who have been deeply wounded, we can be influenced by the thoughts, words and actions of those around us. When we personally take responsibility for keeping our own energy field clean and protected, we can decrease the possibility that we are sending "clogged," "contaminated," "hurtful" or "hateful" energies from our energy field into the energy field of others and the greater collective.

My mother snuggled each of her children into bed at night with a prayer asking that the Guardian Angels be at our side to enlighten, to guard, to rule and to guide. A picture of a very large and beautiful angel, hovering over two small children as they crossed a rickety bridge, hung in my bedroom. Psalm 91 was inscribed beneath the picture. "He shall give his angels charge over you to guard you in all your ways." My mother had no doubt about the existence of her Guardian Angel. When I was very young she told me that during a difficult time in her own youth she had awakened one night to a glow. Her guardian angel, standing at the foot of her bed, assured her that things would work out right. She taught us there were classifications of angels, Archangels being of the highest order. Archangel Michael has the most protective powers since he won the battle of good against evil. He continues to battle against evil, controlling evil with his protective shield and sword.

I ask those who have been deeply wounded to make a sincere effort to increase their awareness of guides and angelic beings, and to request the protection and guidance being offered. I reiterate the prayer my mother taught, for I do believe that angels enlighten, guard, rule and guide us. I stress the importance of a prayerful dialogue with the Archangel Michael, beseeching him to shield with his protective armor.

Virtually all religious systems include celestials in their cosmologies.[1] The belief that angelic messengers were sent from the Divine, to guide and protect human beings, is entrenched in the scriptures of the three major religions of the Western world, Judaism, Christianity and Islam.[2] Numerous patriarchs in the Old Testament, including Abraham and Jacob,[3] received guidance and comfort from angel beings. Revelation was brought to Muhammad, and Mikha'il by Jibril (Gabriel).[4] The New Testament opens with angels foretelling a budding new relationship between God and man, thus creating a bridge between the Old and New, and the framework upon which Christianity suspends.[5] Yet little religious ritual surrounds this belief. When beliefs are not reinforced through celebration, over time they are extinguished.

Even while the world's major religions profess a conviction in the guiding and protective powers of angels, the present resurgence of this dormant belief did not surface from within the traditional religions, but from the earth religions, not from the church hierarchy, but from the grassroots – the people.

Since the dawn of civilization humans have relied on the spirit world for guidance and protection. Evidence remains in the artistic expressions left on cave walls around the world. Carl Jung[6] reminded us that, even in our time, as soon as we get a safe distance from Western Europe and the cultures influenced by it, people live in an enchanted world making little, if any, distinction between the sacred and the secular, between the physical and spiritual realities. In these cultures every act of daily living, from sewing seeds, to hunting, to homemaking, to child birth, to death, is a sacred act. Every act is worship, an act of communion. Daily life is a sacramental re-enactment of their oneness with the spiritual world. They rely on their ability to receive guidance and protection from the spiritual realm during their dream life as well as when they are awake. While deep within each of us is a recognition of the same primordial stories as are re-enacted by indigenous peoples around the world, most of us remain unaware of our close connection with the world of spirit.[7]

When I lived in Hawaii, a Polynesian elder shared with me that he believed his people were closer to the spirits and more readily received guidance and assistance from them because the closeness of the relationship had never been dishonored. He emphasized that we in the modern Western world have lost this refined ability because for too long the sacredness of our connection to the spirit world has been disrespected, disavowed and denied.

Yet each night our dream life provides guidance from the same source that they tap into. We dream in the same archetypal images of death and resurrection, of good and evil, the persistent reality of spirit, and of the hero who is able to triumph over incredible odds, even evil, just as the ancients did, and as primitive and educated peoples around the world continue to do. The hero in archetypal stories shows it is possible to win, despite great adversity, if one has Divine Guidance and protection. Even though the world is full of trickery and malice one need not be overcome by it. In *Dreamquest*[8] Morton Kelsey states, "When the hero stories are understood, they can give us a pictorial anatomy of the human soul and the limitless worlds with which it is in contact."

While many in our world are in desperate need of the guidance, protection and nurturing that should be accessible to them, most of our religious traditions and practices have negated ritual which focuses on the primordial battle between good and evil, on our need as human beings for spiritual guidance and protection, and on ways in which human beings can establish, maintain and strengthen their co-existive reality with the spirit world. Morton reports that the resurgent interest in mythology is because, "Few of our churches are providing the symbolic food human beings need for survival. Contemporary men and women are not adequately nourished on a diet of reason, logic and matter alone."[9]

It was not in error that the invitation to rekindle the human to angelic relationship was given to the earth peoples. Messages from the Divine have always been sent to those not bridled by preconceived notions which interfere with their ability to hear and respond.

Our starving souls long for nourishment. During these difficult times we need once again to tightly fuse our connections to the spirit world. We long for a world where the sacred and secular are interwoven, for in this reality interaction with the spiritual world is an ordinary part of life. The hero stories told in folklore and mythology help ward off the hunger. As in the parables of the New Testament, stories of the Old Testament, mythological stories, fairy tales and folk lore, all reveal multilevel messages, messages we are able to interpret at our varying levels of readiness.

I encourage familiarity with ancient stories. There is much to be applied to our own lives from the lessons learned by the heroes. It is almost impossible to interpret our dream messages if we do not have at least a basic understanding of myth. I ask women to pay particular attention to the Goddess stories. There are many goddesses within each woman, archetypes symbolizing feminine strengths and weaknesses. Studying the goddesses of different cultures can provide women with a better understanding of themselves and their relationships. Recognizing the goddess within, and acknowledging the reflection of her particular abilities, can be an empowering experience.

After listening to a story of woundedness I often ask, "What story does this remind you of?" The answer usually comes quickly, for it comes from the primordial level, the level that holds a remembrance, the level that has heard the archetypal stories before. I ask, "How does that story end?"

Our life stories, our personal tragedies, have parallels in ancient folklore. Knowing that one hero survived, conquered, won over death and evil, can be a powerful model to aspire to, even though in this moment we may feel totally apart from any connection with the world, either physically or spiritually.

When we are traumatized, our soul is robbed of virtues. Soul healing requires a reclaiming of the virtues that have been lost or stolen. Trust is the core virtue from which all others flow. Basic to soul healing is the recognition of how deeply the traumatizing experiences have eroded this virtue. When we have been severely betrayed by the universal order, we have difficulty believing things will ever get better. While we are unable to comprehend how such a disaster could have befallen us, we have an even more difficult time coming to terms with no longer being able to rely on what we had previously and naively taken for granted. We may have once trusted in the many tenants and practices of a particular religion. But now we sense that our beliefs were built upon shaky ground. Unable to feel free of further threat we may lose trust in anything and everything, including the Divine. When we are unable to trust we become fearful and anxious. We know that bad things have happened, and we fear they might happen again. When we are unable to trust, relationships fail (including that with the Divine). We begin to feel separate and apart, disconnected and alone, stalked by pervasive dread.

While smudging, visualization, the sacred use of water, salt and oil, and requesting angelic protection are techniques used around the world to shield people from harmful influences, grounding practices are invaluable in establishing and maintaining balance during difficult times. Grounding is a way of re-establishing our connection to the universe. In grounding we align ourselves with the Earth Mother. We become like a tree. We visualize deep roots moving from the soles of our feet down into the body of the earth. When we are rooted in the Earth Mother we can draw on her strength and receive sustenance. When we are firmly planted, we may sway like a tree but we will remain steadfast. Grounding is a powerful technique to re-establish the balance that is necessary to rekindle trust in the universal order, which is the core for developing trust in all other relationships.

Traditional healers teach the power of using stones to dispel confusion and realign ourselves with the earthing influence that brings balance and serenity. Existing since the dawn of creation, stones have amassed electromagnetic energy from the earth's surface. Their stored energy can be transmitted to anyone who holds a stone and breathes deeply until the nervousness passes.

Rocks used for healing purposes are gathered from river shores or ocean beds. In the washing process such stones have gathered the balancing powers of the waters. Someone holding a river – or ocean-washed rock receives, therefore, both the strength of the earth's energy as well as the balancing energy of the waters. Both strength and the attainment of balance are essential factors in healing.

I keep a basket of ocean-washed rocks. I invite anyone who could benefit from their nurturing and grounding force to pick a stone and keep it close. People who have lived through traumatic experiences often have flashbacks or moments when they re-experience the trauma. This can cause significant emotional pain. Sometimes the experience is so difficult they dissociate from it by emotionally leaving the present reality. Rock medicine is of tremendous assistance during such times. I encourage individuals to keep the rock in a pocket where it can be easily grabbed at the first warning of a flashback. Holding the rock not only prevents dissociation, it also helps in the general reduction of the fear and anxiety associated with an inability to trust the universal order.

An Aboriginal healer taught me that it is each person's responsibility to live in harmony with all of his or her relations. Learning to live in harmony begins by honoring the traditional uses of the sacred medicine objects. Earth Mother has provided all we require. Water, trees and rocks have been placed along our path. These have the power to nurture, to heal, to guard, and to guide our journey. Using the sacred medicine offered by these objects, assists in re-establishing balance within. Only when we have learned to "walk in balance" can we truly live in harmony.

To dream the impossible dream,
to fight the unbeatable foe,
To bear with unbearable sorrow,
to run where the brave dare not go
    Dale Wasserman – *Man of La Mancha*

Soul Energy

The human soul is often described in terms of individual purpose and uniqueness. This belief is based upon the assumption that each person has a unique purpose in life, and that we are endowed with the abilities to achieve that purpose. Our talents are our soul's gifts to the universe. When we are being creative, when we are using our talents and abilities, we are accomplishing our soul's work.

Craftsmen from the Middle Ages conveyed a deep respect for the talent they had been given. They believed the spiral patterns on their fingertips were marks left by the soul entering the body, and they infused what they touched and the things they made with their soul's energy. They honored the sacredness of their soul's gift and deeply invested their soul energy into their labor. Viewing their work as an extension of themselves, and as an expression of their soul, they demanded that each creation be completed to its fullest potential, each piece was an original expression from their soul, a work of art.

When I work with someone who has been deeply wounded I encourage creative expression. In their healing many discover, on their own, the power of using their creative talents as a means of expressing soul pain and as a way to demonstrate the healing taking place. I believe that purposeful investment in developing creative energies can "prime the pump" as it were. Pushing just a little, one's involvement in creative activity can hasten the release of soul pain. With the release comes the invitation for soul healing.

I ask people to photograph what gives them hope. I ask them to draw, paint or sculpt the pain deep within. I ask them to journal, to create stories, poems and songs, to take up pottery, stained glass work, to sing and to dance. All are creative expressions. All release soul pain. All allow for soul healing and soul growth.

I believe that creativity is the expression of the soul. When I see creativity flowering, even the desire to repaint a wall or hang a picture, I see a measure of soul healing.

Developing and using our talents and abilities is an expression of our soul energy. Soul energy is a measure of the depth of our lives.

When we are being creative we are giving birth, as the universe gave birth to the many stars and flowers. The universe is in the habit of making beauty. When we use our creative ideas we multiply the opportunities for ourselves and for others to experience life's fullness.

But all of our covering, while laid down to protect us from the world, interferes with our ability to give to the world. The envelope of clay blocks us from seeing our own light, our own abilities and our own talents. Having experienced hurt, we fear more loss. Our fears keep us from taking risks, from stepping out in faith. Our inhibitions hold us back, blocking us from receiving the tremendous abundance available to us in exchange for the product of our talents.

Some people have even been taught that to show the world their abilities is to be vain or to brag. But each of us is endowed with talents needed for the growth and expansion of All. The Bible firmly teaches we are to multiply the gifts bestowed upon us. The servant who doubled the talents given by the master was blessed. "Well done! You are an industrious and reliable servant. Since you were dependable in a small matter I will put you in charge of larger affairs." The servant, who hid the master's talents, stressing that he did so to keep them safe, was cursed. "You worthless lazy lout! . . . You there! Take the thousand away from him and give it to the man with the ten thousand. Those who have will get more until they grow rich, while those who have not will lose even the little they do have."[1] We are reminded it is not vanity to develop and expand our abilities. It is essential. While sharing our gifts to the best of our ability is required to reap rewards in the hereafter, we are promised that in so doing we will receive abundance in this life as well.

In earlier times, part of ceremonial preparation included face painting. Each painted face chronicled the talents the person was capable of sharing for the expansion and growth of the entire tribe. One only showed the gifts one truly possessed, for one's gifts could be called into use at any time. One would "lose face" if unable to perform in the ways claimed.

To pretend to have abilities one does not have is bragging. To develop and use one's talents for the good of All is productive. In expressing ourselves in creative ways, we share growing potential with the world. This is not only prudent, but healing. As we step out in courage, as we allow even a tiny glimmer of our brilliance to stream through the crevices of our pain, our connection with the sacred is strengthened. We advance our individual soul growth and the soul growth of All.

For peoples who recognize and honor their connection to the Earth, practices and ceremonies were and continue to be an expression of their connection with the sacred. While a Shaman might journey to the world of spirit on behalf of an ill person, the individual "goes on" a vision quest in order to receive spiritual guidance about how to best develop and share personal gifts and abilities.

The place chosen for the vision quest and the sites of other sacred ceremony are points where the human connection with the Earth Mother is strong. The Earth has energy lines which parallel the energy meridians in the human body. When a human being seeks Earth connection, energy begins to flow to that area because our body, like the Earth's, is electromagnetic. By honoring the connection through patience and practice, the alignment grows and the connection strengthens. A power place is created when the Earth Mother's energy is frequently drawn to a site where the energy is requested for healing and guidance.

We commonly refer to "holy places" as sites where miracles have been reported, such as Lourdes or Fatima, and to the "holy land" as the place where Jesus walked and prayed. Yet each part of the Earth is sacred. The sacredness of any area can be increased simply by calling the energy to that place. Abraham went into the wilderness. Morgan Le Fey, the half-sister of King Arthur, went to the mount of the Goddess. Earth People gathered at the sites of stones made sacred by their ceremonies.

Since early times people have understood that the Earth Mother willingly supplies energy when they commune with her through ritual. Singing, drumming and ceremonial dance all gather sacred energy to a site which can then be used for a vision quest, to call rain, to ask for healing or to seek a blessing. The stones at a sacred site hold, for all time, the thoughts and words of each seeker. Medicine people capable of rock medicine can learn from the stones what has transpired in any location.

The worship ceremonies of peoples who recognize and honor their connection to the Earth celebrate the sacredness of their connection to All. This religion is based upon a belief that all in creation must honor and support the life and healing of every other part of creation. When we remember to make ceremony, when we gratefully acknowledge our gifts and when we dance our joy of unity and harmony we draw the sacred energy for our healing, and for the healing of All.

Those of us reared in Western cultures may find the teachings and practices of the religion with which we are familiar more aimed at advancing the religion than at promoting our spiritual connection with All. The worship ceremonies we are accustomed to may or may not parallel the growing needs of our souls. We can become highly religious and yet be deprived of food which nurtures our souls. Rather than assisting in removing our covering of hurt and darkness, and guiding the journey connecting us to the light of All, the dogmas and rituals of our faith tradition may contribute to our sense of disconnectedness by adding further coatings to our covering of fear.

The preservation of any religion results from reinforcing the foundational belief system upon which the religion is based. Many of the beliefs and practices which we in the Western world accept, often without question, have their roots in a Middle Ages hierarchical religious structure. Much of our interpretation of what is sacred, and of our relationship to the sacred, has come to us through a model which throughout the centuries has become tightly fused with political systems which sustain power by disempowering the largest segment of followers. Many of the underlying assumptions and teachings to which we adhere, are rooted in medieval practices which utilize fear tactics to coerce commitment and affiliation to the religion.

Basic to the model is an assumption that human beings are unworthy of any direct relationship to the Divine, and that any relationship with the Divine requires an intermediary. Further to this supposition is the notion that only those in positions of religious authority have the expertise to distinguish what is sacred from what is profane. Only they, therefore, can describe a worthy human-divine relationship of worship, love, hope, trust and forgiveness.

Our fundamental beliefs about our own worth and about our worth in relationships are laid down early in life. Our early beliefs are reinforced time and time again by the religious and political institutions which surround us. These powerful institutions permeate our belief system, strongly influencing our thinking and our behavior. As a result, we hold numerous contradicting ideas which erode our self-worth and interfere with our ability to develop and maintain a personal loving relationship with a Divine Presence. Much emphasis is placed upon the sinfulness of human beings and on the unworthiness of the person. I once gave my son a pencil that had inscribed upon it. "I am wonderful and precious. God does not make junk." How can we be part of the Divine and yet be unworthy of a personal relationship?

Many religions teach that the body is a precious temple, housing the spirit. Yet torment of the physical, not to mention the emotional, body as a means of purification and renewal is a deeply ingrained practice. This idea, coupled with the denial of the feminine aspect of the deity, has led to practices which not only dishonor the individual soul, but which, and most especially, dishonor women and their spirituality. Regulations aimed at keeping women powerless within organized religions have not only excluded women from leadership positions, but have fueled the belief that women are less valuable creations than their male counterparts. While many religious movements are taking steps to eradicate women-excluding practices, these entrenched views continue to permeate attitudes and subsequent actions toward women.

I had not worked long with women who were attempting to survive a life of trauma before I identified the religious and political overtones to violence against them. The issues that women face today are in many ways a result of the history of women in the churches.

During the Middle Ages, and into the decades of colonization, there was a growing awareness of the relationship between religion and power, between power and financial gain. Church authorities recognized that to have the power advantage it was necessary for the priests to establish control over the people and their belief systems. For the Earth Peoples, healing and spirituality were not separate. They celebrated the Divine in all of nature and honored the wisdom and ability of the healer who could connect to the Divine Source of energy and use it for healing. The abilities of a healer were sought during times of physical illness as well as during spiritual crisis. In order to indoctrinate the people into a new belief system, the priests needed to usurp the power invested in the healers and in the Earth Religions. Since many of the priests were themselves unable to render healing, there was a need to separate in the minds and practices of people the long-held connection between physical healing and their beliefs surrounding the sacred.

Teachings and practices related to healing became purposely associated with spiritual healing only. This placed the responsibility for healing solely on Jesus, removing those who claimed to be his ordained followers from their obligation to heal the sick as he had directed, and barring those able to provide physical and spiritual healing from performing their sacred rituals.

Earth religions were banned, and those who continued to practice their spirituality in this way were tortured, and put to death. The meaning attached to words in common usage, such as "witch," meaning a woman with supernatural powers, "pagan," a common word for Earth People, and "voodoo," meaning to search deeply into the meanings of the universe, were purposefully tainted as being associated with evil rather than good. Anyone accused of having healing powers was declared evil, hunted down and hideously mutilated.

During this reign of terror a woman could be labeled "witch" for scolding, nagging, or for talking back to her husband. Both church and state accepted that a woman was less valuable than a man, and that the woman was the property of her husband.

These beliefs and practices were written into laws and continue to influence the laws and practices of our day. Attitudes which project evil qualities onto the female gender have been covertly and overtly used as an excuse to hold women in powerless positions in order to contain their influence. This has marked women as justifiable targets for exploitation and perpetuates violence against them, and against all who are trapped in positions of powerlessness.

Such convictions keep us locked in a belief system that continually supports unworthiness. Feelings of unworthiness cause us to doubt our own abilities. We disclaim our own power and any personal connection to anything that might reinforce a belief that we have sacred powers. These beliefs reinforce our darkness and keep us in a shroud-cloud of fear.

While we continue to hang onto these beliefs as a way to belong and be accepted, these very beliefs keep us separate and apart. These beliefs bar us from knowing our real selves and our connection to All. Living within the confines of such beliefs causes us to be restless, to want, to long, and to search. Inherent in the human experience is a gnawing desire for a connection to the sacred. We yearn for the Divine Presence. We long to burst forth from the clay enshrouding us. We long to let the Divine Light shine from us. We long to give and receive the light. We long to enjoy the exchange, to heal in the exchange, to grow in the exchange.

When our religious teachings and practices support this growth, our journey of healing into the light is supported. But when religion evades or distorts this truth, the pain of further separation is intolerable. When the practices that uplift the sacredness of any people are taken from them, the spirit life of each individual, and of the group, wanes. When religion affirms the spiritual journey, when the sacred in the self, in others, and in All, is supported, religion and spirituality fuse and soul grows.

The only light worth following shines within your soul.
V. Blake

A Road Map of the Soul's Journey

A number of years ago I received a greeting card with the above verse in calligraphy beneath a photograph of a sunrise. The card has long since vanished but the image and the words remain indelibly sketched upon my mind and my soul. The radiance within, as depicted by the sun bursting forth from its resting place, is a powerful reminder of our ability to move our world from darkness into light.

Yet we are only too aware that it is not during our sun-filled days, but during our rainy seasons, that we discover the many layers of clay which surround us. It is during times of crises that we are catapulted into the crevices of our being, there to discover the armor protecting our brokenness. While we know it is only from the darkness that we capture the first rays of light, we also know that during our times of turmoil it would take nothing less than a gigantic crane to budge the heavy casting which has enveloped us.

When I work with people who are attempting to move beyond the darkness, I involve them in activities which help them think in a more wholistic way. In one exercise they begin by visualizing themselves as a full golden circle of light and wholeness. From a sheet of gold paper they cut a large circle representing their completeness. I have them focus on the golden circle which portrays all of their talents and dreams, hopes, feelings, aspirations, desires and abilities to connect and relate to the Divine and to others. I have them try to remember a time when they felt the most whole and complete.

At the beginning of the healing phase many are unable to view themselves in this way. But most are able to imagine, to draw, collage, paint, journal, and describe at least some portion of what is possible.

Unable to see herself as a full golden circle of light, one woman imagined, in hopefulness, what this might look like. She drew a brilliant dandelion with leaves that vibrated in their greenness against a threatening black background. Within the week, she returned with a photo of a dandelion growing in her back alley. The dandelion flourished against formidable odds. It was able to share its full splendor because of its ability to push for the light through a crack in a cement wall. Shortly thereafter, in describing how the dandelion's million seeds were now riding the wind, she whispered, "Just think of all the potential."

The fearless dandelion, which had become for her a powerful symbol, reminds each of us that, with similar tenacity, we too can overcome gigantic obstacles. We too can thrive in the face of great adversity; we too can bloom. We, as Israel, can know deliverance.[1] The Israelites' journey can be our road map. Our desert and parched land can bloom with abundant flowers. We can again rejoice with joyful song. Our burning sands can become pools. Our pain can be turned into joy and gladness. Sorrow and mourning can flee.

I ask those willing to thrive beyond the trauma to reflect upon the impact the loss, the change, the hurt, the torture, has had on their sense of wholeness. I ask that they notice how their view of self has changed. I ask that they identify how their attitudes and feelings toward themselves, toward others, the universe and their God, have changed. I ask that they consider how much of their life energy is being spent focusing on their struggle with these feelings. How many of their resources are spent dealing with their woundedness?

On a sheet of white paper they draw a second circle the same size as the one of gold. Into this circle a pie-shaped wedge, depicting the impact the trauma has on their sense of wholeness, is carved. The wedge is colored using the designs, symbols and color choices which best describe their woundedness. The size of the slice, the symbols and the colors depend upon the significance of the impact. For some, the impact is enormous. Some feel their entire sense of wholeness has been consumed by the change, loss, crisis or trauma. For many there is only darkness. For others the darkness is infused with gnarled designs of angry red. They paste the wedge over the circle of their golden wholeness.

This powerful exercise is done not to emphasize the wound, but as a starting point from where healing can begin. The first step in healing is to acknowledge the depth of our woundedness. Many have denied the pain of hurting, and many have been denied the pain of hurting.

To become actively and physically involved in healing exercises which acknowledge our pain and our desire to grow beyond the pain demonstrates our commitment to ourselves and to the universe. This acknowledgment seems to accelerate the healing process. In completing the circle and wedge exercise, there is a visual and tactile recognition that the golden essence has been buried beneath mounds of fear and hurt. From this recognition comes the impetus to search for tools which will chip away the cover.

As healing strategies are chosen and implemented, a token is placed upon the wedge of woundedness as a concrete reminder of the healing that is occurring. Stars of gold, silver and blue are used; emblems of trees and gardening are used to represent the healing reconnection with nature. Others place music notes and other symbols of the arts to represent their ability to once again express the voice reawakening in their souls. Using a small penknife, one woman slivered the wedge to show the gold that, from beneath her suffering, was beginning to glitter through.

Sometimes, because of a major trauma or because of a "pile-up" of unhealed events, our entire sense of wholeness can be consumed by darkness. Multiple losses can occur in such rapid succession there is little time for healing one loss before the effect of the next is felt. During such times we may even have difficulty distinguishing the aspects of one loss from the aspects of another.

With the loss of a job, for example, one frequently experiences a loss of self-esteem, a loss of role, of status, of power, and of responsibilities. These losses may be compounded by financial and property loss. There may be an associated loss of family support, even a loss of relationships through divorce or separation.

Multiple losses, especially when experienced in rapid succession, can shatter our ability to trust life's circumstances. I often see this inability to trust, or hope that things will ever get better, in older persons who must be placed in long-term care. Upon entry to the facility, many appear confused. When the pileup of recently experienced losses is reviewed, their reason for disorientation becomes comprehensible. In many cases, grief counseling and compassionate support, rather than psychotropic drugs, can more effectively re-establish equilibrium.

Regardless of age, grief interferes with cognitive abilities, causing periods of acute confusion. Because our mind is occupied with trying to "figure out what went wrong" we are unable to focus for any length of time, on anything other than the traumatic event and its effects on us. This interferes with our ability to think in clear and organized ways. We have difficulty making choices, and often do not make good ones. We begin to doubt our abilities, and dread anything unknown, for we recognize the alteration in our thought processes. We experience forgetfulness, agitation and anxiety.

Those who have not experienced trauma have difficulty comprehending the enormity of the impact and the effects on human functioning resulting from a traumatic life experience. Few recognize how ubiquitous trauma is. But trauma comes in many forms. The effects can result from wars, natural disasters, car or plane crashes, train wrecks, kidnappings, assaults, murders, sudden deaths, child deaths and suicide.[2] The traumatization resulting from domestic violence, child abuse or cult victimization is only now being fully recognized.[3, 4, 5] The most serious psychological symptoms and psychiatric disorders occur when the trauma is prolonged and repeated.[6] The most pernicious trauma is that which is deliberately inflicted in a relationship where the traumatized individual is dependent – at worst in a parent-child relationship. The most extreme trauma entails an attitude of malevolent intent on the part of the perpetrator.[7, 8, 9]

Even though we might comprehend that such traumatic events as just reviewed would leave one struggling with a sense of incompleteness, there are numerous other events and times in life, which are often not acknowledged by ourselves or others, which throw us off course and leave us struggling in a state of disequilibrium. We live in a world of change, and with every change there is loss. Change can be developmental, such as sending a child off to college, or situational, as that which we must face following relocation or a house fire.

Some changes are chosen. Others are imposed. Imposed change robs us of our control. Imposed change leaves us as puppets on a high wire, flapping at the wind's whim. The degree of control we have over the situation appears to influence our adjustment. It seems that when we are able to plan ahead, to place time and energy into anticipating the change and subsequent losses, we are better able to move through the experience. This is why unanticipated death, and deaths that are off-time, such as the death of a child, or change that is forced on us, such as being displaced from our country due to war, or sudden and non-chosen job loss has such a profound impact.

Every traumatic event causes change in numerous aspects of our lives. For some, the change may be enormous. For others, the change may be less traumatic. But all change carries with it aspects of loss. For some, the change may herald the loss of a past relationship and a planned future together. For others, the change may include a need to let go of a long-time dream, a goal that can never be achieved.

Loss means endings. Something must end before something can begin. We must let go of the old before we can take on the new. We resist change. We like the status quo. We feel safe with the familiar. Endings mean closure, saying goodbye. Endings cause pain; what has been lost cannot be retrieved. The wound left by what has been ripped from us can be very, very deep.

While the significance of the loss and the long-term effects are unique to each, loss affects us, frequently more than we allow ourselves to acknowledge. Not only are our thinking abilities altered, but the impact is felt in every aspect of our being.

Often, either because we do not recognize the toll the impact of a traumatic event or a pileup of losses is taking, or because we can-not, or choose not, to spend the time and energy required for healing, we place our "healing on hold." We cleanse the exterior, being very careful not to wipe too deeply. We allow only the time it takes for a thin healing layer to cover the surface pain. But like the infected open wound of a compound fracture, if unhealed before the cast is applied, discharge from the festering beneath soon becomes apparent on the cast surface. We cover the ooze with ever increasing bandages. We make them thicker, stronger, more and more clay-like. And we carry on.

But unhealed wounds have a way of refusing to remain dormant. The slightest bump, often when we least expect it, can change the trickle to a free bleed. Bleeding interferes with our lives.

Wounds hidden deeply beneath many layers of covering must be cleansed to the core. The deadened tissue requires debriding. Healing must occur from the inside out.

To visually recognize the need to begin healing at the core, I ask those I work with to return to the exercise of their circle of wholeness, and to reexamine the wedge which depicts the impact of brokenness. The cross-section of the wedge of woundedness is divided into three parts. The top section is labeled "my physical self," the middle "my emotional self" and the base section of the wedge is labeled "my spiritual self." Two circles are drawn around the wedge. The first is inscribed "my social world." The larger circle is labeled "the environment." The circles surrounding the wedge symbolize that as human beings we are body, mind and spirit, and that we are not separate from, but are a part of, and are constantly influencing and being influenced by, our social and natural environments.

This visual metaphor exercise reminds us that when we experience a traumatic life event every aspect of our being recoils in distress. If every aspect is wounded, healing requires that we spend time, energy and resources on healing each of these dimensions. Yet, sadly, most of our personal and professional resources place bandages over the wound, ignoring the festering core. We tend the physical pain and minister to the emotional suffering, but often these resources are put into place and, frequently, already removed before soul's agony oozes to the surface.

The initial responses to trauma are experienced first in our physical body. The adrenaline rush prepares us to fight or to flee. It takes a few days before the insulating shock allows our emotional body to feel the racking torment, but it takes months or even years before the intense soul issues must be grappled with.

When we have been deeply wounded, we respond to soul pain in three phases. In the beginning, we attempt to satisfy the questions arising from our souls with familiar rhetorical answers. We respond from beliefs which have often been given to us by others, but which have never been personally tested. We try to pacify our souls with reassurances such as "It was God's will." "It was all for the best." "I know he is in a better place." "I will see him again some day." "It must be the way God wants it to be." "I must be in this relationship for a reason."

But our souls will not be patronized. The old beliefs are unable to answer the soul's nagging questions. Our souls scream for truth.

By the second phase we acknowledge the challenge. We are forced into combat with our belief system. Each belief, every assumption about life and life's meaning, and about death and death's meaning, must be grappled with.

This torturous time of vacillation is, I believe, what St. John of the Cross referred to as "The Dark Night of the Soul,"[10] and what St Theresa of Avila[11] so aptly described. They wrote that during the soul's dark night we are thrown off course and forced to wrestle the demons that lurk in the darkness, just beneath the surface of our awareness.

We are plunged into the pit of our soul, there to retrace the steps of our journey. We are forced to examine what we have become, and we agonize over what we have yet to accomplish. We become driven in our search for knowing. We can find no reprieve.

Moving cautiously across the rim, we begin our descent into the darkness. We stop and ponder each rift along the chambered walls. The effects of erosion are visible. Bleached by the sun and smoothed by the winds of time, fractures of countless form and size lay in various stages of repair. Each fissure outlines the road map of our soul's journey. Each chip reveals our story.

Progress, while painfully slow at best, is often blocked. Frequently catapulted backwards, we are forced to retrace the steps already taken. While we occasionally soar on eagle's wings to the tips of our peak encounters, for the most part we plod the ordinariness of the flat lands. We dip into the valleys and we trudge the burning sands of our barren dessert experiences. We notice there are jagged cliffs that must be smoothed. There are deep valleys that must be filled. There are barren areas that must be cultivated and watered.[12]

The pilgrimage is not an easy one. The journey within rarely is. It is a formidable path strewn with peril. It is testing time, and our old customary ways of being are proving inadequate. It is a time of barrenness, desolation and depression. It is a time when we feel abandoned by others. But most especially, it is a time when we feel totally and completely forgotten by God. We feel swallowed up by the darkness, and separate and apart from the mainstream of life.

Too exhausted to struggle further, we succumb; we surrender.

We drift deeper. The darkness thickens. We enter the pit. We sink into the silence of the base. The shroud-cloud descends. Our period of cocooning begins.

But our struggle in the darkness is not without merit, for the blackest moment is the moment when the real message of transformation comes. "It is during our dark time, that the eye begins to see."[13] It is in our darkest time that our consciousness mingles with the consciousness of God.[14] Our time in the cocoon is a time of soul purification, permitting our passage to higher levels of awareness.

If we can endure until sunrise, if we can, as Joan Boryshenko asks, "trust and believe that our dark night has come in service of the light,"[15] then we can move through the transition knowing that, if we do the work necessary for our rebirth, we will see the sunrise awaken our soul in welcome of the returning spirit.

We know that we are no longer the same, will never again be the same. The experience of the trauma and the experience of the journey have essentially changed us. But what are we? What kind of butterfly will this worm that is barely able to creep along the hard earth's crust ever become?

Blanketed deeply within the nurturing fibers of the cocoon we begin our transformation. Our groans of agony (steadily and almost without our awareness) become gentle whispers of solace. We dream. We capture glimpses of the grander meaning for our existence. We begin to see some design in the fiber of our cocoon. We notice that the fiber has been stitched and shaped by our experiences. We notice the beauty and uniqueness of our fabric and we see that the filament is being absorbed into the fabric, of our being.

We sleep; we dream; we heal. Our light brightens and it begins, ever so softly, ever so steadily, to pour forth. The outer layers of our fibrous cocoon loosens, the threads fray. The cocoon is worn. The butterfly is about to emerge.

But now we must demonstrate that we can spread our wings. We must show we can fly toward the light. This is a major task. It requires all of our courage. We know little about this new thing we have become. We have difficulty trusting the brightness of this newness.

We have for a long time lived in darkness. We know the darkness. We know how to manage in the darkness. We do not know light.

And yet, we are now keenly aware that in order to fulfill our grander purpose, we must move into the light. We must radiate our brightness.

We must muster the courage. We must overcome the fear. We must risk. We must flutter forward. We must hold onto the truths we have learned in the cocoon. We must share what we have absorbed. We must believe in our brightness.

We are plummeted into stage three of our soul's struggle. We do not have all of the answers, and the ones we do have continue to change as our awareness changes. But we now know which old beliefs we can no longer hold; having been tested in the fires of our experience they have burned away. The beliefs we now hold are beyond beliefs. These have become our personal knowing.

For some, the challenge of moving out of the cocoon and forward into life is too horrific. Unable to accept their own brightness, their own metamorphosis, they choose instead to burrow deep into the cocoon. Unable to receive sustenance from the worn covering, their wings wither. Stuck in the tired fibers they will never know the possibilities of their light.

Others, impatient of the down time, and distrustful of the process, break forth from the cocoon long before they ever discover what kind of butterfly they are to be. With wings too immature to sustain flight, they flutter through life never able to reach the heights to which they were meant to fly.

But, if we do not rush the time of cocooning, and creep into the light before our wings are dry and fully formed, then we too will experience the glory of the butterfly! We too will know what it is to be a thing of beauty. No longer will we need to crawl, for our delicate wings will catch the breeze of God's breath and, following the markers provided to guide our journey, we will soar in the achievement of our purpose.

In the midst of winter
I discovered within me
An invincible summer.
                    Albert Camus

Soul Loss

M ost of us, in both our personal and professional lives, have become pretty good at recognizing the physical symptoms of grief and suffering. We understand the relationship between sorrow and the inability to eat and sleep. We know that abdominal pain, chest pain, headache and backache can be signs that the physical body is recoiling in agony. And we know that the turbulent rivers of the emotions of anger and regret must be navigated. But how many of us have any idea what soul pain, or loss to the wholeness of our soul, might look like?

Indigenous peoples from many parts of the world hold a common belief regarding the human response to life crisis. According to this belief, the psychic shock experienced following trauma shatters the soul. A part or parts of the soul may flee the body to escape back to the peace of the spirit world. Instinctively aware that the traumatic event has taken its toll, shamans and other healers perform various rituals with the purpose of coaxing the spirit to return to its human home.

Even though these practices are not overtly honored within our

Western culture, somehow their legitimacy rings true. Deep within each of us are the roots of our ancient heritage. At some level each of us is aware of this knowing. Our memory is an indelible part of the collective memory, which holds the history of the universe. The history of our soul's journey, as well as the history of the collective soul's journey, the journey of all of humankind, is a part of this knowing. Our ability to tap into what Jung termed the collective unconscious (and which I choose to term the collective consciousness), allows us to piece together and make sense of greater truths than we may have been previously introduced to.

Our language, rooted in the knowing of our ancestors, is a part of the collective memory. We echo the dormant belief about the effects of trauma on our soul when we refer to ourselves as being "dispirited" or in "low-spirits" during the times when we feel broken, disengaged or detached from the animated current of life itself.[1] We refer to ourselves as being "broken in spirit" when we have been robbed of the energy that allows us to feel exuberance and courage. There are times in each of our lives when we would like to "give up the ghost."

As we move through our own personal dark nights we become attentive to the ancient knowledge of soul shattering following traumatic life events. During these times we are keenly aware of the brokenness of our spirit. We recognize that our energy is being focused on the search for the purpose for our existence. We know that we have little useable energy for anything but the search, and, while extremely uncomfortable, we also know that our "stuckness" is essential. We know of our incompleteness. We acknowledge that we must remain still and silent in the deep until we have amassed the energy needed to heal our broken core. We recognize that in brokenness there is no real forward movement.

In September of 1985 my spirit fled. The psychic pain of losing a child forced me to experience the deepest and darkest night of the soul. Like Persephone,[2] I was picking flowers in a beautiful garden one day, and lost in the darkness of the underworld the next. Life had been bright and glorious, but on that mid-September morn all disappeared. I had fallen through a trap door and was held a prisoner in the *oubliette*. Held in the darkness, I was abandoned and forgotten.

For ten long years I wandered dispiritedly, searching in the shadows for a way out, searching in the darkness for what had been lost. Even though I had not heard of the notion of the dark night of the soul, I was keenly aware that my initial response to the shock of my son's death left me hollow and empty, incomplete and disconnected. Engulfed in a heavy dark shroud, I existed in a bewildering state of disequilibrium.

Feelings of longing dominated my thinking. I knew I was searching. I knew I was searching for what was lost. Yes, I was searching for my lost son but, more accurately, I was searching for my lost self, my lost soul and the characteristics that had gone with it. I knew I could not lift the shroud-cloud until I had found the object of my search. I could no longer exist as an empty shell.

Somehow the sinking into the seemingly bottomless pit of agony awakened a voice in the inner most depths of my being. I was being prodded to comprehend. The nagging would not be silenced. My soul's voice, deep within every cell of my body, agonized. Shattered and broken, each cell called out in a desperate need to be refilled with the energy of spirit.

My spirit had escaped an unbearable situation and my life could not get back on course until I had convinced my spirit that its human home had not only been restored, but renewed and strengthened. I needed healing. I needed healing practices that would coax home my sojourning spirit. I needed to convince my returning spirit that its purpose for walking the Good Red Road of physical life could be fulfilled.

Because of my own experience I now recognize and acknowledge soul loss. I work with people grieving the many losses in life. I hear their stories of their souls' emptying and of their need to reclaim their spirit energy. Women, who have been abused as children, frequently tell of escaping abuse by fleeing to the world of spirit. They comprehend that even though "they" return after the abuse, some part of them never comes back. They never feel whole. They never feel complete.

I have been told of escaping into purple. I have been told of being surrounded by purple and of being lifted into purple. I know the spiritual significance of the color purple. It is not difficult to comprehend that these stories are accounts of assistance from the realm of spirit. I have been told of being lifted into purple and then placed under a "Sacred Mother Tree," so great was the need for nurturing. Another told of being carried off by a giant bird, and another of being sustained in the arms of angels. While the body was forced to endure, the spirit was lifted away. But, often, shattered soul parts and their characteristics do not return.

I have studied the way of the shaman. I have journeyed to the world of spirit. Assisted by the shaman and spirit guides, I have retrieved lost soul parts. I have done this using ancient Shamanic practice, but I have also been offered soul parts needed for the healing of the person receiving the energy I was transferring during a Reiki treatment. During these times I have been guided to acknowledge and honor the return of the soul part and to use the Rei (Divine) Ki (Energy) to seal the returning part into the person's crown and heart chakras (energy centers).

Energy healing therapies are sometimes referred to as "alternate" healing methods. This is because we have come to recognize them as alternate choices to pharmaceutical and surgical methods. I prefer, however, to refer to such healing and spiritual practices as "complementary" methods. I believe that both Western medicine and natural and sacred forms of healing must be recognized for the good they can provide those in need. The methods of the natural and sacred world paradigms should be used to complement the best that the Scientific Model has to offer, rather than as a substitute for it.

Many interested in the more natural forms of healing are becoming attracted, as well, to alternate forms of spirituality. They have recognized the close and ancient relationship between healing and spirituality, and have identified a need to recombine the two. While energy-transfer-types of healing are alternate forms of healing deeply rooted in spirituality, Shamanism is an alternate form of spirituality, deeply rooted in healing practice.

Interest in alternate forms of spirituality are causing many to return to the Earth Religions. Shamanism and other Earth Religions provide integration with nature and the natural world along with access to other realms of reality beyond the material world. Tom Cowan, author of *Shamanism and the Celtic Spirit*[3] emphasizes that the word "shaman" comes from Siberian tribes that used the word in reference to a man or woman with a special type of spiritual power. Shamans are visionary, ecstatic healers. In other traditions they would be referred to as "spiritual consultants." A shaman does not, however, guide another based upon personal knowing but rather, by connecting through a trance state to the world of spirit, relays the guidance imparted there.

Cowan, a former Roman Catholic and Jesuit seminarian, found an appealing blend between Celtic spirituality, embodied in its Shamanic practices, and the belief system of Christianity. He writes: "Druids and priestesses, bards and poets, legendary heroes, mythological gods and goddesses, Christian monks and saints, mystics, witches and healers – what separates these individuals over time and space and by the advancing scientific, technological world, is not as strong as what connects them: solid spiritual values that have remained constant over centuries."[3] If we really scrutinize the life of Jesus, and the role he played as a healer and a change agent, it becomes apparent that his actions were more closely associated with those of a shaman healer than with those of a priest.[4]

Shamanism is being revived. The Spirit of the Earth is calling to people to respect nature. God is ever-present in every part of nature, in every part of creation. To dishonor the Earth is to dishonor the Sacred. As Cowan writes, "The more natural way to meet God the Creator is through nature, the seasons, the elements. [5]

Twice in *Living Buddha Living Christ*[6] Thich Nhat Hanh shares a Christian legend reminding us of the presence of God in nature. It is mid-winter. St. Francis calls to an almond tree, "Speak to me of God!" The almond tree responds. God responds. The tree bursts into bloom. This powerful image teaches us that God lives in creation. The coming alive of the tree in mid-winter screams for us to recognize the beauty, the splendor, the glory that is the Creator dwelling within creation.

In his later years, my father-in-law bequeathed to us a sum of money. We chose to spend it while he was alive, and could know how much we appreciated his gift. I love the sun and have for years enjoyed its morning greeting of warmth and promise. I cannot image a finer picture of the face of the Creator than that of the blazing morning sun. Knowing my passion for the sun, my husband used the gift money to add a magnificent East-facing sun-room to our bedroom. Now, each morning as the sun announces another day, I recite the Old Testament Psalm of Glory,[7] a copy of which was penned in calligraphy and given to me by a dear friend.

How clearly the sky reveals God's glory!
How plainly it shows what he had done!
Each day announces it to the following day;
Each night repeats it to the next.

No speech or words are used,
No sound is heard;
Yet the message goes out to all the world
And is heard to the ends of the earth.

God made a home in the sky for the sun;
It comes out in the morning like a happy bridegroom,
Like an athlete, eager to run a race.
It starts at one end of the sky and goes across to the other,
Nothing can hide from its heat."

The psalmist saw, as St. Francis did, the glory of God in all of creation. All is the handiwork of the Maker; all bears the Breath, the Spirit Energy of the Breather of Life.

Shamanism and other Earth Religions are being revived as the call to pay attention to life on our planet becomes louder. But Shamanism is also being revived to meet the healing needs of people. Since the Age of Scientism, and in our efforts to separate religion and health care, we have separated healing from spirituality. Yet, for all of our scientific knowledge, our culture is becoming increasingly a culture of brokenness. Many feel they do not belong. Many feel desolate, alone, separate, apart.

Our institutions are filled with people who have lost their connection to what is sacred, and in so doing have lost any connection to themselves, to others, and to the world around them. When we are broken, when our soul is shattered, when our spirit has fled, we struggle in a Humpty Dumpty attempt to piece the parts back together. Even in our healing efforts, the recall of memories can trigger our need to "leave" and we dissociate. We escape our painful existence and we flee the memory of the cause of our suffering. In our brokenness we are unable to separate the two. The pain is too intense to endure. We must go, and we do go, as one woman said, "far . . . far . . . far away." We escape one more time to the safety of the spiritual realm, but at the expense of our brokenness.

In *Entering the Circle*,[8] Olga Kharitidi, a Russian psychiatrist, describes how a trip into the Alti mountains in Siberia launched her into Shamanic apprenticeship. Through her Shaman-teacher, Umai, she discovered ancient secrets of Siberian wisdom which were given to her to help in her work as a healer.

Umai taught, "Diseases of the mind have only two causes, and they are totally opposite of each other. One way people can become crazy is if their soul or a part of their soul has been lost. . . . The second way people can become crazy is if they are overwhelmed and occupied by a foreign power. There are only two reasons; nothing more."

Umai's diagnosis of the cause of mental illness is identical to the discoveries made by Michael Harner, in his study of Shamanic practices around the world. Harner author and teacher of core Shamanism, is considered the father of Neo-Shamanism in North American.[9]

Both Kharitidi and Harner share explicit examples of the complete healing which results following soul retrieval and the extraction of spiritual intrusions. Olga Kharitidi shares a story of her experience as a healer for a woman in a terminal state of catatonic schizophrenia. Following the brief encounter in which Dr. Kharitidi called for her spiritual-healer-double to "come forth" (and do the healing), the woman recovered completely, able to be discharged from the psychiatric hospital.

I have frequently observed the dullness and lead-like shadow that overcast the eyes of those experiencing mental and emotional strain. I have always believed the eyes to be "the windows of the soul." Of this I am now sure. Following soul healing I have witnessed the return of the brightness and sparkle that belongs in the eyes. It is a declaration of their ability to see more clearly than they have for a long time.

The person receiving soul healing recognizes that something significant has taken place. Even though they may not be immediately able to relate to all that has happened, most tell of the changes they already feel deep within. In a short time they are able to recognize fully the healing that has occurred.

I was called one afternoon to assist with the healing of a troubled young man with whom I was not acquainted. In the "journey" I found a small boy about three years old, wearing blue jeans and a red plaid shirt, hanging upside down on a star. Being new at this work, I doubted my abilities, as well as what I was seeing, but I trusted in what I was being guided to do. When the healing was complete I shared pieces of the story which seemed important for the young man to hear. While he could relate to much of what I had seen and heard, he was unable to make any memory connections with the little boy or the star.

Several days later a gifted teacher told me I needed to hear something to help my learning. The young man had returned to complete the story. When he shared with his mother what had taken place during the healing, she broke into tears, telling him how "upside down" their entire family life had been during his early years. His father had been an alcoholic. One afternoon, while intoxicated, he stumbled into the crib, tipping it upside down. The little boy was left dangling on the star adornment at the top of the crib. His mother told him that for days she was unable to control his terrified cries.

Following my introduction to Shamanic practice I no longer doubted the reality of soul loss. I had personally experienced soul loss and, during Shamanic training, I received soul healing. I have journeyed to the Spirit World. I have retrieved lost soul parts. I have witnessed healing, healing which previous to these experiences I would not have thought possible, such as bringing together the fragmentation of multiple personalities. While I am not a Shaman in the traditional sense, I am a contemporary one. I have learned the value in honoring the Spirit World. I accept its guidance. I am grateful for its assistance. I value this work and, while there is much I do not know, I do know that the journey, not the arriving is my goal.

For a long time after studying and practicing the healing techniques associated with Shamanism, I continued to refer anyone who sought my assistance in this regard. While I saw tremendous value in the work, I did not feel qualified. Yet "Spirit" seemed to be of a different "mind." Shortly after beginning my education and practice in Shamanism, I "received" a soul part as I transferred Reiki energy. Words cannot convey the amazement, yet the reverence and gratitude I felt as the filament-likeness of the young woman. I was working with gently drifted into her heart chakra. Her soul part had fled two years previously when she had received news of her brother's sudden and traumatic death. As in all cases of soul work, this woman now needed to make the conscious decision to integrate the returning characteristics and to develop her soul gifts in order that her spirit could, in this physical body and under these conditions, fulfill the purpose for which it came.

When a soul part flees, the characteristics associated with that part also leave. When a soul part returns, its characteristics return.

If we are able to entertain the notion of soul loss, then we must consider what is lost when the soul part flees. According to Shamanic belief, the soul has characteristics, and it is these characteristics that make us fully alive, fully human, whole and complete. The characteristics allow us to feel joy, and include an ability to appreciate, to be creative, to be independent, to take risks, to love and receive love, to worship, to stand in awe. The characteristics include an ability to connect to wisdom, to understand right from wrong, to gain and impart knowledge, to know and speak truth, yet to be non-judgmental, to feel and convey compassion, to give council, to be courageous, and to know ourselves and our full potential, yet to be humble and just.

In *Welcome Home*[10] Sandra Ingerman described the importance of welcoming the returning soul part(s). She emphasized the necessity of taking the time to acknowledge and integrate the returning characteristics.

Integration of the characteristics is not without laughter, nor is it without tears. It is not difficult to appreciate that if one's independence leaves at the age of three, and returns at thirty-three, some adjustment will be required. If our sense of playfulness or joy flees at a young age, the return, while welcome and necessary for wholeness, will require some getting used to, not only by us but also by those not used to associating us with these characteristics.

If we are able to comprehend soul loss and the brokenness of the soul which results, it is not hard to understand why Shamanic healers view our culture as a culture very much in need of healing. Acknowledging my own soul loss, and the fragmentation of others, and in a search for wholeness, I began to examine strategies which promised more complete healing. Observing the results, I came to recognize the value in the healing methods used since ancient time. As Olga Kharitidi, Michael Harner and Sandra Ingerman affirm, these methods are based on wisdom rooted in the world of spirit. Shamanic healing provides immediate healing, such as cannot be attained by Western methods, even after years of intense psychotherapy.

Olga Kharitidi begins *Entering the Circle*[11] with a hymn which she states is traditionally offered in atonement for possible breaches in the conditions under which Sacred knowledge is allowed to transform. The time has come to join more closely the practices of health and healing. As this happens there is a need for prayers such as the one following to insure we each do our part to covey what is truth.

If there was something in the air
If there was something in the wind
If there was something in the trees or bushes
That could be pronounced and once was overheard by animals,
Let this Sacred Knowledge be returned to us again.
Atharvaveda (VII 66)

The man of intelligence fixes
his gaze on wisdom
But the eyes of the fool are on
the ends of the earth.
                    Proverbs 17:24

Awakening

Karen Martin[1] developed a model in which the pathway through the experience of grief is depicted as a figure eight. The figure eight is used in many cultures to symbolize infinity. Dr. Martin's apparent intent in using this symbol was to describe grief as a journey which may take a long time. And indeed, for some, the struggle to release grief's hold lasts the reminder of their life. When I replicate her model, I like to diagram the figure as becoming smaller and smaller as we are able to find meaning in what has happened to us, and new purpose for our lives. Dr. Martin theorizes that, in grief, some respond initially from their "head" and some from their "gut." Those who begin grieving in their heads, as depicted by the top portion of the figure, try to intellectualize what is happening. The gut responders, those who begin at the bottom of the pathway, respond initially to grief with an outpouring of gut-wrenching emotions. It seems that those who begin by trying to "figure this thing out" soon realize they cannot so quickly find the answers. Their dismay catapults them to the pit of their gut, where they too recoil from the emotional sting of deep sorrow. Those who begin in the gut soon recognize that their outcry has had little effect. Grief continues to hold its grip so, in turn, they attempt head strategies.

I had always placed a lot of faith in my ability to cope. I had always been able to hold my head high as I walked through the storms of life. I had been able to make most things work out by taking control of my situation. I was an intelligent human being. I knew the power of knowledge. I had frequently been able to find and apply solutions found in the wise and written words of others.

Desperate to heal my broken heart, desperate to reclaim my lost self, my lost soul, and urgently needing to feel whole again, I rationalized: "I can fill the empty spaces. I can mend this brokenness, if only I can find the right information on how to make this happen." Others had suffered. Surely there were solutions, directions, formulas, theories, concepts, constructs, frameworks, paradigms. There had to be a way, a road map – a chart for the course.

Clawing and clamoring, I attempted to scale the jagged edges of my brokenness. Educated in both nursing and psychology, I had experience working with others struggling with the hurts of life. I was somewhat familiar with the basic literature on grief and loss but could recall no mention of the notion of soul pain. Like a pilgrim, I sought solace. My retreat centers were bookstores and libraries. I digested the written word, hungry for clues that would provide the answers I so urgently needed. I longed to know how to end this pain. I longed to know how to feel whole again. I craved the information that would provide the key to unlock the oubliette wherein my soul was held captive.

A few authors that theorize on grief and loss, including Karen Martin, describe the need for re-establishing meaning and purpose in life following a grief experience. While meaning and purpose have for centuries been recognized and described as spiritual concerns, the grief theorists discussed these concepts as emotional rather than spiritual. None seemed to recognize the depth of sorrow. None appeared to comprehend the God questions, the real questions, those that plagued me night and day, those that required all my attention.

I turned to others who were suffering. My practice offered the opportunity to combine my experience with that of others. I listened for soul pain. I heard soul stories. In their struggles I heard my struggles; in their efforts, my efforts. They too longed for answers for which I myself was searching. But I was void of solutions. Our souls were chained and I could not supply the key.

Yet the knowing gathered from our collective journey challenged my view of the world, and my view of how the world worked. I grappled with my own notions of health and illness, of curing and healing. I felt apologetic that, even though I had practiced for many years in health settings, where I attended people experiencing extreme suffering, I knew little about suffering. And I knew nothing at all about healing.

Much of my thinking, and therefore the way I cared for myself and others, was primarily based upon formal learning. In my educational preparation, lip service had been given to the notion that human beings have physical, emotional and spiritual components, yet it was generally accepted that these entities were clearly separate. During my education emphasis had been placed on addressing physical needs first and the emotional needs second. Little mention was made of how to recognize or how to meet, spiritual concerns. Any information that was provided on addressing spiritual needs equated spirituality with religion, and religious practice with spiritual interventions.

The framework I had been educated in, and around which I structured my practice, was deeply rooted in scientism. The Curative Model which flowed from this approach had created a pervasive and convincing mindset which assured me that if enough germs were eradicated all of life's ills would cease. Efforts focused on eradicating disease and diseased parts with chemical drugs or surgical removal. Minimal attention was paid to the power of the mind. Few acknowledged the influence of spirit on physical health, wholeness and completeness.

Medicine's ability to hone in with the microscope allowed the reduction of human beings into smaller and smaller pieces. This reductionistic view centered on fixing or curing individual parts with little regard for the whole person. Technological advancement allowed for the replacement of body parts and the creation of specialties and specialists. When this approach did not provide the intended results, new specialists were added to the team so that a human being needing illness treatment could be sub-divided and examined under an even finer lens. Within the Curative Model, each specialty dictated what would be important to assess and, therefore, what interventions would be appropriate to implement.

I had attended the lectures. I had read the texts. I had photocopied the numerous journal articles, but I had not found a vocabulary to describe the effects of traumatic loss and subsequent soul grief. I had not located a model for prescribing curative or restorative action for my broken spirit.

In *Spiritual Dimensions of Nursing Practice*[2] Ruth Stoll defines spiritual needs as "any factor necessary to establish and/or maintain a person's dynamic personal relationship with God (as defined by that individual) and out of that relationship to experience forgiveness, love, hope, trust and meaning and purpose in life." A decade later, Hunglemann's[3] subjects reported that the human spirit longed for connection to others, to the world around them and to a Divine Presence. Both Stoll and Hungleman stated that spiritual distress can result from unfulfilled spiritual needs. While their findings were reported and described in the late seventies and early eighties, their efforts appeared to have had little, if any, effect upon practice. There continued to be no information describing how spiritual concerns manifest or how an individual attempting to survive beyond trauma and loss could reclaim his or her sense of spiritual wholeness.

Yet as I reviewed their work, their findings did apply to my feelings and experiences. I could, as well, see application in the lives of those who were sharing their pain-filled stories with me.

It was clear that in grief we struggle with an inability to trust God or the universal order. I lived with constant anxiety, fearing that more tragedy might befall me. I knew, as well, that my decreased ability to trust myself and others was interfering with choices and decisions which were subsequently hampering my relationships and career. While I often felt extremely alone and disconnected from others and from the world around me, for the most part I was too engaged in the mental and emotional work of trying to figure out what had gone wrong, and trying to discern the purpose for the rest of my life, to make any serious efforts to reach out to others.

I also knew, that I was overwhelmed by regret and a need for forgiveness from myself and my son, and that these feelings were eroding my self-image and self-esteem. I was definitely in need of applying exercises in self-love, yet the guilt and the feelings of futility and hopelessness were too overwhelming for me to convince myself that I was worthy of either self-love or love from anyone else.

I had been taken apart. I had been put together wrong. Important parts had been left out in the reassembling.

There were visible signs in myself, and in those I walked beside, of the relationship between suffering and emotional pain, between suffering and physical pain, and the escalation of chronic and autoimmune diseases. I was becoming increasingly aware that, when the deeper needs of soul are not addressed in ways that honor each person as a unique and marvelous spirit with numerous culturally different sacramental needs, there follows a dramatic increase in social problems such as drug abuse, alcoholism, family violence and vandalism.

In our brokenness we are ruptured from our spiritual connections. When we are unable to heal in ways that help us reconnect to the flow of Divine Energy within, as well as within the collective spirit of others and nature, we become like a volcanic mass – frantic in our need to explode from the confines of our darkness into light. The intense need to reconnect the Divine Spark within to the Divine Energy without can cause us to erupt in numerous unexplainable ways. In our confusion over being cut off, and in our inability to reconnect and feel a sense of belonging to the whole, we strike out. Anger and fears are projected in many directions. Muddled and desperate we attack ourselves, others and even the Earth Mother.

While Western Medicine's approach has clearly advanced the Scientific Model of research and practice, resulting in an ever-accelerating ability to diagnose and treat physical symptoms, it has been less than effective in its ability to relieve human suffering. The fixing of parts and the proclamation of cure, quite in isolation from any real and concrete attempt to provide integrated caring measures, augments the brokenness experienced by human beings. The separation of curing from the sacredness of healing contributes, in numerous and various ways, to the ripping apart that is occurring in our social fabric.

The curative approach has had a powerful and pervasive influence on humankind's own view of itself and its healing needs. The verb "to heal" comes from the Anglo Saxon word *haelan*, meaning "to make whole." The concept of wholeness denotes qualities of order, integrity and balance between and among the parts. It implies, as Plato reminded us, that no part can truly be well unless the whole is well and the whole cannot be truly well unless the parts are well. This means that while human beings are made of body, mind and spirit, and that we exist in social and environmental relationships, we cannot be separated into parts that can be fixed in isolation from the whole.

How could we have become so far removed from the roots of healing?

In many ways we have lost sight of our human wholeness. We have all but forgotten Plato's words. We no longer honor our own need for healing and integrity but join with those who concentrate on fixing parts, piece by piece. We have forgotten that, in our completeness, we are much more. We have forgotten that, even if all of our physical parts are replaced, our souls may be in a tremendous and desperate need of healing. We have forgotten that we can not find peace, feel free of guilt, anger or regret when our spirits are broken. And we have clearly lost sight of our innate need to reconnect to the light of the Divine Spirit lying in wait deep beneath the shroud of our fears.

I had found the Western medical system, in which I had for so long invested so much, inadequate as a system for healing. In continuing to apply the methods and practices of this model, I would be failing myself and desperately under-serving others. We needed more, deserved more. Awakening to the truth heralded the turning point. As my road diverged, "I took the one less traveled by and that has made all the difference."[4]

I searched for you in the oceans
*   and I found you in a stream.*
I lay awake waiting hours
*   and you came in my dream.*
I see you in the star dust
*   and I heard you in the wind.*
I have come to know that you are faithful
and you long to be my friend.
                    Brendalee Boisvert CSM

The Many Faces of God

Unable to silence the prodding from within, and unable to find answers in the scholars and the systems surrounding me, I had no choice but to travel unaccompanied. My chained soul needed to be unfettered. I needed to escape the oubliette. While cognitively willing to journey in hope of finding light, I feared the darkness of the unknown territory. I knew so little about my inner self.

Weakened and bleeding emotionally, dressed only in the tattered sackcloth of a physically exhausted body, I set forth. My quest was to find and drink from the Holy Grail. Parched, I longed to quench my thirst for inner peace.

The scholars of my profession had not provided aid. Perhaps those of my religion could. I reflected on biblical remembrances of those who had journeyed into the darkness and rebirthed into the light. I was reminded of Jonah[1] and his time in the belly of the whale, and of Lazarus and of Jesus[3] who, teachings tell us, were raised to life after their time in the tomb. I began to understand that the fable of Jonah, the miracle of

Lazarus and the resurrection of Jesus manifest the transformation which takes place when human beings reconnect to the fullness of the God presence.

I was encouraged by their examples. I knew the descent into the darkness of my own tomb was necessary to still the voice that screamed to know the answers. I had to discover the truth about why I had been thrown off course, why I had been left forgotten in the dungeon.

In desperation I called to the God I had once felt so close to. I angrily chastised His handling of things. The God I had known, owned and operated an orderly world. In this world view the just were rewarded and bad things did not happen to those who followed the laws of their religion. We were good people. We prayed together as a family; we regularly attended church; we gave freely of our talents and time in support of numerous religious and community activities.

But instead of reward we had received torment. All happiness had been taken from our lives. We existed in a huge gapping hole of black emptiness, an emptiness which was forever present and could not be filled.

We had received simplistic reassurance from friends and family, and cliché messages in sympathy cards, telling us our son and brother was needed by God for a special project in heaven. I witnessed broken families. I was acutely aware of children not wanted by either parent. I knew broken children, children neglected and abused. My wrath billowed. If God so desperately needed a child, why not remove one of these from their painful life circumstances? Why were we, and not some abusing parents, tormented in retribution? Surely our son, a child growing up surrounded by love, would offer the world more than would a child raised in these loveless conditions.

My angry criticism of the universal order engaged me in a continuous dialogue with a deity, but a deity that was unfamiliar to me and who seemed to change frequently and without a moments' notice. In bewilderment I tried to repair the idols that lay broken around me. But none would be mended.

While the God of my past seemed distant and unconcerned, each new expression became more eager to engage in my lament. No longer comfortable reciting the practiced rote prayers of childhood, I began to pour out the unrehearsed torment of my sorrow. While my daily indoor routine became one of silent commiserating with whatever deity happened to be interested, my outdoor times exploded into walks of wailing.

I had been raised in a strong Catholic home and educated in Catholic schools. For most of my life I had felt a loving and close personal relationship with Jesus. I had an image of Jesus as being the Son of God and my personal Savior. For the most part I had relied on him to act as an intermediary with his Father on my behalf. Even though the prayers, songs and scriptures with which I was familiar reminded me that God was also my Father, I had no real sense of any personal connection, nor did I have any particular image of a God other than of Jesus. My understanding of God was very similar to my understanding of Jesus, and my relationship with God was one and the same as my relationship with Jesus. In my bewilderment, I began to realize my understanding of Jesus was, for the most part, not a knowing based upon personal discovery, but a regurgitation of the ideas of others. The teachings I had received flowed from the numerous translations, of the first interpretations of his words and works, which have come to us adulterated, having been frequently altered to suit the religious and political overtones of many centuries.

The adjustment to the teachings of Jesus began early in the formative era of Christianity, with the destruction of ancient Christian gospels considered to be "heretical" (meaning not endorsed by clerical authorities). The Gnostic Gospels, discovered in 1945, include Christian works dated, by Helmut Koester, professor of New Testament at Harvard University, as written some twenty years before any of the New Testament Gospels. These writings, which included dialogues, conversations and visions attributed to Jesus and his followers, were banned as "blasphemy" as they invited each disciple to identify with Jesus himself.[4]

The Jesus of my understanding (the one whose image I had come to know through the eyes of others), the one who had always been so close and so present, had now abandoned me. How could the God-Jesus have left me when I needed him the most?

I received the poem "Footprints." I immediately gave it away. The poem was too true; the truth raked at my bleeding wounds. The unknown author of this poem had also felt abandoned by Jesus during his darkest moments. I was in too much distress to see the resolution discovered by the poet. For me the poem was a bleak reminder that I was now alone, and I was very afraid.

During this intensely lonely time, my mother sent a card which to this day remains on my fridge door. The words, narrating the card's picture of a tiny boat on a raging sea, were taken from the "Breton's Fisherman's Prayer". The words accurately described my life and my life's situation. "Oh God be good to me. The sea is so wide and my boat is so small." I was alone, adrift on the angry dark sea of life. I was out of control. I was drowning. In despair, I screamed, "Jesus where are you? Why won't you help me?"

And Jesus whispered, "Come and meet the Father." I reeled in amazement. I heard it again, and again, and again. "Come and meet the Father." "How do I do it?" I moaned. During the long days that followed the initial invitation, Jesus reminded over and over . . . "I never asked you to pray to me." And I recalled when Jesus was asked, "How do we pray?" he responded. "Pray like this . . ."[5]

I began a repeated recitation of the prayer which Jesus had asked that we pray. While the prayer was familiar "Our Father, Who art in heaven . . .," I stumbled over each phrase. Each word engaged me in conflict.

Jesus said "our". . . he had not said "my Father ". . . he had said "our."

What does "our" mean?

My religious upbringing had introduced numerous confusing ideas. There was so much religious lingo, which like fog was not only difficult to see thorough, but impeded my forward movement. It was unnerving to discover how many religious words I had used, hundreds of times, with little understanding of their meaning. Yet making sense of my grief meant trying to find answers to my despairing soul's agonizing questions. Finding answers meant trying to logically piece together the many conflicting and confusing thoughts that were muddling through my head, my heart and my soul, including thoughts about my relationship with the Divine.

Jesus was God. My religion had told me so. The doctrine had dictated a triune God. Three "Persons" in one God, God the Father . . . God the Son (Jesus) . . . God the Holy Spirit. I had stated this belief probably a billion times. Now I was not so sure.

The Old Testament referred to Yahweh as the wind. I had always loved the symbol. On my long walks, far into the country, I now felt the most in touch with a Divine Presence when I watched the breeze gently blowing through the grass. I recalled W. O. Mitchell's words in *Who Has Seen the Wind*,[6] and was struck with a new reverence for the wind. A familiar spiritual song would not leave my awareness:

Spirit of God in the clear running water,
Blowing to greatness the trees on the hill.

Spirit of God, creation is groaning.
Fill the earth. Bring it to birth, and blow where you will.
Blow, blow, blow, 'til I be . . .
Breath Of The Spirit . . . blowing in me.[7]

I pondered. Could the Spirit of God, be in the water, the trees and the hills? I had been taught that only humans were made in the image and likeness of God. Could the Breath of the Spirit be the Spirit of God, the Holy Spirit? Could it really be the breath sustaining life for all other things? Was the Breath, as in the Old Testament, God?

The Webster's Dictionary reported that breath meant "spirit." The wind blowing over the prairie grass seemed to be speaking, trying to give me a clue. I paid intense attention to the plant life, the clouds and the flying birds. Each had a life-giving and sustaining need for the wind, the breath. The evidence of the breath was everywhere. I pondered the song anew, "Blow, 'til I "be. Breath Of The Spirit . . . blowing in me.

Could this same breath, the wind that sustains life all around, be the same breath that was sustaining me? Could the Breath of the Spirit be within me? Could the Breath be the Energy of God? Could the Holy Spirit be the Breath, the Energy of God? Could this Breath, this Energy, be the Spirit of God, the Holy Spirit? Was the Holy Spirit really God's life-giving and sustaining force within me and within everything that has been created?

A dream offered an assuring glimpse that this new awareness was an important knowing. I witnessed massive padlocked iron doors, blocking the flames, and enormous energy pushing to explode forth from a gigantic glowing red-hot furnace.

A remnant memory of a grade-school poem, chanted as I attempted to interpret the message revealed, "God is at the anvil, welding golden bars. In the scarlet-streaming flame, He is fashioning a frame . . ."[8]

While the dream provided confidence that God was taking a hand in fashioning whatever I was to become, and while I felt relieved to discover fire in my furnace, I ruminated long hours over the source of the enormous energy that was trying so hard to break free.

I found the words of Jamie Sams.[9] "Sacred fire within, place of Eternal Flame. Burn away the barriers in Great Mystery's name." Could there actually be a sacred fire within me? Was the source of energy within, the energy of the Sacred? I had heard that we are a Spark of the Divine, but this was much bigger than a spark.

Were the barriers, the padlocks that were keeping the Divine Energy from bursting forth, my grief, my sorrow? Were these blocks keeping me from connecting fully to the source, keeping me from using my full potential? Was I only using that bit of my Divine Potential that was able to squeeze out, sneak out from around the barred doors?

I could hear the words of William James, "Compared to what we ought to be, we are only half awake. Our fires are damped, our drafts are checked."[10] I did not want to live with my dampers checked. I wanted to let this amassed energy burst forth. I wanted to use it. I wanted to use it to move my life forward. But I could also clearly hear the words of work I had once studied, the source of which I could not locate, "Many men build as cathedrals are built, the part nearest the ground finished, but the parts that soar towards the heaven – the turrets and the spires – forever incomplete."

I had built upon the ground. I had my share of success. But now all that had passed. All the energy and time I had invested into the ground-work seemed very unimportant. I felt a failure. I had much to give, much experience, much education, but I had no purpose. I was stuck and I did not know how to get unstuck.

In *The Illuminated Life*,[11] Abe Arkhoff concludes that few ever live to their potential; that few ever live the life they were meant to. I did not want to belong to that group. I wanted more. This massive energy was within me for a purpose. I needed to know that purpose. I needed to know my purpose. I knew, in discovering this, I would find the key to unlock those gigantic doors.

But now I was more aware than ever that I did not know what I was meant to become. I did not know how the rest of my life should unfold, nor did I know where to begin. And I was wornout from the search.

I had read that the soul loves tranquility. My exhausted body and restless soul longed for such a state. Perhaps the key was in meditation. I tried various forms and various teachers. The masters said the answers lie within. I loved the meditation and the breathing exercises that accom-panied them. I did not find the answers I sought. I found, instead, silence. I welcomed the silence, it was a reprieve. I had not known silence for a long, long time. The nagging, which for months had plagued my thoughts, became less and less intrusive and less and less demanding of my constant attention.

Ever so slowly, and ever so gently from within the place of silence, I came to know the peace of stillness. And in the stillness I heard the whis-per of God. I was being invited. There was no mistake. The voice was barely audible, but the message was clear. "Return to my meadow."

I accepted. I ran to the fields. The discovery was incredible. I ran. I walked. I loitered. I stayed. As the years went by, I delighted in the tender murmur that drifted on the breeze and floated with the raindrops. I was attentive to the whisper, and I heard it again and again and again, in the rustling of the willow branches, in the call of the coyote, and in the moan of the loon. I listened and I heard the song of God. I marveled at the faithfulness of the feathered creatures to their duty. Without fail, their melody reminded the sun when to awaken and when to set.

I lingered and was charmed by God's laughter in the water as it rippled and tickled the rocks along its path in the gully. I was encouraged and attempted to laugh in unison. I had not laughed in a very long time.

My sisters and their families visited. I was drawn to the genuine and hearty laughter they shared as they related the recent life events of their individual families. I had read Norman Cousin's[12] book in which he claims to have twice healed himself of cancer through the use of laughter. Yes, I smiled, although barely, but I could not remember when I had last laughed out loud. And I knew for certain it had been years since I had enjoyed a good out-loud belly laugh, the kind recommended for health and healing. If laughter was powerful enough to heal cancer, surely I could laugh away some of these smothering feelings.

Out in the prairie field, far away from the eyes and ears of anyone who might surmise that I was on the verge of insanity, I forced myself to laugh. I did it again and again and again, day after day after day, until, once again, laughter was able to find its way out of my body of its own accord.

I stayed late in the field and in the meadow. I cherished the opportunity to snatch whiffs of the scent of God. I relished the fragrance as it wafted across the blooms, drifting heavenward. I loved to capture the sweet aroma in the rose petals, and in the sage and the wild grasses that carpeted the prairie. I began to taste God, in the wild honeysuckle, in the sweetness of fresh strawberries, and in the salt of my tears. And I began to feel God in the warmth of the sun's rays, in the coolness of the night air.

I came to know the strength of God in the flash of the lightning, in the powerful voice of the thunder, and in the whirl of the north wind. I came to know the tenderness of God in the bluebells and in the baby lambs. And I began to feel the touch of God, in the caress of my daughters, my husband, and my mother.

I came to see, to hear, to smell, and to feel God in all of creation. I began to notice the magnificent color of God. It was visible everywhere.

God's hue radiated from the purples of the mountains, the cobalt blue in the ocean and from the greens in the forests. I saw the gold of God in the face of the sunflower that hung over my fence and in the orange of the poppy that poked through the stone ledge. Each time I was gifted by the sight of daisies in their fresh, white, crisp dresses, I was reminded of a poem a long-ago dying patient had written about her discovery of God's presence following tragedy:

> I climbed the steep and rugged road,
> grim obstacles to pass;
> When suddenly I spied some daisies,
> peeping thro' the grass.
> They smiled at me with faces snowy white
> and oh, so pure,
> Reminding me anew
> that all God's promises are sure.[13]

I pondered and I probed, and my world view shattered. Personhood could not be ascribed to the God I was coming to know and to love. The God of my now was too large, could not be contained, nor should be. A personified God was too small, too limiting. What need within me had desired a Divinity limited to a personified form? Why had I desired a God just like me, except with some superhuman powers that could conveniently be called forth when I needed assistance?

Why would the Divine Energy, which created and is manifested within all things, only have a human shape, and not the shape of all things? Certainly the "our" was meant for more than the human cry. Certainly the prayer we had been invited by Jesus to use in our discourse with God was meant for all of God's creatures.

*My heart has become capable of every form.
It is a pasture for gazelles and a convent for Christian monks,
and a temple for idols and the pilgrim's ka'ba and the book of the Koran.
I follow the religion of love:
Whatever way Love's camels take,
that is my religion and my faith.*

Ibn Arabi

The Forms of God

The word "psyche" refers to the human soul. It originates from the goddess Psyche, whose name is rooted in the symbols of both "the breath of life" and "butterfly." Psyche was a mortal woman, and while married to Eros, the god of love, was not permitted to see him. When Psyche ignored the order and gazed upon Eros he flew away, seemingly forever. To reunite with Eros, Psyche was required, by Aphrodite, goddess of love and Eros's mother, to complete a series of impossible tasks. Her determination was rewarded with unasked-for aid, and Psyche became a goddess and was reunited with Eros.[1]

The myth teaches us that, although love and soul belong together, and that the union of the two can transform human into divine, such union is only possible through growth and perseverance.

I could no longer contain my God in a personified form, yet I craved the close connection I had once felt with Jesus. But the more I craved, the more his image evaded me. Each attempt to contact my Savior plunged me further into soul debate with the religious tenets of my past. The basic belief upon which all others seemed to rest was that of a triune God, three Persons in one God. Since I could no longer accept the personified concept, and since I was now convinced the person of the Holy Spirit was not a person at all, but was really the Spirit, the Energy of God, the Life Force of the Creator, I began to wrestle with the notion of Jesus in this personified triune model.

Jesus was the Son of God. I knew that to be true. I clearly remembered that God had thus affirmed when Jesus was baptized, "This is my beloved son in whom I am well pleased."[2]

Jesus was the Son of God. Jesus was my brother (but not really). I was a daughter of God (but not really). I had directed the church choir. I had sung numerous songs proclaiming this relationship. I had given frequent lip service to the brother relationship with Jesus, and the daughter relationship with God, yet somehow these relationships seemed very covert. I could never remember any sacred practices which overtly reverenced that I was a sister of Jesus or a daughter of God. Why was that? How had I not recognized the lack of celebration of these relationships, and how could I have been blinded to the absence of the honoring of the sacredness of my femininity, or of any aspect of the feminine in the deity?

I tried to slow the digging. I dreaded to know what else I might unearth. But my thoughts would not heed the red flag. They raced onward.

If God was my Father, if I was a daughter of God, if Jesus was my brother, and if Jesus was God, how could I not have within me the potential to become a god as well? What offspring, what seed did not grow to be of the same form as the parent? A fig seed does not become a birch tree. An aster seed does not become a rose. A pregnant mare does not deliver a puppy.

The logic was mind-boggling . . . and made me very, very fearful. This sounded like blasphemy. What if someone should learn of my pondering? I feared that the theological police might blow the whistle and cry out "pagan heretic." Could I be hunted down and burned at the stake? It had happened in the past.

I had studied logic, and this was indeed the logical conclusion. But somehow things did not fit. Was a part of the assumption wrong?

Drawn to the biblical story of the transfiguration,[3] I mused over the words and the visual images of the scene. I had learned that each fable, each story, each parable in the New Testament, was meant not only for the people of that time, but for the people of all times. What lessons was

I to learn from the transfiguration?

Jesus had said that everything he was doing his followers could also do, and even greater things.[4] Was the transfiguration to show that we each can be transformed as Jesus was? Are we on earth in our physical form to manifest the glory that is God that is within us? Are we all part of God, each of us given the task to brighten the God Light within? As we each brighten our light, our God Light, the Fire Within, do we become more and more of the God Light? As we use the source of Divine Energy within, as our fire burns brighter, making our light more visible, do we move closer and closer to becoming one with the God Force that is within us, and fuller and fuller with the expression of the God Force that is a part of all that has been created? Are we the created, a part of the Creator, called to be sparks for igniting, for co-creating with the Creator? What spark does not have the potential to become a full-blown flame?

I had been taught that Jesus was both God and human. Could it be true that each of us is both God and human? Was Jesus an advanced expression of the co-creative expression each of us is called to be? God had said, "This is my beloved son, in whom I am well pleased."[5] Was the role of Jesus to show us this truth, to tell of our own ability to transform, transfigure? Was the mission of Jesus to provide an example for all of us, showing us how we each can move toward our own transfiguration, our own transformation, at which time we too would hear "This is my beloved son/daughter in whom I am well pleased"?

Jesus said he came to set us free.[6] Were his intentions to set us free from ignorance, and from the short-sighted views we hold of ourselves individually and collectively? Had Jesus come to lift us from our meager existence? Were his teachings calling us forth from beneath our blanket of fear, of hurt and disillusionment? Did not all the teachings of Jesus call us into the light?

In the Old Testament, Yahweh lured those he loved into the wilderness. "I will lead her into the desert and speak to her heart."[7] We are reminded that God's gentle whisper is easily obliterated when we are submerged in the noise of the world. Was the purpose of my dark nights, my purpose in the dungeon, to discover the truth of my own ability to transform, transfigure? Was the shattering of old views a key to unlock the padlocked doors that kept the fire of molten lava from flowing forth in a full glowing blaze?

Were my dark nights preparing fertile ground for my own enrichment? Was I remembering my own unique magic? In *Real Magic*[8] Wayne

Dyer emphasizes that magic is no more than a change in consciousness. Could my magic manifest itself? Could I find and use my gifts, my talents, my abilities? Could I break the chain across the furnace of my soul?

Was I a unique creation, yet a part of the Eternal Flame, on this earth to discover the Divine Flame within and to brighten and extend the Divine Flame throughout the earth?

But I had learned Jesus was the only begotten son of God. How could I even think I could identify with the Eternal Flame, the Breath of Life? This was certainly contrary to what I had been taught.

Oh Jesus I wailed! Where are you? What is truth? I do not want to believe heresy, to speak heresy.

I struggled. Do I share or do I avoid this truth?

I dreamt. Once again, I was a registered nurse working the midnight shift. I was attempting to complete morning care for a very large old man. Somehow I was unable to "clean him up." Even though I tugged and fussed, he seemed completely oblivious to my efforts as well as to his entire surroundings. I summoned help. My aide indicated there were now other tasks requiring attention and she was annoyed at me for continuing in my futile efforts. I glanced at the clock. It was seven in the morning. I had to leave. As I turned to do so, I noticed two nasal cannulas, both lying near the old man's face. I tried to reinsert one into his nostrils, but the lines were tangled, and the tangling had made them too short. In my attempt to free one of the lines, I discovered they had both become disconnected from the oxygen source. I was unable to complete the task. My report was due.

Jung emphasized that a non-interpreted dream is a letter from the gods that we have not bothered to read. Jung taught that during the dreamtime we tap the collective knowing, the place where ancient wisdom lives. The symbolism in the dream was too clear.[9]

In folklore and mythology, the archetype symbol of the old man is seen as authority, and often associated with old views, old attitudes. The authority holding on to the old attitudes was oblivious to what was going on around it and was nearing death.

Oxygen symbolizes breath, the breath of life, the source of life. According to Tom Chetwynd in *Dictionary of Symbols*,[10] breathing in dream or myth depicts the vital masculine spirit. The vital spirit of the heavy, weighted authority was dying. The authority had become disconnected from the source, from the Breath of Life. The lines leading from the source had become too tangled to untangle. Time was running out. There were other things to pay attention to now. The time was seven. In the *Dream Dictionary*, Boushahla and Reidl-Geubtner emphasize that "seven is the combination of three (heaven) plus four (earth) and is related to the dual nature of man, which is associated with spiritual development, awakening."[11] It was time for spiritual awakening.

I pondered Jung's words. "The necessity is imposed of perceiving the error in what was previously our conviction, of sensing the untruth in what was our truth, and of weighing the degree of opposition and even hostility in what we took to be love."[12]

How had the source of the Breath of Life become, over the centuries, confused by the authorities, mixed up, tangled in such a way that we had lost our connection to the source?

Have we focused so much on the messenger, Jesus, that we have not heard the message? Have we lost sight of the real source of the Breath of Life to which we must be connected?

In *If God Does Not Die*,[13] Bernard Martin shares that from his deep personal loss came the realization that it was necessary to kill the God of his conception or remain permanently with sterile thought. "This God that I had imagined must die. It is necessary to kill the God of my faith." I anguished in the truth that had unfolded. Had I created an idol in Jesus? Had I been worshiping an idol? Was it time and necessary to break the idol? Had Jesus purposefully remained out of touch so I could discover the real source of life?

But how had I come to believe this distortion of the truth in the messages given by Jesus? Had I developed a sheep's eye view of the shepherd, or had I been purposefully blinded from the truth of my own relationship to God, the relationship that connected me to all of creation and therefore to all of the power contained therein? Were the teachings of my upbringing, rooted in a philosophy of disempowerment, to keep me subservient by blinding me to my birthright?

"But Jesus, you promised when we seek we will find you, when we seek with all our heart."[14] "Jesus, all of my thoughts, all of these conclusions seem so unchristian. They challenge the Christian views you established?"

Jesus whispered. "I was never Christian."

My desire to reconnect with Jesus was propelling me further and further into territory that was less and less familiar. I feared the unexplored terrain. I wanted to feel the safety and comfort I had once felt when I walked and talked with the familiar Jesus. I longed for the parameters of our relationship to be the ones I had grown up with. The searching, the stretching, was threatening. The truths I was unveiling were isolating. Few wanted to discuss such possibilities. Few wanted to consider such ideas. Few wanted to challenge their firmly established world view. Few wanted to budge from the safety of the familiar.

I needed more support, more help, more direction. My religion had taught me that the "good book" would provide answers. I reviewed well-known texts.

Numerous times in the bible Jesus had called for guidance, for direction, for support from his Abba. I cried, as Jesus had. "Abba . . . father." The voice within me screeched. "What had Jesus meant when he used the word father?"

I attended a presentation by a biblical scholar. His translation into English of the words spoken by Jesus awed me. The information filled my deep need to understand the discourse of Jesus. "A more exact translation for the word 'father' as used in the context spoken by Jesus would be, 'O breather of life'." I recognized the truth in the scholar's words.

It was spring. New life was birthing in response to the nurturing warmth of the creative breath that enveloped the countryside. Signs of new beginnings were everywhere.

My child had been in the springtime of his life. He would never know the full bloom of summer love. He would never hold a woman in his arms; he would never father a child. I would never see his gifts, his talents, his abilities in their summer or autumn seasons. I would never know his fullblown potential. I hungered for the years of mothering and of grandmothering I had been denied. Each sign of new life, reminding me of the son I had given birth to but could no longer nurture, ripped at the feminine aspects of my being. A breast biopsy revealed the hurt within my body. Festering was apparent in this organ for sustaining new life.

I longed to share these sorrows. I begged for a confident. I needed to converse about these matters. I cried for a deity that could comprehend.

My son had died. He was still so young. I was his mother. A mother is supposed to nurture and comfort, and keep her child safe and warm. I did not know where my son had gone. Was he safe? Who was caring for him? What did he have to face all alone? What was it like where he was? What dangers lurked for him? I needed an ally. I needed someone on the other side, someone who could understand such matters – someone who could parent. I needed someone to provide the caring, the hugging. I needed someone to read him stories at night and listen to his corny jokes. I needed someone to know he preferred oatmeal for breakfast. I needed someone to know he liked to sit on the stair, in the warmth of the heat duct, as he dressed on winter mornings. I needed someone to know how much he liked to hunt and fish and catch minnows. I needed someone on the other side to know he played hockey, and that he was a good hockey player. I needed someone to know he had just won his first golfing trophy. Someone needed to understand he really did not care much for school, that he found it took too much precious time away from discovering the wonders to be found in the natural world. I needed someone who could see his bright, just developing, beautiful spark. I desperately needed someone to provide him mothering, at least until he was a bit older, a bit safer, at least until I could be there to take over.

My longing drew me to the only remnant of a feminine deity I knew. After all, I reasoned, she would understand. Her own son had been taken in a cruel way at a young age. She must know my feelings. I begged Mother Mary to nurture my son, to care for him, to be his protectoress. She consented and, out of my gratitude, an immense bond developed. But this deep relationship with Mother Mary forced me into an even more ferocious struggle with my world view. How could I have ever voiced a belief in only the male aspects of God? Could the God of my now have only a masculine gender, even have a gender?

I searched for evidence in the splendor surrounding me. The natural order in all of creation is a process of birthing and rebirthing, a process of mothering, of nurturing. There was clearly evidence that this order flowed more from the energy of a feminine deity than of a male deity.

I realized that, within myself as well, there was a developing and ever-expanding blend of both the masculine and feminine. I had many characteristics traditionally associated with being a woman. I had been creative. I had loved to sing, to dance, to garden, to decorate. I was a nurturer, to my family and to the many patients I had cared for. But I also possessed many talents much more associated with the masculine. Though I felt less than capable now, I had once been a strong leader. I had received promotions in my profession because of these skills and my abilities as a clear thinker and problem solver.

I observed the lives of others. Many of those I was now seeing professionally were older. My gerontological studies proposed that in successful aging there is a coming together of the masculine and feminine characteristics. The theories suggest that in later adulthood a major developmental task facing the male is to develop more of his latent nurturing aspects, and for the female, to develop more of her masculine potential in order to bring a sense of wholeness and completion to life.

Listening to older adults as they shared their struggles, I heard this theme again and again. The evidence substantiated the theory. In their stories these older people identified a longing to expand their undeveloped or underdeveloped aspects.

Their accounts reminded me of my father. In later life he participated in tasks which, in younger years, would have been, not only uncharacteristic, but would likely have been self-tabooed because of the image he held of himself as provider and protector. My children still joke about how, in contrast to when their grandmother gardened and they would delight in helping themselves to her produce, when grandpa took ownership of the raspberry patch he strictly barred young feet, scolding that they would trample the canes. He took immense pride in this new-found joy, and loved to see the full product of his newly discovered ability. As my father's physical strength declined, the necessary role reversal allowed my mother to more fully demonstrate her abilities as manageress and protectoress of their living, and of my father's dying.

Reviewing life, determining if the gods are pleased with the life that has been led, and the talents that have been developed, is not only a process of aging, but takes place, regardless of age, as preparation for imminent death. It is a process of determining and completing unfinished business to the best of one's ability, and within the time left, so a satisfactory closure may be brought to life.

As I listened professionally, I identified personally. I witnessed in their brokenness, my brokenness. In their healing efforts, I found lessons for my own life. I too was reviewing life. Where had I gone wrong? What had angered the gods? How could the gods be appeased?

"Every valley shall be filled in, every mountain and hill shall be made low."[15] What within me needed to be filled? What was it that needed to be made low? What needed attention? What masculine, what feminine characteristics required nurturing in order that in wholeness I might more fully develop and manifest my unique talents and abilities?

While I was not facing physical death, much of the old me had already died, and much was in preparation for burial. This was my opportunity to pay attention to the neglected areas of my life, to catch up, as it were, with what was really important. This turning point, this time after which life would never again be the same, was affording me a chance to make the changes while there was still time to do so.

It was clear, the life review process I was privileged to witness in the older adults, dying younger persons, and in myself, while stimulated by a need to come to terms with our mortality, affords opportunity for soul growth. The soul's need for wholeness, for completion, demands full attention to the development of the underdeveloped masculine and feminine aspects of our personhood.

While cognitively accepting the challenges to my life proposed by the life review, my inner voice staggered beneath the weight of the obvious inconsistency between the new information and my previous understanding. Why would a deity possessing only masculine characteristics plant a deep need within human beings to develop more fully both the masculine and feminine aspects of their humanness in order to enter the afterlife? Why would a God possessing only maleness want his human creatures to more fully develop both their masculine and feminine characteristics?

New and deeper fissures were appearing in my already fractured belief system. My grief need to have my son nurtured by someone on the other side who could understand mothering, had led me to discover and bond with the feminine aspects of God. But now my image of the Father-God lay in ruins. I could no longer relate to a God portrayed as Father-Son, and the God of Abraham, Isaac and Jacob. I longed for a God of Naomi, Sarah, Ruth, Rebekah and Rachel.

While lip service was increasing with the goal of raising awareness that, implicit to my faith is a belief that God possesses characteristics of both genders, the obvious signs that the maleness of God is intrinsic to Christianity were visible everywhere. I could find in my faith tradition only a masculine metaphor for the Divine, and in the language of worship, a lack of pronouns for communicating any feminine aspects of God.

I felt violated as a woman as I recognized the diminished roles of women in the ritual of my faith practices, and in the lack of women in authority positions within the religious hierarchy. I felt shame for my years of blindness to such practice, knowing that gender power imbalance is at the root of violence against women, and those in positions of powerlessness. I had studied power and its uses and misuses. I had worked with many who were victimized by the misuse of coercive power. I had recognized in suffering the decreased sense of personal strength and worth, and I had recognized that the more traumatized and more victimized a woman is, the easier it is for a perpetrator to re-victimize.

I had witnessed the insatiable appetite of coercive power, the desire to control another, to leach out the power of another to feed the deep pit of insecurity. I had seen this desire to gain more "self" through the disempowerment of others in political situations, in work situations, in professional helping situations, in family situations, and in situations of power misuse by those deemed to be representative of God.

These covert and overt messages convey to women that they are less worthy in the eyes of their church than their male counterparts. These messages, coupled with an ever-increasing recognition of the flagrant misuse of power by clergy over women and children, and most frequently against those who have already experienced significant trauma, have created a mushrooming awareness of the inconsistency between the behaviors, values and attitudes of the leaders and those who represent the leaders. Nowhere in the gospels are we given an image of Jesus as one who shows superiority over another. Nowhere in the sacred text do we witness the usurping of the power of another by Jesus, or of his re-victimization of those who are vulnerable.

We see, instead, how Jesus showed compassion for the women less accepted by the social standards of the times.[16] Jesus did not re-victimize. He did not rob the women of the little power they had. He empowered them. He rekindled their flame, filling them with the power of unconditional love.

I felt outrage at the discovery within the texts, foundational to my religion, of linguistic bias not found in the original texts. It was shocking to find that church patriarchs had given sexist interpretations to texts and events that could have been described in non-sexist ways, and that they include numerous descriptions of woman as subordinate to men, and as the embodiment of evil and temptation.

In her study of women's roles in religion, Nimira Lalani[17] found many interpretations in text considered to be sacred, which cast women as less important, including the notion that woman was created last to show dominance by man. She stressed that these situations could all be interpreted differently, especially since the order of creation indicates progression, not regression. She further emphasized that since God caused man to fall asleep before the creation of woman, man was neither a spectator nor a participant, and neither was he a consultant during her creation!

I longed for celebrations of the sacredness of woman, and an honoring of woman's creative, life-giving and nurturing potential. I hungered for ritual that marked the important changes in my life as a woman and mother. I thirsted for opportunity for reflection on my changing and growing relationship with the Divine. I needed a religion that would bring a new sense of celebration to my life and to my experiences with the nurturing and supporting powers of the feminine deity growing within me.

I investigated other faiths and faith traditions. Did other women feel as I felt? Did other religions include, segregate, or negate women and their worship needs?

Through my research and travel to countries where the Islamic and Hindu religions are practiced, I concluded that in these traditions, as well, women are excluded from authority roles in the practice of their faith. Nimira Lalani indicted that, to feed their spiritual hunger, Hindu women build female solidarity and find alternate sources of religious power by participating in life-cycle rituals which focus on the health and prosperity of their families.

Lalani also noted that, even in Buddhism, while considered around the world to be more egalitarian, since Buddha emphasized in enlightenment a complete oneness of the masculine and feminine aspects of personhood, there remains a cultural gender bias. This bias still prevents women from the overt acceptance of equal participation in religious community life.

How had this disempowerment of women in their religious communities happen? I examined religions of the past and unearthed deep sexist roots to religious practice. Most striking was the discovery that most cultures had once been Matriarchal. The power which women have because of their close ties to nature (through her co-creative abilities) has been traditionally feared. This fear of women's power, especially during her moon time (menstrual cycle), became over the centuries the catalyst for introducing traditions which steadily, but surely, stripped women of power.

One such power-stripping strategy was to equate, in the minds of men and of women alike, the notion that women and women's sexuality is not sacred, holy and powerful, but is sinful and dirty.

I recall, as a young adult, attending a baptism. The words, "this child conceived in sin," still resound.

I reeled in disbelief. Were sexuality and birthing and mothering not sacred in the eyes of my church? A woman was capable of conceiving and birthing a God – God who is love,. Yet the love union of a couple was sinful? Was this another message of woman as temptress, as the embodiment of evil? What guided the thinking that shrouded, in evil, the sacredness of sexuality and the co-creating of life from the love of a man and woman?

I needed a religion that did more than tolerate women. I needed a religion that did not turn away from women in pain. I needed a religion that honored and venerated the feminine and the goddess aspects of the deity and of myself. Like Patricia Lynn Reilly, in *A God Who Looks Like Me*,[18] I could no longer accept a shame-based religion shaped by men, for men and based on men's experience. I needed to feel connected. I needed to feel grounded. I needed to restore my foundation.

Long before religions became male-dominated, women connected with the Goddess within themselves, within nature and within All. I searched for the Goddess and found in the ancient religions a Goddess image, representative of female power, as beneficent and independent. I discovered that, since early times, women have connected with the Goddess for spiritual fulfillment and solidarity with other women. Today, within the sanctuary of the Earth Religions, any woman, at any stage of life, can find herself reflected in the Goddess depicted as maiden, mother, or wise older woman.

Long before power and religion became partners, people had found the sacred. The Earth Religions have maintained connection to the Sacred. During my dark nights I had captured a glimpse of the sacred, that glimpse had shone light on the profane.

I was reminded of my many experiences with the Kahuna Healer in Hawaii, and my visits to the Sacred Heritage sites. I recalled the Moon Lodge and the honoring by the entire tribe of each woman's need for nurturing and for reconnection to the Earth Mother and the Sacred Sisterhood during her monthly barren time, in order that balance and rhythm might be maintained in her life.

I longed for balance and rhythm. I longed to reconnect to the sacred cycle in my life. I needed once more to feel my heart beat in synchrony with the heartbeat of the Earth Mother. I needed to belong to the whole. The growing sacred within needed a voice, needed expression.

The masculine God in the religion of my childhood had become too staid, but yet I could not relate solely to a Goddess image. My sense of wholeness, my need for completion demanded more. I needed a relationship with a Divine Presence that could help me recognize and expand both the masculine and feminine aspects of my being.

I had witnessed the Creator in the wind. I had tasted and smelled and touched the Creative Spirit. I longed for a religion that understood this form of God Energy, and could help me celebrate the ever-increasing expression of the Divine Growth within me, and within All.

Heaven is above all yet; there sits a judge
That no king can corrupt.
     William Shakespeare – *Henry VIII*

Heaven

My son had died in autumn. Once again it was autumn. Watching the gathering of the fruits of nature reminded me of a biblical passage quoted in a song that somewhere in my past I had loved and frequently sang. "Unless a grain of wheat falls to the earth and dies, it remains just a grain of wheat. But if it dies, it produces much fruit."[1]

The song's message is that death is necessary for rebirth and growth. My path to the prairie field was becoming etched. I was daily gifted by the splendor and the lessons gained from the natural world. The field, the meadow and the lake shared numerous tales of the continuing process of life. The perennial rebirth whispered that life goes on despite visible signs of death. Seeds of evidence shared the time-honored truth that loss and rebirth are an inevitable part of living. They are not separate entities, but come in Gemini, the twin form. I was reminded that loss is as natural as the shifting of the tides. I noted that a beautiful sunset must sink into the ocean in order for the night to be born, making the sunrise of the next morn possible. The sunflowers, which I came to so appreciate as they turned their faces in full radiance toward the summer sun, also revealed they must gradually drop their seeds and die in order that in the following spring new life might burst forth in the same splendor I was now witnessing.

Yet, while the lessons gained observing the natural order reinforced hope in the process of rebirth, and offered some assurance that, somehow, somewhere, life continued even beyond death, I was still acutely sensitive to the fact that loss had other meanings. In comparison to the traumatic and sudden death of my son, and the significant losses I witnessed others experience, these reminders were barely perceptible.

I had developed strong bonds of affection with my child. The severing of these, and the attempts to heal the wounds, had left me deprived, stripped, robbed, divested, denuded. I felt apart from everything and everyone, even from life itself. I was wanting, lacking, consumed. The precious priceless treasure of my child, our relationship, and all the promise of any future moments together was gone. There was no way of getting it back.

My entire sense of self had been destroyed. My self-esteem, self-respect, pride and dignity had dwindled. I no longer knew what I represented, what I stood for, or what I believed in. I could not assume to advance using my abilities since I no longer knew what they were. I was filled with self-doubt and plagued by dread and anxiety. I had lost my sense of security. I vacillated in my ability to trust myself, others and the universal order.

While the signs around me, most especially those of autumn, supported the notion of rebirth and new growth following dying, the season itself and all the painful anniversary memories it conjured caused me to struggle, more than ever, with the questions surrounding the "why" in relation to my son. I could see that, as the wheat in the song, the experience had caused me to "fall," to be laid barren. I had seen myself, the views I held of myself and what I believed in, die. I could even see beginning signs of new birth and growth within me, but I could not accept that my son had fallen. My son was in the springtime, not the autumn, of his life. He had not been given the time to show the world his ripened potential. Why had he been taken? How could the loss of life at such an early age be a growth experience? Where was his life being fulfilled, being rebirthed? In what field was he bearing much food? I had once had a simplistic acceptance of life after death and of heaven. Now I was plagued with numerous challenges to this unquestioned endorsement. "Is there a heaven? Where is heaven? Is he in heaven?" "What is heaven like" "What is he doing there?"

Trying to be helpful, people offered cards and prayers. "May the souls of the faithful departed rest in peace." I wanted to scream, and often did. I could not bear to think that my son would be resting for all of eternity. He had loved life. He had so much to accomplish, to see, to discover. He was creative and active. My tormented soul needed answers to heaven and the activities that went on there.

In anguish, I lamented. "O birther of life who art in heaven." "Heaven!" "What is heaven?" "I need to know about heaven."

I discovered in *A Guide to Walking Meditation*,[2] that Thick Nhat Hanh believed the world we live in right here, right now, contains all the wonders we can expect to find in heaven. I was awed by his discussion. But most especially, I was grateful for the satisfying visual images he created as he shared his beliefs about honoring the sacredness of this earth-heaven. He emphasized that because of the sacredness of the Earth, when we stroll upon it, we should do so with the dignity of The Buddha, of Jesus.

I was aware of the power of walking. I knew that besides strengthening stamina and physical strength, walking helped to improve self-esteem and decrease depressive feelings. I knew that walking allowed sorrow to fall away, making room for peace to enter. And I had discovered that my worn path into the field had led me to know the Sacred in all of creation. Thick Nhat Hanh shared the importance of paying attention, of being fully present to the beauty of the sights, sounds and smells surrounding us. In doing so, we begin to see the infinite potential in each.

Once again I turned to nature, this time to the ocean's shore. The waves gladly moved toward me, pulling from me all that was hurting. In gratitude I watched the tides drift outward, carrying my fears and hurts, anger and regrets to the "nursery of creation," there to be revitalized and rebirthed. I reflected as Thich Nhat Hanh prescribed and found that there is possibility for Oneness with all of creation and with all of the possibilities of creation.

I found the ocean, like the meadow, mystical and holy. Both hold secrets for those in retreat from the torments of their usual circumstances. Both are full of sun, full of abundant possibilities, and both blend into the sky in a way that often makes it difficult to distinguish where one begins and the other ends. Both give a different perspective to life and to reality. Both provide a view greater, grander, than we are accustomed to, a landscape bound only by the limits of our senses. Far from shore or far from habitation we gain a different perspective of our own importance. Amidst the vastness we shrink and the might of creation envelopes. Wrapped in the sacredness of our surrounding, while alone we feel less alone – while apart we feel more apart. We notice more clearly our relationship to the whole. We acknowledge the importance of each blade of grass, each coral. We honor their existence, knowing their necessity in the magnificent chain of life, their importance in holding order in the universe.

Breathless I beheld the splendor, the immenseness. I felt the wind and filled with the breath that gives abundant life. I paused. I wondered. A verse from Ecclesiastics reverberated: "What now is has already been; what is to be already is."[3] I wondered if this place is what has been, what is, and what is yet to come. Was it here, right here, that I had found what I had come for?

I had come craving the possibility that somehow, somewhere, my son continued to exist. I had come searching for the truths about heaven. The ideas I was incubating and the conclusions I was drawing were dramatically altering my perception of the world and my place within it. The world I was coming to know was vastly different from my world of yesterday. The world surrounding me had become more immense, grander, more unknown, and yet more Sacred.

My view of the world had changed, and in the changing of the view I had been changed. What was once so important was now of little importance. What used to be of little importance was now paramount.

The loss, the turbulence of the struggle, and the reality I now knew existed had altered my perception. I knew I was not the same, nor ever again could be, for I had seen in the meadow and in the ocean, and in the changing of the seasons, and in the recycling of the moon phases, an order I could not ignore. Loss followed by rebirth was all around and in all life forms, even in the continual process of the rhythmic pattern of my life. I had lost many yesterdays and gained many todays. I had lived through many changes. I had adjusted to starting over many times. I knew that change involved letting go of what was and replacing it with what is.

I resisted. I feared the unknown territory in the land of the new beginnings. I longed to return to the safe and simplistic yesterdays. I grieved for what used to be. I grieved for what had changed, for what had been lost. I grieved for what I would have to leave behind if I allowed myself to move further.

As usual, my heart and head would not work together. My heart struggled in accepting what my head was comprehending.

I wanted to heal. I wanted to feel whole again. Yet healing seemed to be as painful as the hurting had been. I knew I could no longer live with the old views, ideas, attitudes, yet if I moved forward would I be leaving my son behind, and dishonoring the preciousness of his life and our lives together?

The discoveries in nature had proven a definite key for unlocking the formidable doors confining my soul's energy. But did I really want to open those massive portals? I was familiar with the icy waters of grief, and knew how to navigate its angry current. I feared the movement into the unknown and the treacherous river of healing. Would I drown in the flood of my own painful emotions?

Noah had moved through the greatest flood of all time. It was only after the flood that he had been gifted with the rainbow. Each time the rain rewarded me with a rainbow I was reminded of Noah's experience.[4] I deliberated over the mixture of rain and sunshine needed to make the arch of color. I pondered this mixture in my own life.

I was drawn to the vibrancy of the rainbow. I had read that people use color for healing purposes. I wanted to know more about that. I studied color and the psychological and spiritual associations of color. I was fascinated to discover that each color has its own frequency, that the frequency of each color holds the same frequency as a musical note, and that both music and color frequencies can be used in healing – used to increase our own energy frequency. I learned that particular colors call to us when we are in need of them in our life. I found this fascinating. I was wearing a lot of purple, a color which I had never before preferred. Now I recognized the significance. Purple represents the spiritual realm. I was struggling with numerous spiritual questions. I was in great need of the energy from this color. I was grateful for purple. I needed its energy. I needed purple to support me in my search for truth.

Prior to the death of my son, music had been a vital part of my life. I sang continuously both for personal pleasure and for the enjoyment of others. Arranging time for all that was involved in teaching children music had been a part of my routine. My son had played the saxophone, both daughters played the piano. I realized there had not been music in our home for a long time. I no longer sang, and I was unsure of the last time the piano had been opened. I could not remember when the lessons had ceased. I sat at the piano. The music would not flow. I tried to sing.

The words were flat, meaningless, expressionless. My soul could not so easily be fooled. I lacked the soul energy to create.

If I could not produce the effects I needed for myself, I would use the works of others. I had studied that loud, harsh sounds may increase anxiety and fear, but that sounds of wind, ocean waves and peaceful classical music can pull our energy frequencies into synchrony with these more calming vibrations. I added chimes and a windsock. I introduced musical sounds as barely audible background in my home, office and vehicle. I filled decorative bottles with colored water and set them in an east window. Here the sun reflected the color to me as I worked. I added purples, and green and blue, the important colors for healing and for balance, into my home and into my wardrobe.

The anxiety and pervasive dread that had become my constant companions decreased. Convinced that more positive mental health was, at least in part, a result of introducing healing and balancing sound and color into my life, I incorporated the research on these nontraditional methods into teaching and practice. I encouraged those who were themselves feeling restless and anxious, as well as those who provided care for older and dying persons, to try these interventions and determine if the addition would decrease restlessness and increase peacefulness in these circumstances. The positive responses were remarkable.

After seeing the improvement in sleeping patterns, and the decrease in night wandering, attributed to the nighttime playing of taped ocean waves, and seeing the positive effects of introducing healing and balancing colors in even small amounts, one eager long-term care staff chose to dramatically increase the amount of blue in the environment of older agitated residents. Not only did they begin to use this color in linen choices and for decorating, they used it in various ways at mealtime, including using dinnerware etched with blue and putting the drinking water into blue jugs. They were convinced that this change in color helped to decrease restlessness at mealtimes as well as throughout the entire day.

As I studied color, I discovered that by increasing beauty in our lives, not only through the use of color and music, but in numerous ways, such as by adding flowers and fragrance, we can stimulate endorphins, the body's own morphine-like substance. By stimulating endorphins we can lift depressive feelings and improve moods. It became important to linger and smell the wild flowers along my path.

When my children were little, spring always arrived in my kitchen with a bouquet of dandelions. How many days had passed since I had received those treasured momentoes of love? When did those little hands stop offering me golden lion faces?

My daughters were no longer children. When had they grown? I had been away for a long time. It was time to return, time to awaken. It was time to place some flowers on my windowsill.

My aunt sent me a tape. The songs had been written, arranged, played and sung, by one of the sisters in her religious community.

I Am in the rainbow and I am in the rain.
I Am in your broken dreams and I am in your pain.
I Am in your sorrow and I come to show the way.
I Am in and part of everything and I'm in you to stay."[5]

I recalled again the rainbow and began to breathe in the colors. I invited red, orange, yellow, green, blue, indigo and violet to enter. I gave each color permission to permeate my being, to fill each cell and replace the darkness of sorrow lodged there. I needed the healing energy of each color. I asked each cell to be open to receiving the color, and to resonate with the peaceful frequency of each color's vibration.

I inhaled the vibrant colors that surrounded me. I invited the blue of the sky and the green of the forests and grasses to balance and heal my emotional pain. I asked the reds and oranges to connect me to the earth and heal my physical pain. I inhaled yellow for courage, and asked the majestic purples of the mountains to heal my wounded soul.

Breathing in the rainbow, I discovered that I too was a rainbow, that areas of my body picked up the various colors in the universe and, in turn, reflected them back. I could feel my body flood with color and surround me with color. I could see colors move through me and from me, blending with the colors that surrounded me.

Finding the color meditations healing, I began a regular morning color ritual. At the top of a distant hill, arms outstretched to the universe, I begged the Spirit Energy of the Creator to fill me with gold light. Gold is the color most frequently associated with the Divine. As the light flowed, I discovered within me energy centers, each center filling with a vibrant color of its own, yet blending into the next and extending beyond me. As the gold light entered my crown it turned immediately to a vibrant violet, filling my entire head, yet blending into indigo as it moved from my forehead down into the throat. Here the light became cobalt blue, only to meld into vibrant green as it saturated my heart center. Green became yellow at the solar plexus, and on into orange just above my pubic bone. Orange fused with the brilliant red that flooded my legs and penetrated the earth.

Grateful for the energy, I asked to be filled with the gifts of the Spirit so I might use them to move myself from the confines of my hurt, for my own good and the good of All. I found that the gifts of the Spirit were within my body. I discovered wisdom in the violet of my crown center, understanding in the indigo of the third eye at the front of my forehead, and knowledge in the blueness of my throat. I found compassion in the green of my heart center, courage in the yellow of my solar plexus. I discovered creativity to be used with humility in the orange center of reproduction. I stood in awe and love of the Creator, and all of creation, as I grounded to the universe in the redness of my root chakra.

The universe was in me and I was in the universe. God was in me and I was in God. I was a hologram. I was fascinated to learn that others believed similarly and began to find evidence to support Bohm's[6] conviction of the entire universe being structured like a hologram.

In the *Holographic Universe*[7] Michael Talbot quotes Karl Pribram from an interview in *Psychology Today*. Karl commented, "It isn't that the world of appearances is wrong; it isn't that there aren't objects out there, at one level of reality. It is that if you penetrate through and look at the universe with a holographic system, you arrive at a different view, a different reality. And that other realities can explain things that have hitherto remained inexplicable scientifically: paranormal phenomena, synchronicities, and the apparently meaningful coincidence of events." My world was not the world I had belonged to. The world was Sacred and I was not separate from it but connected to All.

If I was a part of the whole, my unhealed self was interfering with the healing of the entire universe. I had a responsibility to heal. I searched for healing methods. I studied energy-transfer healing techniques, first for self-healing, and then to be able to assist others.

I studied reflexology. I practiced being able to touch each organ in the body by massaging only the soles of the feet or the palms of the hands. I studied iridology. I spent time with a physician newly arrived from China. He used a voltage meter to test the energy in the ear. As he touched with a fine probe, a particular acupressure point on the ear, the gauge on the monitor registered the voltage. When the voltage fell below the normal range, indicating a decreased energy flow, he would refer to a chart of a huge ear. The picture of the ear had transposed upon it a diagram of the entire body. The physician accurately diagnosed the affected organ based on the decreased energy flow to the organ as indicated by the meter and corresponding chart.

These practices are based on a belief that everything in the universe is a replication of the whole, and that the whole is contained within any of the parts. If you treat any of the parts you treat the whole. The eye, the foot, the hand and the ear – each are used in treatment, based upon knowledge of the hologram. All of the treatments are based upon an understanding that energy flows along energy lines, known as meridians. The Universe, the Earth and the human body are all sustained by energy which flows along meridians.

I discovered that I too was one with the energy of All, and connected to all other energy fields in the entire universe. If I was one with the universe, was the universe, and perhaps even heaven, in me?

I was fascinated by Albert Einstein's theory[8] that energy can not be created nor destroyed, only changed. I needed to know more about energy. I needed to discover for myself whether the energy of life, so profoundly viable in a young life, and then so obviously invisible in death, could indeed be changed. Could life indeed go on after death? Could the vibrant energy that was my son be transformed?

Over the years I listened to dying patients describe visitations they had received from family members who had predeceased them. These experiences were usually diagnosed as hallucinations, but my inner knowing had always challenged such a simplistic "easy out", within-the-comfort-zone explanation.

My willingness to "hear" stories of the paranormal brought into my professional and personal life people eager for the relief which comes from being believed. Following resuscitation, a young man confided he had felt his spirit leaving his physical body and was saddened when "he" was shocked into returning. A friend told of seeing a light move from her father's body at the time of his death. Students and colleagues shared their observations of "evidence" of the spirit departing when a patient died.

Movement into exploring this terrain, led me to the research on near-death experiences conducted by Elizabeth Kubler Ross,[9] Raymond Moody,[10] Melvin Morse[11] and Kenneth Ring.[12, 13] Documentation of the descriptions of the "death experience" of individuals brought back to life after long periods of clinical death (medically confirmed absence of all vital signs) have shown considerable consistency. Their findings speak convincingly in favor of a spiritual existence after physical death.

In *Life At Death – A Scientific Investigation of the Near Death Experience*, and *Heading For Omega*, Kenneth Ring describes a particular pattern to the near-death experience. The person senses a separation from the physical body and becomes aware of a feeling of tremendous peace and well-being. The person begins to sense that his or her consciousness – the real self – is now above the physical body, and is able to see it objectively, almost as a spectator. The real self begins to move through a dark tunnel, propelling rapidly toward a bright and beautiful white or golden light. The light beckons and is extremely comforting as it pulsates and suffuses the person with love. The individual is given a panoramic life review which contains virtually every experience. He or she sees life objectively – as it really was – and sees the effects of his or her actions upon others. The measurement of a life well lived was made according to how well he or she had loved.

The person might also meet a relative or a religious being of some sort, and be asked to make a decision whether to go further into the experience or go back to physical life. The choice often seems to be up to the individual. In some cases the person is told by one of the beings present that he or she must return, that it is not yet time.

These researchers emphasize that while near-death experiences have been studied primarily in the West, they are by no means limited to Western people. People of all cultures have reported similarly.

As I sifted the literature, I discovered that the perceptions described by those who have near-death experiences cannot be explained by normal means and suggest that profound paranormal events take place during near-death experiences. People often return from such an experience with information they had no possible way of obtaining. Some have reported seeing deceased relatives whom they had no idea had died; others report meeting relatives, such as a baby sister, that they had never been aware of.

The numerous reports, and the consistency of the reports, suggest that something very real happens. In the opinions of Doctors Kubler-Ross and Kenneth Ring, people who survive clinical death afterwards possess the total inner knowing that death does not exist in the way they had imagined it to exist. The message they convey is that we have nothing to fear in dying, that dying is peaceful, beautiful and a transcendent glorious experience.

Dr. Melvin Morse has presented hundreds of cases of children who have had-near death experiences. All of the children speak of heading for a light that seems to be "all-knowing, all-forgiving and all-loving."

As a mother I needed this assurance. I longed to know that what my son had to experience as he left his physical body had not been terrifying, that he had not been alone in the process and, most importantly, that he was in a place of love.

Dr. Morse reports that following resuscitation children frequently describe how everything in the world fits together in a glowing light. In interviewing these children later in life, he discovered that they rarely touched drugs or alcohol for they understood these substances somehow dimmed, rather than led closer to, the light. He, as well as Doctors Elizabeth Kubler Ross, Kenneth Ring and Raymond Moody conveyed their deep conviction in some form of consciousness existence after death. From their findings I garnered that consciousness is soul.

My sojourns by the ocean, my meanders in the meadow, and my experience with, and study of, near-death experiences convinced me that nothing exists separate from Oneness, separate or apart from creation, from the Whole.

Could our souls belong to a larger soul, a larger consciousness, a heavenly place?

In the fourteenth century, Hildegard of Bingen[14] had a vision of consciousness. She saw consciousness, rather than being in her, as residing outside of her. She envisioned that the consciousness that moves from us connects us person-to-person, and person-to-all things, and brings us in each moment fully in communion with the sacredness in each moment of creation.

Five centuries later Carl Jung[15, 16] supported her vision. He and others have contributed to creating an awareness of a much bigger reality, a reality that at any moment each of us is a part of. This reality, which contains the knowing of all time, exists because our consciousness blends into the consciousness of the collective. The collective consciousness is made up of all the hopes, dreams, aspirations, knowledge, healing strategies, miracles, etc., that have existed, do exist and will exist. All that exists in consciousness is the relative now.

Could the soul energy of a loved one be as near as the vibrations of other invisible electrical and sound waves? Are we walking side by side with our loved ones, unable for the most part to see or hear them? I had read and been told of visitations, during both dreaming and waking states, by loved ones who had died.

A terminally ill young man had been receiving regular energy transfer treatments. I had left him in the care of another while I spent several restorative weeks near the ocean. Toward the end of the vacation I woke up shaking with the realization offered me.

The man was being taken upward on a gigantic people-mover type of escalator. As he passed the area where I stood behind a window-like structure, he turned, smiled and waved goodbye. Part way up, a platform appeared to the right of the escalator. As the cloud-like filament that surrounded the platform dissipated, I saw my son standing beside a large glowing presence. The presence communicated that "because you have given unconditional love, you are being given an opportunity to one more time hold your son." I embraced my son, surrounding him with all the love I was capable of extending. The sensation was real, undream-like. For one moment I held my son in his bodily form. I had prayed for this experience. I had begged for this experience. I continue to relish the gift.

I was shown that I had finally learned the powerful effects of unconditional love – love without strings attached. As a parent I had not always given love without expectations.

I had glimpsed heaven. I no longer doubted this reality. I knew that my son was there. I knew that he was being guided and protected.

I had seen the Universe within me, and around me, and I had seen the escalator going up. I knew that something of heaven was in me and around me. I also knew that something of heaven was outside of this dimension.

Infinity, when all things it beheld,
In Nothing and of Nothing all did build,
Upon what base was fixt the lath, wherein
He turn'd this Globe, and riggalld it so trim?
Who blew the Bellows of his Furnace Vast?
Or, held the Mould wherein the world was Cast?
Who laid its Corner Stone? Or who's Command?
Where stand the Pillars upon which it stands?
Who Lac'ed and Filleted the earth so fine,
With Rivers like green Ribbons Smaragdine?
Who made the Seas its Selvedge, and its locks
Like a Quilt Ball within a Silver box?
Who Spread its Canopy? Or Curtains Spun?
Who in this Bowling Alley bowld the Sun?
                    Edward Taylor – *The Preface*

Hallowed Be Thy Name

Prior to the Second Vatican Council, rituals of worship in the Roman Catholic tradition were performed with little involvement of the congregation. This practice flowed from the belief that only ordained priests were deemed worthy of direct dialogue with the Almighty. Speaking in Latin, and with his back to the people, each priestly act represented the need for a mediator between an unworthy people and their God. While the choir joined in the Latin chant of a "high" mass, their involvement was also separated from the commonness of the congregation by language, distance and the physical structure of a loft.

But on very special occasions, such as Confirmation Sunday, and the Feast of Corpus Christi, the entire congregation stood in reverence as we joined in an English version of "Holy God We Praise Thy Name."[1]

Lord of all we bow before Thee.
All on earth Thy rule acclaim, all in heaven above adore Thee.
Infinite Thy vast domain, everlasting is Thy Name.

In the simplistic way of childhood, I rationalized that on occasions such as these, God could receive our devotion even if it was conveyed in a language other than Latin, which I assumed to be the language spoken in heaven. Awe swelled as my voice joined in unison the hundreds declaring admiration for the name of God and the handiworks of our Creator. To this day I am touched by the sacredness of those moments of communal worship as I reclaim the reverence of that glorious song spiraling from our tiny church dome to the cathedrals of the Kingdom.

Music and song has always been my clearest channel for sending and receiving messages to the Divine. Since early childhood, I had loved to sing, and did so whenever and wherever the slightest opportunity arose. The times of praising in song, either alone, or with my entire church community, and declaring admiration for our God, and for all of Creation, have been throughout my life, the holiest of experiences. Yet for years following the death of my son I was unable to sing. The numerous tapes and records which I used to play almost continually rarely left their jackets. The words would not come; the melody would not flow. The words were wrong; the melodies did not fit the expressions of my soul.

A large growth on my thyroid gland was discovered. The throat is associated with communicating one's voice, one's truth. It is an avenue of expression, especially creative expression. The thyroid gland is responsible for growth and progress. I was blocking my own growth. I had been given a gift. I was not using that gift. I was not expressing who I really was, or that which I really believed in. I was not praising in ways that were right for me. I was not sharing either in word, or song, the Sacred Truths that I was coming to know more clearly. Lodged within the lump in my throat was blocked creative energy. The abnormal growth manifested a need for change.

A familiar psalm hauntingly reverberated. While my throat could not give it voice, every cell moaned my feelings.

Hear Lord the sound of my call;
hear and have mercy.
My soul is longing for the glory of you;
hear lord and answer me.[2]

My work with people from various cultures had been increasing. An instinctive awareness and reverence of the sacredness of traditional practices and the power of traditional healing methods could not be ignored. I was discovering a connection between what I was experiencing as I journeyed inwardly and what I was witnessing in their practices. I longed to know more about the sacred relationship between humankind and All of Creation.

I leafed through a booklet inadvertently left behind by a student, colleague or client. I registered in a course and many glorious summer sage-filled days studying ancient Shamanic practice followed. Powerful helpers and guides from the world of spirit had been waiting. They gladly accepted my invitation. For it is only upon being summoned that they make their presence known. The Creator has given free will to humankind. Spirit guidance respects our choice.

Dragon surrounded me, directing me, and became visible in numerous ways and in numerous places. Most people raised in Christianity view dragons as maleficent, since we know only of the dragon slain by St. George. The dragon is a complex and universal symbol, seen as both frightening, yet manageable. Dragon is traditionally the Guardian of Power. There is a heroic part in each of us, which must face dangerous conflict in order to overcome the lower side of our nature to reach our inner resources. Dragon allows this conflict. The symbology to be discovered in the story of Saint George and the dragon is that in managing the dragon spiritually, we become custodians of our own power, of our own future.

Owl came to guide my travels to the underworld. Owl is associated with strategy and wisdom, and can see in dark places. I needed the protection and wisdom, and the good darkness-vision that owl could offer. Owl hovered as I studied soul loss, and guided my awkwardness as I practiced soul retrieval. Knowing my inexperience, owl completed, unaccompanied and unencumbered by my lack of skill and knowledge, the soul retrievals. Leaving me safely in a protected area, my owl helper sought out and returned with the lost soul part(s), entrusting me with only the task of sealing in the treasured find.

Reindeer spirit entered, directing my experiences as I learned to extract soul intrusions. With antlers held high, connecting us to the upper world, and with four feet firmly anchoring us to the physical plain, we journeyed in safety. My spirit and the spirit of the reindeer fused as we tore at the intrusions holding others from fulfilling their life's mission. The reindeer enabled me to learn, not only the extraction of soul intrusions for another, but to recognize the soul intrusions within myself. From the reindeer I learned the importance of being connected to the spiritual world, and also the importance of being grounded to the Earth.

When I first used color meditation to visualize the colors within my own energy centers, and when I began to identify the colors streaming into my aura, the purples, colors associated with the world of spirit, were visible, but the reds and oranges, colors connecting me to Earth, were absent or, at best, dull. My life was not working. I could not put my thoughts into clear words, nor could I make my ideas manifest in reality.

We are meant to be connected to the Earth. We have been assigned earthly duties. We have been asked to increase the heavenliness of activity upon the Earth. We cannot do this if we are not firmly a part of the Earth and deeply rooted within it.

A gifted teacher taught me to become as the standing people, the trees, to send my hair, as branches, into the sky, there to draw spiritual energies. I learned to guide the energies through my body, and to ask that they carry along all that was not working for me. I learned to firmly plant my feet and direct the energy into the large roots which extended from the soles of my feet deep into the Earth Mother.

I learned that, without being grounded in the Earth, I was unable to make manifest in reality the ideas of the mind. Without this union we are disconnected from the source which feeds our Sacred Fire. Yet when we firmly establish and maintain our connection with the Earth Mother, fears and hurts are drawn from us, and we receive in turn the fuel required to fully develop our talents and abilities.

When we return gratitude for the sacred gifts we have been given, when we give unconditionally and to the fullest of our potential, and when we celebrate in joy our Oneness with the Universe, we hallow the co-creative force within, the Eternal Flame of the Great Mystery, the Creator, of which our Sacredness is a part.

Within months of welcoming my reindeer guide, I discovered Linda Schierse Leonard's *Creations Heart Beat: Following the Reindeer Spirit*.[3] From her I recognized that the reindeer's ability to find its way through dangerous wilderness, and to survive the starkest winters, was a guiding example for me to follow. Reflected within the peaceful eyes of the reindeer was an image of what I should become. I needed to reclaim and to rely upon my own instincts. My reindeer guide was encouraging me to believe as the reindeer people do. If I allowed the reindeer spirit to guide me, perhaps, as Leonard promised, "images of hope and peace" could once again inspire me, and I would be able to once again "honor and affirm life."

Dr. Leonard emphasized that, "The image of the reindeer moving in the wilderness points to the possibility of survival and a rebirth of trust and confidence. Nothing except extinction can stop the reindeer in their purposeful annual migration. The images emphasize the saving grace of silence, space, and solitude. It gives us a vision of another realm, one not yet infected by despair, in which we too might move forwards with freedom."[4]

Cave drawings indicate that man has probably always relied on animal helpers and other spirit guides for direction and protection. By their life patterns, habitat and natural instincts, animal guides can draw us to and along our spiritual path. Living in a symbiotic existence with animals, our ancestors learned to recognize that nothing exists in isolation. Every part of creation is an essential and interwoven part. As each part gives and receives to its greatest potential, All exist in peaceful and abundant balance.

The more I learned, the more I recognized how sacramental Shamanism was. The more I practiced, the more aware I became of the Sacred within myself and within all of creation. The more aware I became of the Sacred, the greater became my relationship with the Creator. The more connected I felt to all in creation, the more connected I felt to Jesus and his teachings. I saw in his words and works, contained within a framework of love, a desire to communicate the traditional wisdom of the Sacred within all.

When I first began to study the Earth Religions I was immediately drawn to the holiness enshrined within these traditional practices, yet I wonder where Jesus was in all of this. I journeyed.

I was a traditional healer, encircled by a crystal clear light which flowed from an enormous circle of Sacred Beings that hovered high above me. Jesus was in this circle. Buddha was in this circle. The circle of Sacred Beings to which Jesus and Buddha belonged was in like manner encircled. The golden radiance shining upon them came from above them.

I received Shamanic healing. This time not only my world-view, but also my world, exploded. For three days the magnitude of life surrounding me became more real, more grand, more alive than I would have previously thought an earthly possibility. I was a part of the trees, the rocks, the lake. I could see, I could hear, I could feel the trees, the rocks, the lake. Their energy surrounded me and was within me. I could see, hear and feel my energy, my aura, within the trees, the rocks, the lake.

I was no longer alone. I was in the Universe and the Universe was in me. I was a part of All. Yet I was free.

I had been freed of spiritual intrusions. My sojourning soul parts had returned, and they had brought with them the characteristics that had gone away. My shattered soul had been mended. I could reclaim my wholeness. I could reclaim my soul's gifts. My talents and abilities had been released from the chains of the oubliette. My unfettered soul could fully express its creative voice. Once again I could receive guidance through the songs that gently drifted into my awareness. Once again I could proclaim in song the glory of the Lord. I had found as had St. Irenaeus that "the glory of God is man fully alive."[5]

I was alive, more alive than I had been since early childhood. There was work to be done. Time was of the essence. I had gifts to share. I could no longer hide my talents under a bushel, or behind a throat lump. I had to make manifest the glory that was within me.

I had begged Jesus to show me the way. Jesus had invited me to penetrate the reality of God. I had accepted the invitation. Looking deeply and listening attentively had freed me from the bonds of blindness created by the fear and hurt coercively applied by a religious tradition more focused upon reinforcing a belief in their monopoly of the truth, than in guiding each and every individual in a process that would fan and brighten the smoldering embers of their Eternal Flame.

As Thich Nhat Hanh in *Living Buddha, Living Christ*[6] emphasized, it is not Buddhism, nor Christianity, but the lives of Jesus and Buddha that are most important to us, because as human beings they lived in ways we too can live. Jesus and The Buddha had come into Oneness with the Godness within them. When we become fully human we come into complete solidarity with the humanness and the Godness of Jesus. Of the Buddha, Thich Nhat Hanh states, "He was human, but, at the same time, he became an expression of the highest spirit of humanity.". . . "When we are in touch with the highest spirit in ourselves, we too are a Buddha, filled with the Holy Spirit, and we become very tolerant, very open, very deep, and very understanding."

I had dreamed of the Eternal Flame within me, blocked from exploding forth by gigantic padlocked steel doors. Jesus referred to himself as a door and The Buddha is referred to as a door. Both are teachers who show the way. They showed how to open the door. They modeled love, understanding, courage and acceptance.

A gifted teacher instructed us that as we journey to the East we are provided opportunities to find the Golden Door, the door leading to all levels of understanding and awareness. The East is where Grandfather Sun greets us each morning, bathing us, if we allow, in the goodness of the new dawn. Grandfather Sun gives the golden rays of masculine energy which we require (whether we are male or female) to live in wholeness. As our male aspects develop we utilize more fully the abilities of the left side of the brain. We think more logically, are able to understand and apply concepts. We function in an organized manner, and we see more clearly how ideas can move from the world of thought into the world of action. As the masculine energies surge through our body we become warrior-like. We become good leaders and protectors, and we move forth in courage to tackle fears of limitation.

Jamie Sams[7] is a gifted teacher who guides our journey along the three paths which lead to the illumination found beyond the Golden Door of the East. We move along the first path by using any talents and abilities we have. Every effort to develop and share our gifts is rewarded with energy which expands their further development. We progress along the second path by shedding the poisons of past hurt. Old resentments create toxins which fester and keep our wounds continually raw. Purposefully and intentionally finding and using healing strategies aids our movement along the second path toward the Golden Door. The third path toward illumination is sharing. We must share what we have. We must share our time, our energy and our talents. We must give in gratitude, in thanksgiving, for all we have been given.

To pass through the Golden Door is to move into the Golden Light of Knowing. Knowing is the melding of wisdom with the understanding gained from experience. The Golden Light of Knowing radiates from the glow of the Sacred Fire within. To pass through the Golden Door is to pass through the Door of Truth. It is to come to a place where there are no limitations, no fears, no doubts.

To pass through the Golden Door of Truth is, I believe, what the mystic poet William Blake referred to when he wrote, "If the doors of perception were cleansed, man would see everything as it is, infinite."[8] Our perception is made up of the thoughts and feelings, beliefs and attitudes that are unique to each of us, and which are based upon our past experiences. Our perception can give us an altered view of reality. Blake believed that the more we cleanse the clouded lenses of our perception from expectations, the more we are able to move from the mundane, and the more able we are to tap the source of infinite creativity.

To move beyond the threshold of limitations, fears and doubts is to live with spiritual courage as described in *Fire in the Soul*[9] by Joan

Borysenko. "Spiritual courage grows through our willingness to keep on remembering, to keep on searching for the sacred behind all the seemingly mundane and even terrible facets of life." Spiritual courage is more than faith that we are ultimately safe. It is the inner knowing that this is so. That knowing is the composite of all our experiences, dreams, serendipities and practices of remembering – which is part of our soul-knowledge.

I believe that as we make conscious efforts to move toward the Golden Door of Illumination, we are given peeks of the reality contained beyond. The closer we move toward the threshold the more the serendipitous delights increase, and the more conscious we are of the truth in the time-honored saying "coincidence is God's way of remaining anonymous."

In the moments when we are fully present to life we experience the infinite. In these moments we know no fear. When we experience love, joy, gratitude, compassion, peace and beauty, we touch the greater reality. When we stand amidst the rapture of a morning sunrise, or gaze at the stark beauty of a flock of geese winging their way to their Northern nesting ground, we transcend our little selves and know the Oneness of the greater self. When we stand in awe we hallow the maker of each awe-filled moment.

We can learn to apply the lessons of the East whenever we need to begin again. When a path is new it occupies all of our attention. One of the most important lessons of the East is to learn to focus our attention. As children we instinctively know how to do this. We become completely absorbed in examining each new aspect of our surroundings. Our total awareness becomes submerged in the butterfly, the leaf – the stone. Our "little mouse sister" does what she does with all of her tiny being. We can learn from her guidance how to pay attention to the moment. When we are fully present in the moment, all of our senses become involved in what we are doing. It is this heightened alertness, this complete giving of ourselves to what we are doing, that increases our capabilities. It is the practice of mindfulness.

Mindfulness is better known, however, as a Zen meditative practice for shifting consciousness from the mundane to the infinite. But regardless of what traditional method we use, paying attention, pulling ourselves into the very present moment of an action, of an experience, is a very healing strategy. Keeping our focus in the now, draws us from the pain of the past, and keeps us from leaking precious energy on future dreads. Mindfulness moves us toward the Golden Door of Illumination.

While for a long time I had been convinced of the healing potential of mindful-practices, it was not until I witnessed my mother in the rose garden that I fully understood the "aweness" of the mindful-moment. As my mother, then in her late eighties, lingered in her examination of a rose, I was suspended above the reality of the experience into the sacredness of the union that was unfolding between my mother and the flower. I knew that she was beholding her Creator in the handiwork of creation. And I knew that in the beholding she was hallowing the name of her God. In that moment I witnessed the Oneness of our human condition with the fullness of our true reality. In that moment I learned the lesson of mindfulness, a powerful lesson of the East.

It is no accident that the twin teachers of the East are the mouse and the eagle, one of the humblest creatures and one of the noblest. We must journey to the East of the Sacred Medicine Wheel many times in life in order to acknowledge our own vulnerability and that of others. But until the journey is made to the South, the place of the heart, there to learn of sacrifice, of sensitivity, and of love that expects nothing in return, we are too full of a false sense of personal greatness to be of real assistance to the People. Until we journey to the West in search of personal power, and the correct use of power, and until the wisdom of the North is gathered, we cannot truly be of service to the People. Indeed the essence of what it is to be human is to be of service. This is the greatest lesson of the Medicine Wheel.

Like the stone circles and labyrinths, and other forms of the sacred circles found around the world, the medicine wheels are linked to peoples' cosmology. These circular forms show us how to move toward the centre of our own beings. They help us align with the forces that created and maintain the earth.

Wheels also provide a model for achieving balance in any endeavor. By using the wheel to guide activities those activities come into balance.

Sacred Wheels are based on the four directions and each of the directions represents a particular quality. The directions are archetypal symbols of the diverse qualities that combine to make a whole. Wheels symbolize these qualities in a variety of ways (colors, spirits, animals, weather and zodiac symbols) but they all show that different qualities combine to create a whole. The four directions can be subdivided into other multiples of four, which create eight, sixteen or twenty-four sections to represent more diversity. Since these diverse qualities are all on an equal footing around the wheel, the wheel offers a system for integrating diversity into a harmonious whole.

While, in North America we generally associate the Medicine Wheel with Native American Teachings, cultures around the world have used and continue to use the wheel to explain the workings of the universe. Some examples include the Celtic Wheel, the Roman Wheel of Fortune and the Tibetan Kalachakra.

The Celts, a tribal people of the British Isles and Europe in the fourth century B.C.E., created a Sacred Wheel to represent their belief that the universe rested on a wheel and the four directions.[10] An extension of this wheel can be found in the Celtic Goddess teachings. Arianrhod, known as the Goddess of the Silver Wheel, became associated with the wheel the Celts found in the sky.[11] We know this wheel as the Milky Way.

The Aztec calendar, dating from 1011 C. E., is associated with the Aztec Indians of Mexico. This wheel has eight divisions on its outer layer and four primary divisions on the inner ring. The wheel reflects the Aztec view of the cosmos, with the sun god in the middle. The four symbols around the sun god represent the four elements, earth, wind, fire and water.[12]

The Roman Wheel of Fortune was central to the ancient Roman concept of justice. This wheel was based on the twelve signs of the zodiac and showed the relationship of events on earth to the movement of the constellations in the stars above.[13] The wheel follows the rule of using multiples of four to determine the points on the circle. The quality of the signs of the zodiac metaphorically demonstrates the energy that goes into making the whole.

Another wheel that orients peoples to the universe is the Tibetan Kalachakra. The Kalachakra, also known as the Wheel of Time, is a detailed sand painting created by Tibetan Buddhist lamas and monks. This sand painting is a model of wheels within wheels. Eight wheels contained within the broadest circle. There are four central divisions on the inside of the wheel, designed in the colors red, yellow, white and black.[14]

The Darma Wheel of Tibetan Buddhism depicts the process of personal development. This wheel shows the cycle people pass through in their pursuit of inner clarity.[15]

The Yoruba are a tribe in western Africa in the area now known as Nigeria. The Yoruba Wheel is similar to the Roman Wheel in that it is a divination tray. Their wheel is divided into four primary divisions, based on the four directions, with four additional subdivisions. The Yoruba Wheel conveys the unity of the Yoruba cosmos and is used to call on spirits of that direction.[16]

The Lakota and Tsalagi wheels are probably the best known of the North American Indian Medicine Wheels. The four directions are the basis of these wheels. Words, animals, seasons and colors are used to symbolize the qualities of the diverse points on the wheel.[17]

A number of years ago, I had a vivid dream which lingered in the forefront of my awareness. With each new experience, with each subsequent dream, added wisdom followed. But it was not until I had studied the Medicine Wheel that a full understanding emerged.

A cock had entered, transforming in an instant to a peacock. Boasting a brilliant tail, it strutted unto the stage. The resplendent plumage, emerging from its very center, bathed it in a luminous glow of passion and energy. As suddenly as it appeared the magnificent creation burst into flame. From the core of disintegrating ashes appeared my face.

I was haunted by the need to understand the symbolism. I had little knowledge of mythology and had never heard of the phoenix, the mythical bird that sprang forth from its own ashes. Yet I knew that this dream was too important to go without interpretation, that this dream was somehow transformational. I undertook dream study. I promised to forever after be a model student if, during the very first day, the instructor would decipher the mesmerizing images.

The cock is generally depicted as a symbol of a new day. To have one appear in a dream forecasts a new beginning, a journey to the East. To have the cock change to a phoenix indicates a growth of understanding from the plain and unadorned to the beauty of the fully plumed bird. The phoenix symbolizes a need to die in order to live fully, a need to let go of the old before the new can burst forth. The phoenix represents rebirth, immortality, resurrection, all symbols of the East. All remind us that from the darkness comes the dawn.

When my days contained little more than lamenting and searching and begging, I had cried out "O God help me. Show me the way. I do not know what you want of me, but whatever it is I will do it. I have tried it on my own and I can not move forward. My life is not working. My life is a mess. Whatever you want of me I will do. Just be clear with what it is that you want, I seem to be very blind and very hard of hearing, but I give up. I can not do this alone. I desperately need you to show me what you want of me, and show me how to do what you want of me. Please bring the people into my life that I need, and please lead me to the people that need what I have to give."

From within the bleakness of that dark existence I was unable to recognize what I much later came to know. The giving up, the total letting go of control, the recognition of how little control I really had anyway, heralded the first rays of morning. I now recall that I had attended a lecture on the meaning of the word "Amen." The scholar translated Amen as a falling back into the arms of God. I became as a trusting child thrown into the air by a loving father. I had come to the point where, while I knew not how, I trusted that I would land in the open arms of a loving Creator.

I now know that the phoenix dream is not uncommon among those attempting to live beyond catastrophic circumstances. I ask those I work with to monitor and journal their dreams. I hear their phoenix stories. I offer the hope and promise that the phoenix dream brings.

We each have the capacity to create ourselves anew, to begin again to journey to the East. We can transform ourselves and our lives regardless of what we have been through.

Maybe the true purpose of our suffering is that out of our pain we will rise again like the phoenix. Maybe the true purpose for our suffering is that in our transformation we receive new vision, new hearing, new insights, new awareness. And perhaps the real purpose of our suffering is that as our burning experiences leave our previously conceived notions in ashes, we can hallow the Creator in ever new and wondrous ways. For only then, can we be of true service to the People.

There is an inmost center in us all
Where truth abides in fulness.....and
"to know"
Rather consists in opening out a way
Whence the imprisoned splendor may escape,
Than in effecting entry for a light,
Supposed to be without.
Robert Browning – *The Imprisoned Splendor*

Thy Kingdom Come

In 1945, a young boy digging for lime fertilizer near the Upper Nile discovered an earthenware jar. The jar contained ancient manuscripts. From their translation we receive a dramatically different picture of Jesus, his teachings and the early Christian church than that of the New Testament. The writings include dialogues, conversations and visions attributed to Jesus and his Disciples, as well as a number of Christian gospels, including the Gospel of Phillip, the Secret Book of John, the Apocalypse of Paul, and the Gospel of Thomas.[1] The manuscripts had been hidden, for preservation, against the third-century destruction order of the Archbishop of Alexandria. In the *Laughing Savior*,[2] John Dart shares the significance of the Nag Hammadi Gnostic Library. He shares that the teachings contained therein reveal a, "religion forgotten for over sixteen centuries, a religion related to, but radically distinct from the Judeo-Christian tradition."

In the Gospel of Thomas we read that when Jesus was asked about the kingdom of God he responded: "If those who lead you say to you, 'look the kingdom is in the sky,' the birds will get there first. If they say, 'it is in the sea,' than the fish will get there first. Rather the kingdom is inside you and it is outside of you. When you come to know yourselves then you will become known, and you will realize that it is you who are the children of the living Father. But if you will not know yourselves, then you will dwell in poverty, and it is you who are that poverty."[3]

Jesus clearly stated that the kingdom is within and it is outside of us. Jesus directs us to learn the truth about ourselves. He does not claim to be the only begotten son of God, as the New Testament Gospel of John insists, but reveals instead "it is you who are the children of God." We all are the children of the Creator, and as children we each have God potential. And when we come to know this we will come to know of our true heritage.

It is not only the words of Jesus that steer us inward for the truth, but the message resounds from all corners of the world and is spoken by the masters of various cultures and traditions. Folklore, fairy tales and stories of mythology remind us that since early times sacred ritual has guided the journey through the internal portal. World religions continue to teach this important theme. Those who honor the path of Confucianism know that what the under-developed man seeks is outside. What the advanced man seeks is within himself. The Shintoist is reminded not to search in distant skies for God, for in man's own heart is God found. Hinduism teaches that God abides hidden in the hearts of all. In Sikhism, the *Guru Grant Sahid* instructs that God is concealed in every heart; His light is in every heart. And a Buddhist knows that if you think the Law is outside yourself you are embracing not absolute Law, but inferior teaching.[4]

Healers, clairvoyants and seers, such as Edger Cayce[5], and Emanuel Swedenborg[6] have likewise taught much about the truth contained within our own hearts. In numerous ways they encourage us to pay attention to what we think, how we speak and how we behave, for it affects us in this life, in the life after death, as well as in future incarnations. Data gathered from subjects, who have had near-death experiences, as well as from those who have regressed to a past life and to life between lives, supports the teachings of the masters and those shared by Cayce, Swedenborg and others.

Dr. Ian Stevenson, head of the Department of Psychiatry at the University of Virginia, School of Medicine, has documented thousands of cases in which children spontaneously remembered past lives. His academic writings, including *Twenty Cases Suggestive of Reincarnation*[7] and *Children Who Remember Their Past Lives*,[8] are revolutionary. Dr. Stevenson and his team adhere to the strictest research methodology as they examine in detail every aspect of the claimed past-life experience. In each of his reported cases a child, usually between the ages of two to four, and without prompting, spontaneously recalls explicit details of a past life. In order to be examined by the Stevenson team, the "past-life" remembrances must be so specific and so detailed as to provide the team with enough information to begin an investigation of the validity of the former identity. The team begins its research by verifying that the child could not have found out about the remembered experience by other means. Such is the case of Sukla of India, who at one and a half years would cradle a block of wood and call it "Minu", her daughter. Over the next few years Sukla remembered enough details for her family to take her to the village of her remembered former life. Sukla led them to a home where a girl named Minu lived. Minu's mother had died when she was but a baby.

In another case, three-year-old Michael Wright of Texas amazed his mother with accurate details of an auto accident in which he had previously died. The life he remembered was that of his mother's high-school boyfriend. While neither his mother's relationship with the boyfriend, nor the accident, had even been spoken of, the three year old was able to describe the accident in precise detail.

Dr. Stevenson's publications[9, 10] provide evidence that his subjects had lived a previous life. Similar findings are reported by researchers Brian Weiss in *Many Lives, Many Masters*,[11] and *Through Time Into Healing*,[12] Roger Woolger in *Other Lives Other Selves*,[13] Helen Wambach in *Reliving Past Lives: The Evidence Under Hypnosis*,[14] and Edith Fiore in *You Have Been Here Before*.[15] In the words of Dr. Wambach "If you are sitting in a tent on the side of a road and 1,000 people walk by telling you they have crossed a bridge in Pennsylvania, you are convinced of the existence of that bridge in Pennsylvania."[16]

While each of the above researchers had set out to disprove reincarnation they, like Dr. Alexander Cannon, an Englishman awarded degrees for his work, by nine European universities, accepted the testimony of regressed subjects only under duress. In *The Power Within*,[17] Dr. Cannon writes. "For years the theory of reincarnation was a nightmare to me and I did my best to disprove it and even argued with my trance subjects to the effect that they were talking nonsense. Yet as the years went by, one subject after another told me the same story in spite of different and various beliefs. Now well over a thousand cases have been investigated and I have to admit that there is such a thing as reincarnation."

As previously discussed, researchers examining the experiences of those who have been resuscitated following a near-death experience conclude that consciousness continues in the realm of spirit. Reincarnation researchers conclude that not only does consciousness continue as a spiritual essence but that emotions also survive the grave. Regressed subjects reexperience both positive and less-than-positive feelings associated with events from previous lifetimes. While the majority of recalled past-life experiences are painful, with the remembering comes healing. Dr. Edith Fiore, a clinical psychologist from Saratoga, California emphasizes, "If someone's phobia is eliminated instantly and permanently by the remembrance of an event from the past, it seems to make logical sense that event must have happened."[18]

In *Children's Past Lives*,[19] Carol Bowman reports that not only do children's unexplained fears and phobias dissolve, but even physical symptoms heal following remembrances of former lives. She shares case studies in which physical illnesses and injuries of one lifetime manifest in the physical body of the next, appearing as the same illness, a rash, or even as a birthmark located on the identical place where a previous wound had been inflicted. She and other researchers conclude the rapid physical and emotional healing which occurs following the reexperience of the past-life illness or injury is because the subject is now able to view the rootcause from a distant and more objective viewpoint.

Our wholistic nature as human beings is supported by the incredible findings of regression research. While our physical body disintegrates, our physical experiences and our emotional responses to the experiences are "assimilated" into our consciousness. Indelibly engraved upon our soul, these "markings" are carried into future incarnations. They remind us of where we have been, of what we have accomplished, and of what we have yet to accomplish.

Regression therapist and researcher Joel Whitton, a Toronto psychiatrist, has learned much about not only the emotional and physical restorative value of regression therapy, but in *Life Between Life*,[20] he and Joe Fisher describe the spiritual value of previous-life time viewing. By accident, Doctor Whitton discovered that people can not only be regressed to past lives, but that they can also revisit the life that occurs for the soul between its earthly incarnations.

In the Tibetan *Book of the Dead*,[21] the time when soul resides outside of a physical body is referred to as the *bardo* state. In the bardo, plans are made for future incarnations, and the soul studies what it will need to know and understand in order to advance. The bardo is the school of theory; physical incarnation is the clinical experience. Life on earth provides tests which determine the degree to which the lessons have been mastered. We ourselves design the tests. We ourselves determine how well we will use our time in the bardo and in physical life.

Regression therapists and theorists write that entry to the interlife begins before the karmic judges. The life that just ended is reviewed and the soul is able to see how the most recent past life fits into the bigger picture of the soul's development. The soul witnesses the tests pass, and reviews where lessons still need to be learned. The soul makes choices about its spiritual evolution.

Under hypnosis one woman described to me her intense desire to discover the path to God. "There are many higher planes and the idea is that you must come back, many times, into physical form in order to become more godlike so that you can one day reach the plane where his spirit is."

The planes are often described as varying in intensity of beauty and brightness, and as having cities, universities, large halls of learning and libraries. In *We Are Not Alone*,[22] Robert Marsh writes of his Eckankar experiences in soul travel. "With little ceremony, he ushered me in the Soul body to the spiritual city of Agam Des." . . . We arrived at a huge vaulted temple which shone brightly with creamy hues." Following another journey he writes, "the schooling we received was in a huge academy, with the same high levels of discipline and obedience. We were like second graders in a vast enlightenment that ran up to fifteen or twenty grades." On a subsequent search for spiritual knowing, Marsh journeyed to the fifth soul plane. He describes his joy at, witnessed there, the Swans of God.

No wonder we are instinctively drawn to the fairy tale of the ugly duckling. We recall our own glimpses of the fifth plane, our own view of the swans. Our souls know that to advance into the ever increasing levels of brightness we must shed our dowdy duckling feathers. We must become swan-like.

Our love for the swan flows not only from remembrances of life between incarnations, but also from primal memories of tribal life. We recognize the swan as the guardian of surrendering to the dreamtime pull. Our souls remember that in previous embodiments we could journey from a waking state into the dreamtime, the reality where our souls travel as our body doubles, to "see" with unlimited vision, and to bring back information required in the physical world. Our souls seek to rekindle the memory of their predetermined and self-designed missions which have become clouded, during life, by a smokescreen of fear. Our souls long for the knowing, but have forgotten how to journey.

Dreamtime experience in the waking state is different from the dreams experienced during sleep time. In a journey from the waking state the vision is clear. If the need to know is strong, messages from the dreamtime reality will infiltrate our sleep time dreams. In these lucid dreams the scenes are vivid, We are not in the usual passive dream-like state, but are actively involved. These are the dreams we most often have when we have "seeded," or planted, during a sacred ritual, a question to which we request a dream answer.

During my long sorrow-filled days I had seeded many dreams. I had witnessed the glowing fire within. I had viewed the Eternal Flame locked behind doors created by hurt and fear. I had marveled at the potential of the phoenix. I had been shown the possibilities of the Eternal Flame of creativity and passion in my life, the possibilities of the kingdom within. But I had also been shown that pride and cockiness must be purged before I could rise like the phoenix from the smoldering ashes and "face" the kingdom without.

I began to understand that death of the body or death of the ego were still the first steps to rebirth. I began to recognize that the ego builds us a disguise for lack of self-love, hope, trust and courage. The dreams had propelled me into the crevice of my being, the crevice of the universe where there is neither time nor space, where all is one, with the raw energy of creation coming from the Eternal Flame.

Through the crack in the universe I had glimpsed pure creativity. I had viewed my embryonic abilities and talents. Peering beyond the darkness, I garnered courage to confront my fears and move into who and what I was to become. But yet the raw potential lay dormant, for I did not know how to turn the potential into reality, nor in which direction to tiptoe forth.

My dream life implored me to pay attention to what was really important. My wounds were healing. I longed to be in the reality of the new beginnings, but the old ways of being no longer worked. I knew I was called to do something more meaningful than I had ever done before. I had no idea what that might be, yet I believed that I should know, that I had known for a long time. The anguish of the vacillation, of the searching, and the longing made me fretful and anxious. Waking frequently with palpitations, I knew I was having yet another reminder that time was running out.

As a child, I had learned to seek the assistance of the Saints, especially the Patron Saints. I had learned that St. Anthony was the patron saint for helping to find lost objects. St. Anthony had assisted me numerous times throughout life. I now needed his help more than ever. I could not locate the important information, the valuable details. I had once had numerous talents and abilities, now I had only raw potential. I had lost direction. I was a different person now. I needed to find out who I was and what I was good at. St. Anthony gladly joined my daily treks and listened as I beseeched. "Help me find in me what it is that I am to do. . . . Help me find my gifts and abilities. . . . Help me to discover ways to share my abilities with the world. Let others find in me what it is they are looking for."

St. Anthony led me to a Shaman. I journeyed to the beat of the drum. I learned to cross the barriers of time and space where both realities can be viewed. I discovered that all reality is parallel. The kingdom within, the reality we create – first in our thoughts and subsequently in our behavior – is the reality we experience while in physical incarnation, as well as in the afterlife.

St. Anthony brought me to teachers on self awareness. Jesus had said the "kingdom is within you and it is outside of you." I understood that what was splashing around in me was affecting my reality. What was splashing around in me was a result of all of my behavior – all of the deeds, all of my actions. Most importantly, I now recognized that all reality begins first in the world of thought, and remains there as attitudes and beliefs. My destiny was determined by my ability to change my thoughts. My ability to move my life forward, to pass the tests I had set for myself, was in my power. The results would depend on the choices I made.

The Tibetan *Book of the Dead*[23] asserts that the soul's surroundings in the bardo state are produced from what is "within." James Van Praagh[24] reported that the environment of the interlife is a reflection of our thought forms. Goodness of thought results in goodness of action. Goodness becomes reality in both this life and the interlife. One woman found music beyond anything ever heard in this world. For others it was, splendid palaces and beautiful gardens.

But lack of goodness of thought also results in lack of goodness in action, and manifests in both this reality as well as the next. The authors of *Life Between Life*[25] cite the case of Victor Bracknell who, as the past-life personality of Michael Gallander, was a pious seventeenth-century puritan. He was convinced he was doing God's will and that his ruthless crusading actions would rewarded at death by the sight of Jesus. But the life between life brought him no Christ-like vision. Instead, he was confronted with the suffering he had inflicted on others.

Numerous past life regression therapists and reincarnation philosophers remind us that the course of our soul's evolution cannot be altered by the simplistic notion of being saved.

The Buddha taught that the path to enlightenment[26] (to brighten the light within) is walked by right thought followed by right action. Jesus taught the beatitudes.[27] Give food to the hungry. Give drink to the thirsty. Welcome in the homeless. Tend the sick. Visit the prisoner. For what so ever we do to the least of the brethren, we do in solidarity. What we do to others we do to the Collective. What we do to All we do to ourselves, as our time before the karmic judges reveals.

I often find that when someone has lost a loved one to death, they struggle with the numerous times their loved one had not fulfilled the religious mandates, prescribed as necessary for entry to the kingdom. I ask them to ponder the beatitudes. I ask that they reflect on the loved one's numerous efforts to give love and caring to others.

Love in thought and deed is described not only in Christianity and Buddhism as the way to find the kingdom within and without, but love of God, self and others also guides the path of those who follow the numerous and various other traditions. The message conveyed in Confucianism is to employ all your heart in whatever you do. The Koran teaches that riches are not from an abundance of worldly goods, but from a caring heart. Those who follow the Jain tradition learn to master their senses, to avoid doing wrong, to do no harm to any living being, neither by thoughts, words nor acts. And a student of Taoism is taught to extend help without seeking reward.[28]

When Jesus said the kingdom is both within and outside of you he was likely referring to the totality of soul growth that has taken place in the multiplicity of human forms in which the soul has been housed, and to the notion that we create, by our thoughts, words and deeds, our own internal and external kingdom, not only in this lifetime, but in the after life as well. He was likely asking us to pay attention, to slip into the crevices of our being, for there we will rediscover what we already know, for we ourselves have written the script.

The Sacred Road, which allows the seeker to view those aspects of the self that lies below the surface of physical reality, and to discover the universe of consciousness is built of lessons gained in the West. The authors of, *The Sacred Tree*,[29] write that "The West is the direction from which darkness comes. It is the direction of the unknown, of going within, of dreams, of prayer and of meditation. The West is the place of testing, where the will is stretched to its outer limits so that the gift of perseverance may be won." Everyone who has tackled the difficult realizes that, the closer we come to our goal, the more arduous the climb. Yet the capacity to stick to the challenge is within each of us, if we but receive the energies of the West.

A gifted teacher directed my focus on the energy of the bear, the animal of the West, and invited me to spend quiet time in hibernation. One day as I watched the "cloud people," I witnessed the bear lumbering toward me. The bear reminded me that thunder and lightening often come from the West. These are the bringers of power and of useable energy – energy to heal and energy to defend and protect, energy to create and energy to move our goals to completion. But the energy of the "thunder beings," can only be amassed when, like the bear, we retire into the silence of our being. The insight gained can only be found by shutting out the clamor of the world and going alone to pray and be tested.

Returning to the darkness of the cave, or returning to the womb, both bring new birth. The West is the place where we amass feminine energies. Through introspection, new ideas, like babies, can be fertilized, nurtured, given life. In the West all future begins. When we, like the bear in the autumn, enter into hibernation, we gain the insight of what is important to harvest and what must be blown away as chaff.

The turtle also symbolizes the West. Our rebirth can be painfully slow. The turtle models perseverance, and it is only through perseverance that we can gain the gifts of our autumn experience, which is the season of the West.

When I needed it most, a colleague gave me a poem by an unknown author that clearly describes the journey to the West and the need to persevere until we discover the kingdom within:

> Above all, trust the slow work of God.
> We are quite naturally, impatient in everything to reach the end
>   without delay.
> We should like to skip the intermediate stages.
> We are impatient of being on the way to something unknown,
>   something new.

Yet it is the law of all progress, that it is made by passing through
   some stages of instability – and that it may take a long time.

And so I think it is with you.
Your ideas mature gradually – let them grow
   let them shape themselves, without undue haste.

Don't try to force them on, as though they could be today
   what time will make them tomorrow.
Only God could say what this new spirit
   gradually forming within you will be.
Give our God the benefit of believing that his hand is leading you,
   and accept the anxiety of feeling yourself in suspense
   and incompleteness.

When we journey to the center of our being, we experience directly the connection between our soul and the universe, and between our spirit and the Spirit of the Creator. We come to know more fully who we really are and what we are really meant to become. These are the gifts we receive as we graduate from the West. When we have penetrated the kingdom within, we have learned the lessons of the West. When we have learned the lessons of the West, we are ready to permeate the universe without. These are the lessons to be learned in the North. These are the lessons of wisdom.

Our birth is but a sleep and a forgetting;
The soul that rises with us, our life's star,
hath had elsewhere its setting,
And cometh from afar,
Not in entire forgetfulness
And not in utter nakedness,
But trailing clouds of glory do we come
From God who is our home.
Heaven lies about us in our infancy!
       William Wordsworth –
       Ode: Intimations of Immortality

Thy Will Be Done

People removed from our world of biological theory believe that we are directly influenced by seven generations of ancestors, and have a direct responsibility for the next seven generations. Contained within this belief is an assumption that we inherit not only physical characteristics, but also the unfulfilled hopes, dreams and even memories of our ancestors. In other words, we inherit not only their physical attributes but their emotional and spiritual ones as well, and we "promise" to carry on and accomplish their unfulfilled aspirations in order to move forward, in an evolutionary way, those who follow behind.

A graduate student colleague shared with me an experience which seemed to support this belief, at least in part. During summer recess she visited Scotland. On an outing to see historic sights in a town unfamiliar to her, and much to the chagrin of the tour guide, my classmate felt compelled to leave the group and follow a cobblestoned path to the doorway of a small shop. Forced by an unaccustomed boldness, she pushed open the door, knowing even as she did so exactly what she would see. The shop, once a home, contained a stone hearth and many smaller details with which she felt keenly familiar. Upon hearing the description and the location, and recognizing the link to the names of the present owners, her mother believed the present-day shop had once been the home of my colleague's great-grandmother. My colleague had not known of her Scottish roots. Her Scottish great-grandmother had come to Canada in mid-life, bearing her English husband's name. She had always yearned to return, and spoke frequently of her life and home in Scotland. Her daughter, my classmate's grandmother, had married a Canadian of Irish descent. My classmate had, therefore, always considered herself to be of English-Irish ancestry. She now not only treasures her Scottish heritage, but firmly believes that within her genetic make-up are the fond memories of her great-grandmother's life in Scotland, and her unfulfilled desire to revisit the home of her birth and happy childhood.

Those who argue against the possibility of past-life experiences would be satisfied that the inherited memory theory could completely explain my classmate's experience in Scotland. Others would prefer to believe that she recalled these memories by tapping into the collective consciousness, where the memories of All reside. But do either of these explanations negate the possibility that my classmate was indeed recalling a past-life experience, a previous experience indelibly inscribed upon her own soul?

In *Ageless Body Timeless Mind*,[1] Deepak Chopra maintains that transplant patients report uncanny experiences following organ transplant. Unaware of whom the donor was, the recipient begins to participate in the donor's memories and experiences. "Associations that belong to another person start to be released when that person's tissues are placed inside a stranger. In one instance, a woman woke up after a heart transplant craving beer and Chicken McNuggets; she was very surprised, because she had never before wanted either. After she began having mysterious dreams in which a young man named Timmy came to her, she tracked down the donor of her new heart, which had come from the victim of a fatal accident; when she contacted his family, it turned out that the victim was a young man named Timmy. The woman was stunned to discover that he'd had a particular fondness for drinking beer and had been killed on his way home from McDonald's."

Chopra goes on to remind us that "because experience is something we incorporate (literally, "make into a body), our cells have been instilled with our memories; thus to receive someone else's cells is to receive their memories at the same time."

Within each of our cells is a complex protein called deoxyribonucleic acid (DNA). DNA holds genetic information. Its twin partner, ribonucleic acid (RNA), is responsible for transferring genetic information within the cell. DNA gives us our inheritance and is considered to remain unchanged, as it was inherited, throughout life. RNA changes, however, in response to life circumstances. Chopra shares that at exam time medical students "show a decrease output of interleukin2, a critical chemical in the immune system that fights cancer. The production of interleukin2 is controlled by messenger RNA, which means that the student's anxiety over passing his exams is speaking directly to his genes."

When we grieve, when we feel hopeless, our biochemical profile alters in response to our emotions. When we smother beneath a shroud of hurt and depression there is a decreased output of electro chemicals at the neurotransmitter sites. Our hormonal levels drop and our immune system becomes less effective. Our immune cells and endocrine glands contain the same receptors for brain signals as our neurons (specialized nerve cells). They function, like an extended brain, in their ability to pick up information. They are equipped to register and respond to each bit of data that either nurtures or threatens our survival and wholeness. Even our skin receptors register a lack of nurturing touch differently than loving touch, and our tears contain traces of different chemicals when we are sad, as compared to when we are joyful.

These measurable physical changes, in response to spiritual and emotional distress at the cellular level, influence RNA. RNA is the twin partner of DNA. A child inherits DNA. Is the DNA that we pass on influenced by our own responses to life, as demonstrated in our RNA? If the recipient of an organ also receives the memories contained within the cells of the donor, it is reasonable to assume that our children also receive our memories in their cells. If they receive our memories, why can they not as well receive the memories of their grandparents which were passed to us and which we pass to them?

Measurable physical changes, even at the cellular level, in response to spiritual and emotional distress demonstrate in one more way the interconnection between body, mind and spirit. When I use energy for healing purposes, the person receiving the exchange will sometimes have an overwhelming emotional release, often demonstrated by crying or sobbing, followed by intense feelings of peace and calm just prior to the decrease in physical symptoms.

Every aspect of physical functioning, and every physical change within our bodies is a process of energy exchange. This energy is not contained within us but radiates beyond us. Our energy field contains the intermingling of our physical hurts, our hopes, our dreams, our aspirations, our joys, our sorrows. Our energy field is the sum total of every vibration released through the creation of our every thought, word and action. As previously discussed, near-death researchers conclude that our human essence, our consciousness, continues to exist following death. The consciousness that resides outside of us, but that is a product of what goes on within each aspect of our being, does not die. Those who have been resuscitated report having seen how our consciousness intermingles with the consciousness of All.

If our consciousness does not die, and if our consciousness is the result of all of our lived experience, and if it intermingles with the greater consciousness, the greater consciousness must, therefore, also contain the wholistic lived experiences of all who have lived. It is very reasonable, therefore, to assume that not only can we tap into the collective memory, but it is also comprehensible that we pass on to our children not only our physical, emotional and spiritual characteristics, and those of their immediate ancestors, but because our consciousness "bumps" into the consciousness of All, we have within our very make-up the collective. We each inherit and we each pass on the wholistic essence of the collective.

But does the acceptance of tapping into the collective consciousness, or of inheriting from the collective pool, interfere with our ability to be reborn? Or, could it be possible that, rather than interfering, both of these suppositions highly support the theory of rebirth?

When we reexamine my classmate's profound experience in the Scottish town, do we confine our thinking to asking whether she inherited the hopes, dreams and aspirations of her great-grandmother? Do we ask whether she tapped the collective pool for such information, or do we honor the truth in both of these and ask a third and more profound question? Did my classmate inherit the collective hopes, dreams and aspirations, and even physical properties garnered by humankind throughout our history? Did she inherit a part of the collective, but inherit most specifically from her ancestral pool? Were these "tapped into" tendencies inherited and infused with the individual hopes, dreams, aspirations, even physical attributes of the soul that had once existed as her great grandmother, which was now housed in the body of my classmate?

Therapists and past-life researchers present numerous findings from individual and group research to convince even the staunchest one-life supporter that we do indeed become our own ancestors. In *Children's Past Lives*,[2] Carol Bowman shares that when children are shown old family pictures, it is not uncommon for a child to have a flashback memory, and to emphatically state "That's me!" as a particular person is pointed out.

We do indeed influence the next generations for we become the next generations. We move through numerous lifetimes meeting the same people over and over. According to regression therapists and theorists, group reincarnation, in which the same set of souls evolve, through constantly changing relationships in different lives, recurs frequently. In the words of one of my clients who felt compelled to make compensation, "I didn't treat her too well in my last life, I have to work off the debt."

Carol Bowman[3] gives numerous examples of child subjects who spontaneously, without hypnotic techniques, describe past lives shared with the same siblings, the same parents. Children subjects have also remembered lifetimes when they were the parent or grandparent of their present parent.

During one five year old's regression, Carol reports how the child explained the soul's interaction within its group. "As you die, you have choices as to what you can do. You can go back to a scene from the life you left and get any information you want to answer questions to finish up your life there. You can see what happens with the people you left behind. You can go back while you are in spirit and say goodbye and see what happens to them in the future. If you see that all is well with them this frees you to leave the Earth plane' (his words exactly)."

According to Dr. Whitton, sometimes the karmic need to return to the same relationship situation is so strong that a soul will choose, or be advised to choose, bodily affliction. One woman, knowing that there was a high incidence of Alzheimer's disease in her family chose to reincarnate anyway, believing that her karmic links with her mother were more important than any genetic deficiency.[4]

When we consider the possibilities being communicated by spiritual teachers, seers, clairvoyants, poets and researchers, as well as through our own instinctive knowing, we begin to view reality and our relationships in a much grander way. We see life differently – in a more continual form. We comprehend as Dr. Morris Netherton in *Past Lives Therapy*.[5] "It took nature ten million years to build the Grand Canyon. I can't believe it takes just seventy or eighty years to build a man's soul." And we ask, "What of the children who have only one year, eight years or thirteen years of life?"

All too frequently we relate to our loved ones, especially our children, in ways that communicate disrespect. We are often inattentive when others speak. We may talk in condescending ways, or sarcastically. We may command them, without consideration for their feelings or their likes and dislikes. We often do not use the same common courtesies, such as "please" and "thank you," that we extend to a stranger. Yet if we but consider that this loved one, this sister, this child might indeed have been our own mother, our own grandmother; if we but acknowledge that our four year old may actually be a great and ancient, and highly evolved soul, we would respond differently, with a greater respect – with admiration. If we recognized that the father we mourn may be the child we conceive; that the brother we argue with may be our husband of the past, we would appreciate more fully the grander scheme of things.

If we were to move from the paradigm that has blinded us into viewing our lives and our relationships in such a confined and narrow way, we would begin to observe our loved ones and their behaviors differently. We would ponder our relationship with them. We would value who they really are. We would encourage what they are to become, for we would acknowledge the reasons for their life and for our time together. We would see their birthmarks, illnesses, phobias, fears and mistakes in different ways. We would ask where the behavior originated; we would explore the cause in order to relieve the symptom. We would see beyond the physicality of one life. We would awaken our silenced memory of the grand process, of our connection to all that we have been, and of our connection to all others who have and continue to be.

A while ago I joined my husband as he thrilled to the movie *Sharp's Regiment*,[6] based upon the book by Bernard Cornwell. A sergeant in a long-ago war was trying to motivate his men to follow a change in plans which stemmed from a change in philosophy. His words captured my attention. "It is not a sin to be born in the dirt, but it is a terrible sin to want to remain there." It is not a sin to have come from whence we have come, but it is a terrible sin to want to remain there.

Were we not fogged by an ideology, supported by those who hold firm to the belief that we live only once, we would not close our minds to the information explosion confirming the opposite. We would behold differently if we were not kept unaware by those who hide behind their methodologies which, instead of building a theory to fit the circular evidence, desperately continue to squeeze the findings into the square holes of their preconceived reality.

Wherever we look, whatever we touch, there is evidence of an ever-evolving, ever-expanding reality. We are more. Our cells are not just lumps of matter that direct physical processes.

In the bardo state we choose, with the guidance of our karmic teachers, the lessons that will assist our soul's evolution. As we pass the tests, we progress not only toward fulfilling our own purpose in life, but our personal evolvement moves forward the entire collective. Joel Whitton reports that while we are at liberty to reject the judges' planning advice if we do not heed the counsel of our karmic teachers, and enter this life without a karmic plan, we set ourselves up for a life of unproductive and unnecessary trials and hardship for, with no script to follow, the soul becomes a victim of fate rather than a participant in destiny. Those who are living out their karmic scripts have an inner sense that life is unfolding as it should. Those who are not, feel, instead, that everything is out of control.[7]

When we are not following the plan that we have selected for our soul's advancement we have a pervasive sense that we are off course – a ship without a rudder. I knew that my entire body had faltered during those bleak days of struggling to find the meaning in what had happened to me, and trying to determine the purpose for the rest of my life. I lived in fear, and struggled with overwhelming dread.

I now frequently hear others describe similar, often identical, feelings and experiences as they attempt to regain mastery of their existence. For many, it is only during the darkness that follows a traumatic life event that we begin to pay attention to the nagging from deep within our unlit souls. Like a beacon, the crisis warns us that unless we get back on course disaster will result.

Pondering Joel Whitton's subject's descriptions of the karmic script, and how they had created their lessons for this life based upon what the soul needed for advancement, I question whether DNA is actually a soul factor. If consciousness does not die, and is rebirthed, and if consciousness carries physical, emotional and spiritual memories, it would also carry our karmic plan for this lifetime. The twin partner, RNA, could then be designed to record soul's progress in achieving its individual and collective mission. Since RNA changes in response to thinking, and since our entire body chemistry alters as RNA changes, it is no wonder that when we struggle with purpose we feel the effects in every body system.

From the details shared by Dr. Whitton's subjects we glean that the planning process in the between life state is rather like a stage rehearsal for the next life, and sometimes for the next lives. In 1897, Ralph Waldo Trine was one of the first to describe how we create our reality first in the unseen world. In his book, *In Tune With The Infinite*[8] Trine wrote, "Everything is first worked out in the unseen before it is manifested in the seen; in the idea before it is realized in the real, in spiritual before it shows forth in the material. The realm of the unseen is the realm of cause. The realm of the seen is the realm of effect. The nature of effect is always determined and conditioned by the nature of its cause." Trine reminded us that we fulfill on earth what we design in heaven. We fulfill in reality what we create in our minds. We receive in heaven what we create on earth.

Each experience moves us either toward the accomplishment of our life's commitment or moves us further from Oneness. As human beings we are given free will, the power to choose. Is God's will, therefore, really God's will as we describe it, or is the will of God in support of our free will? Do we blame God when the experiences we have in life are really based upon choices we have made, some in this lifetime, others based upon many lifetimes and even interlife times of free choice?

Prior to my own tragic experience, I could point out the numerous manifestations of experiences resulting from the choices made in this life. In both my personal and professional life, present circumstances could often be traced to the origin of personal choice. But somehow, through the tears of my own pain, life was no longer so cut and dried, so black and white. Looming large were many examples in which the cause as personal choice and the effect of painful life circumstances could not be joined. I saw around me those born into abject poverty, and others born into the torment of war-torn countries. I witnessed infant abuse. How could their life experiences, at the very beginning of life, be based upon personal choice? How could a child's sudden and tragic death be based upon choice? How could hundreds on a doomed plane have chosen to die all at once, each of them living in very different circumstances?

And yet, I could plainly recall the comment I made to a psychologist just days after my son's funeral, curtly informing him, "This was the way it had to be; this was the way it was decided." I knew he was bewildered, yet as sure as I was of the truth in what I said, I was unable to say more. My response, spoken during a time of personal crisis, came from a place of intuitive knowing. During crisis our need to survive is great, yet the shock of the experience shuts down our ability to manage life's circumstances in our usual and learned ways. During such times we tend to respond from a deeper more instinctive level. My response to the psychologist's query, coupled with the following experience, nagged me to determine if and how such difficult life circumstances could possibly be a result of choice.

During the early days of grief, the bishop, whom we greatly respected, traveled from the neighboring city to offer condolences. His presence meant a great deal to my family. Attempting to explain the details of the accident I felt caught in the confusion of knowing that in order for this accident to have happened many details had to be in place at exactly the right time, but his simple, gentle comment "There are no accidents," froze my ability to say more. While I had never heard of such a notion, here again was the proclamation of another deep truth, the proclamation of a belief that haunted me for explanation. While the bishop may have been referring to the generally accepted notion of the "will of God," his remarks rekindled an ember somewhere in the yet unexplored crevices of my soul.

Have we "contracted," prior to birth, with others? Is it possible that we perhaps arrange and exchange with others in our ancestral soul group for the particular lessons that our soul needs in order to advance its particular evolution, as well as the growth of the entire collective?

Such pondering compelled me to explore the possibility of previous lifetimes. The thought of rebirth, of reincarnation, threatened the fundamental core of my belief system. I was a Christian. Christianity, which stems from resurrection,rejects reincarnation. The Council of Constantinople in the sixth-century condemned the theology of Origen and his notion of reincarnation as unfitting for Christians since it challenged the belief in resurrection.

My son had died at such a young age. He had not had the opportunity to experience life fully, completely. I wanted to believe that he could have another opportunity, that he could know the joys of love. Yet I also wanted to believe that someday our family, his dad, sisters and I could again all be together. It scourged me to envision the possibility that he could be a part of some other family while we were robbed of the happiness of seeing him grow and develop.

Yet the idea of living more than one life made a lot of sense. Since early childhood I had mouthed a belief in a just God. Now I challenged how, in justice, a god could judge for all of eternity the life of someone who had been given thirteen years. How could the accomplishments of one so young be compared to those of someone given ninety years? How could a just god allow some a life in the slums of Calcutta and others life in Buckingham Palace? How could some live with the inconveniences of the fourteenth century while we live with the conveniences of the twentieth? How could someone suffer an entire lifetime serving the will of another, and never get a chance to experience the earthly pleasures and joys known by others?

Rebirth could certainly be a way to justify the injustices I was witnessing. Reincarnating into a different set of circumstances in order to accomplish what the soul yet needed to accomplish would allow for soul growth, and it would be a way to live the unlived experiences of a previous life.

While sorting through these conflicting notions I pondered my numerous childhood déjà vu experiences, experiences when I had sensed that I had already done something before, been here before.

I wondered about the frequent childhood battles between my brother and myself. They almost always began because I would challenge his comments "I'm the girl and you're the boy." Had he been the girl and I the boy in the last life we were together?

I remembered my parents' laugher at comments made by my mother's young brother to his father. "When I was big and you were little." Was this a childhood memory of an earlier time when their roles had been reversed? Why would I now remember these episodes? What was stirred within me at that tender age, so powerful as to indelibly engrave those words into my memory?

I recalled, as a junior-high student, writing a paper on Hinduism. Now distant from the experience I marveled at that. How was it possible that I, a child raised in a strict Catholic home, attending high school in a girl's academy run by Catholic nuns, would even conceive of the notions needed to write such a paper? Why had I chosen this subject? In my entire sixteen years I had met only three people who were not Catholic, and they were surely Christian. My research of the literature was difficult. There was little available information on Hinduism. I was struck by the idea that some people actually believed that we have more than one lifetime. Yet, I set my heart to the task with such focus that I won an opportunity to present the paper at a public forum.

Were these triggers of remembrances from what had gone before? Were they reminders of previous experiences? Were they forecasting what was important to pay attention to?

Yet it would be many years, and only following tragedy and the relocation to Hawaii in search of self healing, before the idea of reincarnation would resurface. A university faculty colleague in Hawaii shared numerous stories of her firm conviction that she had lived previously in Hawaii. California-born, she had come as a nurse to Hawaii. The moment she deplaned she "knew' that Hawaii was her "home." She married, and since her husband was of Hawaiian descent, their children were permitted to attend Kamahamaha School, a school originally funded by Queen Kamahamaha to ensure education for Hawaiian children. While delighted that their children could gain admission, my colleague told me that throughout the many years of her children's schooling, each time she entered the grounds she was overwhelmed by uncontrollable sobbing. What memories were aroused? What experiences were recalled? Had she perhaps been rebirthed, with a need to reconnect with her "family," in order to learn the soul's lesson assigned to this lifetime?

Rebirth implies reincarnation, and reincarnation implies a reentrance of the soul into the physical body. The third-century Christian theologian Origen taught about the pre-existence of the soul from all eternity. As Thich Nhat Hanh in *Living Buddha Living Christ*[9] indicates, this belief is similar to reincarnation since, if we are incarnated once, there is a possibility of being incarnated again. Thich Nhat Hanh reminds us that the soul is immortal. It is the body that needs to be resurrected.

Aware of my quest, a friend called to share her discovery of Carol Bowman's *Children's Past Lives*.[10] The inner voice reasoned – if a child as young as two blurts out, "I remember when I died before, or "My other mom had curly hair,". . . . you need to pay attention.

In the first chapter of her book, Carol related a story of her own five-year-old son who was terrified by loud sounds. When asked to close his eyes and relate what he saw when he heard the loud noises, he immediately described himself as a soldier – an adult soldier – a terrified adult soldier forced to kill other men in an attempt to stay alive. He described the clothing he was wearing and drew pictures of the battle scene where his life ended.

Eagerly, I studied the reams of past-life research. I discovered that while it is only recently that children's past lives have been researched, there exists incredible, ever-expanding documentation to indicate that memories of past lives are recalled naturally by young children. Freely, under hypnosis, or during self-induced trance states, adults in virtually every culture and in all countries of the world also share memories of having lived before. It appears to matter little whether or not the religious beliefs of the person who recalls the past life include reincarnation.

As I pondered the words of Carol Bowman's young subjects who spoke of being rebirthed, often into the same ancestral group, I reasoned: If we are rebirthed into the physical body, and if we reincarnate to move our entire soul group forward, we could easily re-enter a physical body that bears much similarity to the one we have now. We would be drawing from a similar genetic pool of physical characteristics. Yet I debated. I had witnessed myself in a different culture.

One morning, while riding the elevator to my fifth-floor office, the door opened to admit a young woman. We smiled and shared a friendly good morning, the kind you give to a familiar acquaintance. As we stood staring at each other, both of us acknowledged that the other looked familiar, but that we had not met previously. About a year later we met again, this time at a conference. We both remembered our unique earlier exchange. Deciding to become better acquainted, we agreed to meet at lunch. Barely had we begun to converse when my new acquaintance momentarily "changed" into the likeness of an American Indian woman. While her facial features remained similar, her hair turned from blond to black and was held in place by a band hosting three feathers. From the braids which outlined her face dangled feathered jewelry. Courageously, I dared to share what I had witnessed. She confided that for a long time she had felt an "intense need to understand more about the life of aboriginal women."

Months previous, I had attended a drumming ritual. The ceremonial building was located near a small river in a semi- treed area. At the ceasing of the drum, and during the quiet that surrounded the invitation for individuals to share in the Sacred Circle, I "saw" through the open doorway hundreds of tepees situated along the riverbank. I was there, in the midst of the activity taking place in the center circle. I was carrying wood to the fire, careful not to disturb, but all the while paying close attention to the dialogue.

Had this new acquaintance and I shared life as aboriginal women? What lessons did our souls learn then? Why had we been thrown together now?

Soon after this cosmic reminder of a tribal life and as if to reinforce the lesson of the continuity of life and my need to focus on the messages being provided, I began having a series of experiences where, from a waking state, I would feel "myself" lift from my physical body. During these moments I witnessed myself as an Egyptian slave involved in a love relationship with a Roman soldier who had a likeness to my present husband. My husband of today had saved me from sexual slavery centuries ago. My husband of today had been a lover in the past. Our forbidden relationship then was sanctioned now.

A number of decades ago, Martha Rogers,[11] a famed nursing and quantum physics theorist, proposed that from birth to death each human is evolving. At the same time that each human being is evolving, the entire collective is moving forward in an evolutionary way.

As one's soul group evolves, therefore, so too would the entire collective. Could it be possible that the entire soul group moves through each evolutionary change together?

Could the models provided for us in the natural world also apply in the world of spirit? Human beings evolving as the soul group evolves, and the entire collective evolving as the soul group evolves, is a modeling of the critical mass theory of learned behavior. According to this theory, the behavior of an entire species changes when enough members of that species begin to behave in a certain way. The energy that goes into creating the action by one member is projected into the collective. From the collective consciousness the energy is picked up by another, and another and yet another. When enough members of any one species are performing a certain behavior, a critical mass is reached and the entire species now acts in the new way.

In *The Hundredth Monkey*,[12] Ken Keyes provides support for the critical mass theory. He tells of a group of monkeys being studied off the coast of Japan. One day a monkey began washing a sweet potato in a certain way in salt water. Soon after, other monkeys began to model the behavior. When a certain number (the critical mass) were washing their potatoes in this way, monkeys hundreds of miles away, having had no physical contact with the first group, began washing their potatoes in exactly the same way.

Wayne Dyer[13] emphasizes the significance of this theory for human development and world peace. If we clearly understood the effect we as individuals have on the collective, we would be more conscious of the thoughts we think, of the words we say, and of the actions we perform.

We each have the responsibility to monitor what we send into the collective consciousness. If we truly realized that our behavior is contributing to the total behavior necessary to reach a critical mass of behavioral change, we would be more aware of our individual potential to create either peace or war, to maintain the earth or to destroy it.

My thoughts raced. We do create our own reality in this world. Our consciousness is the sum total of our life experiences. Our consciousness does not die. Our consciousness blends with the consciousness of All. It is reasonable, therefore, to assume that we create our reality in the world of spirit as well. As we evolve, so does our soul group, as our soul group evolves so evolves the entire collective. As we evolve we draw to us the lessons and the relationships which allow us to advance.

Consistently, researchers reporting on the experiences of those who return following clinical death emphasize that the most important thing in life is love. The second is knowledge. Those who receive a second chance to live, come back with a conviction that life is so incredibly important that we ought to have a feeling of tremendous gratitude for all that life offers, even for the sufferings inflicted on us, for they offer an opportunity to express love and compassion both toward ourselves and others.

"Thy will be done." I had mouthed the words frequently. Yet, in suffering, I had challenged the will of God. Now I debated. Was it God's will that I suffer, or was it really my choice to suffer? Was my suffering God's will, or had it come as a result of my free will?

Our son had died. Had we made this choice, the choice that he would die young and that we would suffer? Had we prearranged with our son and brother, and he with us, for the lessons that he and we needed to learn in this lifetime in order that we might more fully and more freely express love and compassion toward ourselves and others, in order that we might advance our soul growth, and the soul growth of All?

Are the immediate surroundings and circumstances into which we are born based upon choices we have created for our soul experiences? Are the joys and the sorrows in life based upon the choices we make? Are we responsible for our life experiences? Does each experience offer the potential to advance our ability to love ourselves and others? Does each experience offer us the potential to increase our knowledge of love . . . of God . . . of God that is love . . . of love that is God?

And still her grief would not abate.
At last she bore another child, and great
Was the father's joy; and loud his cry" "A Son!"
That day, to thus rejoice – he was the only one.
Dejected and wan the mother lay; her soul was numb . . .
Then suddenly she cried with anguish wild,
Her thoughts less on the new that on the absent child . . .
"My angel in his grave and I not at his side!"
Speaking through the babe now held in her embrace
She hears again the well-known voice adored:
"Tis I, – but do not tell!" He gazes at her face.
                    Victor Hugo – *What is the Message*
                            from this Gentle Spirit?

On Earth As In Heaven

"On earth as it is in heaven." I pondered. I had heard preaching on this phrase only in relation to the notion of the divine authority of the pope to create dogma, to decide what writings were sacred and which were not, to declare what actions were sinful and which were not, and in relation to the sole ability of the clergy to interpret, to dispense and to administer sacraments. I had frequently heard that Jesus invested in his male apostles a promise that he would bind in heaven what they chose to bind on earth, and he would unbind in heaven what they would unbind on earth.[1] Yet, I was aware that over the centuries this phrase had been used to captivate, to humiliate, to torture and to slaughter. This phrase had been used to exploit and to coerce others into inflicting untold suffering in the name of Jesus. Since nowhere in the words and works of Jesus was there any evidence he had ever taught, or modeled, such autocracy, and since my personal pain had created within me a sensitivity to the suffering of others, I could no longer identify with such extreme rationalization.

What had Jesus intended by this teaching? What was the real message being given to those who would follow? What was Jesus telling me now? What was in this teaching that I needed in order to heal my pain, to brighten my spark, to move me into knowing and loving my Mother-Father Creator?

"Ye shall know the truth and the truth will set you free."[2] These words of Jesus are frequently echoed. Yet, I believe, that the truth which most profoundly tells of our soul's eternal journey has been purposefully withheld from Christian doctrine. Christians, and all the citizens of the world that have been influenced by Christianity, suffer in both this life and the next from the blindness created through the manipulation of the real truths taught by Jesus.

Karma and reincarnation are the most important concepts to know and understand in order to discover the meaning and purpose of life, to answer imponderable questions of life, death and suffering, and to truly understand the teachings of the Old and New Testaments. The Law of Karma is recorded in scripture. When we are willing to set aside our preconceived mindset, we are able to easily and clearly recognize the important truths contained within this law as revealed by the patriarchs, and by Jesus and the apostles. When we remove the blinders of indoctrination, created over the centuries by those who stood to benefit financially and politically by shielding the masses from the truths contained within the Law of Karma, we realize that Jesus did teach reincarnation.

When we truly desire to move deeply into a love relationship with our Creator, we open ourselves to knowing. This knowing does not come from theological theory or from the words of others. It comes from the Divine Spirit deep within each of us. The journey of our soul, our spiritual journey, is a never-ending, and ever-escalating journey of loving and of knowing. When we truly desire to know, we begin to remember and to recognize the little hints that inform our brain of what the soul already knows.

At some point in life each of us faces an experience which causes us to struggle with the questions of the meaning and purpose of life, of suffering and of death. Facing crisis turns us inward. The movement into soul forces us to examine, in depth, the bedeviling questions which we have, up to this time, only glimpsed. But in turmoil, in our attempt to make sense of what has happened, we examine the possibilities of good and evil, of heaven and hell, of resurrection and rebirth.

A 1982 Gallup Poll indicated that 23 percent of Americans believe in rebirth.[3] There are strong indications that those responding affirmatively to this question have since increased (Check your local bookstore). The awakening spiritual consciousness stems from the depth of our core. Here lies the seed of awareness.

While the curtain of forgetfulness is drawn as we enter this life, we are sometimes given a flash of the distant past, a moment as real as if we are once again in another reality, but as concrete as the one we are presently focusing upon. We may have fleeting memories of moments of goodness that we must learn to build upon; we may perhaps witness an event in which our actions hurt us or another; we may glimpse the actions of another which hurt us – actions that we have refused to forgive. Hurtful behaviors, thoughts or words interfere with our movement into Oneness with the Creator. Such behaviors carry karma needing to be balanced.

We have little recollection of former lifetimes for we need to be locked into the here and now. We have an assignment for this life, and we cannot get anywhere today while we are mired down in yesterday.

Recently, an older woman sought to be guided on a "journey." Because of plaguing dreams and various waking experiences she held a realization that something from a past life was interfering with her progress in the present. Something from the past needed to be resolved in order that she might live out her numbered days in the peaceful feeling that she had accomplished the predetermined purpose for which she came to this lifetime. Following the journey, she told me that as the drum began to beat, she was immediately lifted by an eagle into a large tree. From this vantage point she was shown an encampment of tribal peoples. Her immediate and overwhelming sense of belonging changed in an instant to feelings of fear and horror. She witnessed a betrayal and saw the massacre of many of her kin. She was propelled into the midst of the slaughter and allowed to feel again the excruciating emotional and physical pain of the fatal wound which ended that life.

As quickly as she had descended, she was lifted from the scene of the massacre back to the safety of the tree perch. As if to reinforce what had taken place, an eagle commanded: "That is past! Do not dwell on the past! You have a pearl of wisdom. That wisdom must be imparted."

Obviously shaken, but grateful for the experience, she was now aware that much of the pattern in her present life was based on an intense fear of once again being betrayed. She had much wisdom to impart, but her inability to trust had been interfering with her ability to complete fully her soul's assignment.

Understanding the Law of Karma is key to understanding the soul's journey. The soul is eternal. The aim of the soul is to achieve oneness with its Creator. Our soul does not necessarily have the ability, or opportunity, to fulfill this mission in one lifetime. If we need another life time and another, and yet another, the same soul is rebirthed into new circumstances, with a new assignment, which will help the soul move forward on its spiritual journey of reunion. I once heard a mystic say. "Our body is like a car; we get in; we use the car; we leave the car; but we are not the car." Our body is like a garment. We wear the garment. The garment wears out, often before the soul finishes its travels.

Prior to the influences of Christianity, the notion that the eternal soul re-entered a physical body was a part of the belief systems of ancient peoples worldwide. Plato taught that the soul was immortal and its disposition in this life carried the disposition from past embodiments. What parent has not recognized the numerous variations in reactions and responses by his or her children to life's situations and experiences?

Numerous tribes of indigenous peoples in North America, in Central and South American, Africa, Australia, Siberia, as well as many peoples of the Pacific, including the Hawaiians and Tahitians have believed and continue to believe in reincarnation. Reincarnation was a part of the spiritual beliefs of many of the early dwellers in Europe, including the Lapps, Finns, Icelanders, Norwegians, early Saxons, Swedes, Danes, Germans, and the Celtic peoples of Britain, Ireland, Scotland and Wales.[4, 5]

Today, reincarnation is mainly associated with religions originating in the Far East, including Hinduism and Buddhism. In these traditions reincarnation is linked with the Law of Karma. Karma is a Sanskrit word meaning thought, word and action.

Every thought, word and action creates energy, energy that moves from us, becoming our consciousness and blending with the consciousness of All. The energy created affects our lives and the world in the form of good Karma, if the action, thought, or deed was done with the right actions and with the right intentions. Negative Karma is created in our lives and in the world if our actions, thoughts or deeds are evil, or done with ill intent. The Law of Karma requires that what is sent forth returns in like manner. The Golden Rule says to do unto others as you would have them do unto you. The Law of Karma states as you do unto others it shall be done unto you. The Old Testament teaches: "life for life, eye for eye, tooth for tooth, foot for foot, burn for burn, wound for wound, stripe for stripe."[6] The message continues throughout the New

Testament. Jesus said, "Put your sword away. Those who use the sword are sooner or later destroyed by it."[7] Jesus was reinforcing the words of Yahweh to Noah and his sons "Who so ever shedith man's blood, by man shall his blood be shed."[8]

What is sent from us in thought, word or deed will advance, or interfere with our ability to move into Oneness. Because we are not separate, but are a part of All, what is sent forth from us also advances or interferes with the movement of the entire collective toward Sacred Oneness.

One fall day when I was a little girl, I sat in the yard watching as my mother made new feather pillows. She was reusing the feathers from the worn pillows to complement the new goose down. After recycling the feathers into their fresh crisp abode she shook the old casings to get rid of any that remained. I was delighted to see the freed feathers drift where the breeze would have them go. Responding to this opportune moment, my mother explained that our words are like the feathers. She warned me that we must be careful of what we say. For as it is almost impossible to pick up the feathers scattered by the wind; it is almost impossible to reclaim the words set free from our tongue. We never know who will be touched or where our words will land. We must speak only those words that, regardless of where they land, will yield only good results.

My mother was providing guidance for Christian living. But she was also instructing me about the effects of karma. My father, although he had perhaps never heard of karma and reincarnation, provided an important message about karmic law, which I frequently share. One misty morning as I tagged beside him on his jaunt to herd the cattle homeward, I learned the lesson which I have come to call the Law of the Echo. I had never before experienced an echo, but as my dad called to the cattle I clearly heard his words return. Fascinated, I tried. What I sent, I received.

Numerous times throughout life I have pondered the Law of the Echo. What we send out returns to us. When we holler hello, into a rain barrel, hello comes back. When we holler "love" into the rain barrel "love," comes back. When we holler "hate" into the rain barrel "hate," comes back. The universe is a giant rain barrel from which the echo returns in the form that it is sent forth from us.

The Law of Karma teaches that what we send we receive. We may receive it in this lifetime, or we may receive it in future incarnations. We carry the good karma we have accumulated and we carry the negative karma that has not been balanced by the effects of good. We cannot become one with our Creator until we have no negative trailings, no negative karma. All negative karma must be balanced by good actions, thoughts, words. The Law of Karma requires that the thoughts, words and deeds of a past life that were unbalanced during that lifetime determine the assignment and the lessons of this life. The thoughts, words and deeds of this life determine our destiny in future lives.

There is no injustice in the universe. There is only continuity of being. Our thoughts, words and deeds return to us, as our teachers, so we can sense how it feels to be on the receiving end of what we send out. The lessons following a negative action can happen very quickly, or they can follow in another lifetime. The rapidity with which we receive our lessons increases as our level of consciousness increases (and consciousness increases as love and knowledge increase). In *We Are Not Alone*,[9] Robert March states "The further we travel along the spiritual path, the quicker the return." The lessons are provided so we can self-correct and move forward in our ability to love. Our journey to the sacred, our search for ways to ever increase our ability to love and to know love moves us forward into Oneness. We long for Oneness. We long to end our feelings of separateness, feelings of being apart from, broken from.

The Law of Karma is for everyone. It operates automatically and without prejudice. No one is exempt. No one gets away with injustice. Karmic law guides our journey and the journey of All. We choose what karma we will work out. We request what burdens of our karma will descend at birth. We choose how far we will advance on our journey to Oneness. When we pass the tests of the lessons, recognizing that each lesson is an opportunity to lead us forward in love, eventually to a complete and unconditional love of God, self and others, our soul responds in joy.

We have not been conditioned to think in terms of karmic retribution, and in terms of accepting our lessons and passing our tests as movement toward unity with the Creator. We have instead been taught that it is fatalistic to believe in karma. And we have misused the teachings of Jesus to perpetuate a belief that someone else carries our burden. In his letter to the Galatians Paul writes, "Every man shall bear his own burden."[10] Jesus did not say I will carry your burden for you. Jesus said "My burden is light."[11] He carried no karma. As Clare Prophet in *Karma, Reincarnation and Christianity*[12] states, Jesus was speaking about the burden of karma. He did not say if you accept me as your lord and savior I will negate the Law of Karma. He did not nullify the law. He reinforced it. Jesus said "I assure you, on judgment day people will be held accountable for every unguarded word they speak. By your words you will be acquitted, and by your words you will be condemned."[13]

Centuries ago, Jesus' direct teachings on the Law of Karma were removed from sacred text. The Gnostic gospel of Pistis Sophia[14] quotes Jesus as saying the "souls are poured from one into another of different bodies of the world."

It was not until the fourth century, when Christianity evolved to an institution ripe for political manipulation, that opposition develop to reincarnation in Christian theology. The new Church-State alliance, felt threatened by those who believed in reincarnation because such Christians tended to be self-reliant, free thinking individuals whose sub-servience could not be guaranteed.

Nevertheless, it took until 553 A.D. before Emperor Justinian issued an ecclesiastical edict condemning as "monstrous" the belief in reincar-nation. A campaign of terror followed. Those who refused to surrender their convictions were slaughtered. Yet, because the rebel Christian bands, primarily the Cathers, held so tenaciously to their belief, it took until the thirteenth century for the belief in reincarnation to be all but purged from Western thought. Only the smoldering embers of the dampened flame of reincarnation remained within the sacred fire pots of the Alchemists and the Rosicrucians. During the Renaissance, and the Age of Enlightenment that followed, the embers were fanned. But the faint glow was not sufficient to sway the masses that were swiftly mov-ing from things spiritual to things mechanical and scientific. Not until the mid-nineteen fifties, and on into the sixties, did the influence of Eastern thought penetrate in any serious way the formidable Western fortification built centuries-strong against the belief in reincarnation.[15]

In the early 1950's, psychiatrists and psychologists began to "trip" upon the benefits of hypnosis to stir deeper memories of troubled clients. Published cases of the recall of past lives, increased public aware-ness and interest. Those troubled by what they considered to be an inconsistency between their beliefs and Christian doctrine began exam-ining sacred text. Many found that the Law of Cause and Effect, the Law of Karma, is firmly rooted in Judeo-Christian scripture.

The Old Testament, beginning in the Book of Genesis, is filled with stories of strict punishment for wrong actions and rewards for good actions. The stories of Adam and Eve, of Cain and Able, and the flood of Noah, all inform us of this law. We are reminded that what we sow we reap. The accounts reveal that, as our indigenous cousins believe, the blessings as well as the sins of one generation are bequeathed to succeeding generations. We are reminded in Exodus that horrendous Karma can descend, not only on individual, but upon a people moving in a direction away from Oneness with their Creator.[16] In the Book of Obadiah, we read: "As you have done so shall it be done to you, your deeds shall come back upon your own head."[17]

We are reminded over and over that it all comes back to us – our good deeds as well as our bad deeds.

Clare Prophet[18] reminds us that, like Abraham and Solomon,[19, 20] we too are tested. She emphasizes that our tests are opportunities to receive blessings.

We are given abundant occasions to build upon the good karma we bring into this lifetime and remake the negative karma. We are given many chances to turn even the most negative trail into a blazing trail of glory. This is why karma is not fatalistic. As with any prophecy we can alter the prophetic path by changing our lives, and by changing the energy sent from us. When we make a commitment to grow in the love and knowledge of God, and move steadily in that direction, we are given opportunities to balance even the heaviest load of karma. We can change the course of our lives by changing our thoughts, words and deeds.

We have free will, the will to choose good or evil, the will to choose to change the karmic energy sent from us. Everything we do, everything that happens to us, is based upon a choice we have made. Free will, however, does in no way wipe out karmic law. We can live miserably by sending forth, and receiving in return, hurtful thoughts, words and actions. We can shorten our lives by choosing a lifestyle which damages our sacred temple. We can choose to lengthen our life and our happiness by balancing our karma. We do indeed have free will. We are responsible for the choices we make.

This, I believe, is the most sacred of laws. Jesus said "Do not think that I have come to abolish the law and the prophets. I have come, not to abolish, but to fulfill. I tell you solemnly, until heaven and earth pass not one jot and one tittle will pass until all be fulfilled."[21]

Yet Christians study the bible, oblivious to the Law of Karma clearly written into the scriptures. A mindset created by centuries of religious, social and political indoctrination, which blocked the early teachings of Jesus as recorded in the Gnostic texts, has created a paradigm which blinds many from seeing that Jesus spoke of the reality of karmic law.

Those of other religious persuasions, those not hampered by the Christian mindset, are able to plainly identify what Christians themselves are often blinded from seeing. Those of other theologies are able to quickly point out the numerous references to karma and reincarnation in the Old and New Testaments. In *Living Buddha Living Christ*[22] Thich Nhat Hanh, a Buddhist monk, does just that. He further reminds us that Buddha means to "wake up." To become Christ-like, we Christians need to become more Buddha-like. We need to wake up.

In *Karma, Reincarnation and Christianity*,[23] Clare Prophet reminds us that the Sermon on the Mount was Jesus' doctrine on karmic law. "With what judgment ye judge yea shall be judged and with what measure yea meet it shall be measured to you."[24]

Jesus stated his reason for being. "I have come to set you free."[25] If we do not understand his teachings, and follow the examples provided to guide our journey of love, we will remain caught on the cycle of birth and rebirth.

Jesus was perfect love. He said the Father and I are One. As perfect love he was One with the Creator God. Jesus came to show us how to brighten our own Divine Spark and how to move our Sacred Flame into Oneness with the Eternal Flame. Jesus came as our role model. He said "learn of me."[26] We are told to love.[27] We are retold in the New Testament what we had heard in the Old. Love the Lord thy God with all thy heart, mind and soul. Love others as self.[28]

Jesus said I have come that you may have abundant life.[29] If we continue to believe that what we send from us in no way affects us or the entire collective, we will continue to live surrounded by our blanket of fear and hurt, never knowing our true potential, never receiving the abundance which is our heritage right. But if we have eyes to see and ears to hear, we will recognize the truth and move steadily in the direction of reclaiming our responsibility, and ultimately our place of Oneness with our Creator.

The disciples of Jesus knew the laws of karma and reincarnation. They knew that a man could be born into difficult circumstances to make up for past karma. They also knew the Old Testament law stating that the sins of the father could be visited on the son. They believed, that the good works as well as the sins of one generation could be visited upon subsequent generations. It was only because of their deep understanding of the Law of Karma that they were able to formulate the question they asked Jesus about the cause of the man's blindness from birth.[30]

Jesus replied "neither." He did not negate either of the possibilities the apostles had proposed, but he offered a third. Jesus was stating that nothing in life is black and white. He was reminding them, and us, that we are not in a position to judge the conditions of another. He was reinforcing that the Laws of Karma, which direct both individual and group karma, are real. Were they not, Jesus would have made a clear and profound statement denying the very basis of the apostle's question. But he did not. He told the apostles these were both possibilities, but not all who are born into difficult life circumstances are repaying their karma or the karma of their soul's group. Some born into difficult life circumstances may be great spirits, ascended masters, coming to teach love and compassion, coming to help advance this world. Jesus was teaching us that in some circumstances (including the one before the apostles at that moment) people are given difficult life conditions in order that the Glory of God may be revealed. But this does not separate choice from the life condition, from free will. The choice was made to have the glory of God revealed in hardship. Jesus himself was a prime example. His life and his death were enmeshed in difficult circumstances.

While in this circumstance, Jesus was emphasizing the glory of God, he was also acknowledging karma, ancestral groups, choice and free will. He was reinforcing that the thoughts and actions of every person contribute to the good or evil of this world.

Each day we use our free will. Each day we choose to add to the good or interfere with the good in the world. Although we each carry the limitations of character as determined by our past thoughts and actions, at the same time we each choose to follow the tendency as it has been formed, or to struggle against it.

Astrology is the writing of karma. Our natal chart tells what good and what negative aspects, from former lives, we bring into this life. The magi came to pay homage. They had studied the positions of the planets at the birth of Jesus. They had seen his natal star. They knew the birth of this Child was incredible. They knew the Child born under this star had perfectly balanced karma. They knew he came into this word to do good deeds. He carried no negative karma needing to be balanced. His glory was revealed in the universe. It was written in the stars, in the positioning of the planets.

We can learn from our astrological chart as well as from the study of Numerology what strengths we have to build upon in order to balance the negative momentum of the karma trailing us. Astrology and Numerology are tools we can choose to use to master our lives. We can learn from what the ancients have left for us, or we can ignore it. These, and prophetic dreams and visions, forecast what will happen if we do not do something to stop the karma heading us toward a calamity.

A prophecy provides information. Through the use of free will we can make choices for change.

In *Life Between Life*[31] Joel Whitton shares that from his subjects he has learned that karmic tests are built into our karmic script. Whether or not we pass these tests determines how, and how far, we will progress in this lifetime. A dramatic example exemplifies the point:

As a young man Steve felt extremely negative toward his abusive father and rarely visited him in the nursing home. On one occasion, however, Steven felt drawn to visit. He found his father very ill and connected to life-sustaining devices. As he stood at the bedside, Steve noticed the respirator tube had become dislodged. He could either call for help or turn a blind eye. After a moment's reflection, he ran for a nurse who hastily replaced the tube.

Some years later, Steve had a serious bicycle accident. He later discovered, under hypnosis that if he had allowed his father to die, he himself would have been killed in the bike accident. If he could forgive his father the transgressions which had extended over several lifetimes he would bring an end to the karmic plan.

Remember that during early childhood, during the dreamtime, and when regressed under hypnosis, we are not bridled by social and cultural values, by our belief system, or by any indoctrination. Our unhampered soul is independent of earthly programming and so we see and speak out of the depths of the wisdom of the soul.

In *You are Not Alone*,[32] Robert Marsh shares that prior to the adoption of twin daughters both he and his wife had similar dreams of a lifetime in which twin daughters were taken from them by an invading army. In the dream, one of the twins chided the father, "I hope you do a better job this time than you did last time." Marsh knew they were being given another chance and they were being asked, "not to mess up this time."

I too had a dream in which I was reminded that I had "messed up." I had promised to attend a performance held by my daughter's class. I came running frantically into the concert hall just as the curtain was drawing on my daughter's act. Dressed in a business suit and carrying two briefcases it was clear that I was "on the run" between "important" contracts. I asked if my daughter would be appearing again. The teacher responded, "There are no second performances." My son was standing on the opposite side of the stage. He gazed at me, shook his head, and as he slowly turned and walked away he said, "Mom, you are still not paying attention to what is really important."

The words jolted me to consciousness. The realization of the source of those early words with the psychologist came crashing down on me. "This was the way it had to be." I had not paid attention to what was really important. I had messed up. I had not understood.

Could I have changed the karmic script had I "wakened" sooner? What was bound on earth was bound in heaven. Could I have changed the prophecy? Had I not changed on earth what could have been changed in heaven?

But I was still messing up. I had come so far. I had made so many changes. I was not at all the same person. But my son was warning me. "You are still not paying attention to what is really important." But what was it that was so important for me to pay attention to?

I was led to a man with clairvoyant vision. "Your life is out of balance." He suggested a woman who taught divination. I learned to pay attention to the numerous ways in which I could receive Divine Guidance. I learned to trust the feelings in my body and use a pendulum, like a dousing rod, when seeking direction. I learned that fear comes not from spirit, but from ego. Spirit knows it is limitless. Ego fears the loss of self-esteem, and encourages us to hide behind a "painted face." When we hide our truth, when we do not speak what we know is right, we do not give to others what they are most needing from us.

I had been hiding what I knew deep within to be an important truth. I had been sharing only what I had learned in the classrooms, and only what could be quantified and measured by science. Yet even as I did, I knew that I did not believe in the effectiveness of the methods. I practiced little of what I shared with others. The healing strategies I personally used were from models far removed from those I taught. Perhaps it was time to take off the mask . . . to speak from an inner knowing.

I needed the courage of the Shaman. Again I was to hear that I was not "walking straight." I was reminded to "talk my walk." I was encouraged to pay attention to the lessons of the South.

In the South of the Sacred Medicine Wheel we learn to live in balance with ourselves and with all of creation. In the South we learn that Great Mystery created each creature with gifts and abilities. Human beings often do not know of their unique talents, for they have been covered by fear. Until we shatter the expectations we have placed upon ourselves, and allowed others to place upon us, we will not find what is uniquely ours to give. It is only when we drop the masks of fear do we see who we really are and come to understand the beauty of our original essence.

From the Shaman I learned that when we are stressed out, when we are running in all directions, we must stop and reconnect. We must plant our roots firmly and be still like the "standing people" so we can see what is growing in our forest. Only when we are firmly rooted, and receiving energy to strengthen and sustain both the masculine and feminine aspects of our being, while acknowledging in gratitude the root of every blessing, can we Walk in Balance. Only then are we able to manifest fully our creative gifts and abilities.

While our relations in the plant kingdom are the givers who continually give to the needs of others, the rocks are the holders of energy. The trees and the rocks balance each other as holders and givers.

I received from the mineral kingdom. A rose quartz crystal over my heart brought healing and absorbed fear. A clear quartz crystal carried in my pocket provided clarity and insight. I received from the plant kingdom. I asked each tree and plant to share their unique gifts. From the pine I requested peace and serenity. I asked the willow to teach me to bend so that I could be fruitful in the use of my abilities. I asked the oak for strength and courage. From the mountain ash I begged protection from harm.

When thou dost ask me a blessing,
I'll kneel down and ask thee forgiveness.
William Shakespeare – *King Lear*

Our Daily Bread

"Give us this day our daily bread" had, for me, always been a prayer of both requesting and of gratitude. Among my fondest memories of childhood are my memories of smell. Primary of these are the aromas that wafted from mother's homemade bread. Enshrined deep within the recesses of my brain are the sights and sounds that encompass those delectable whiffs. Growing up in a large farming family, we had limited material wealth, but of bread we were assured. Bread filled the Roger's Golden Syrup pails that mother secured into the little red wagon to insure their safe delivery, by my brothers and me, to our father and his harvesting crews. Bread, which filled those same Roger's Golden Syrup pails, fed our hungry bellies during our school days. And warm newly baked bread greeted us as we arrived home on frigid prairie winter afternoons. Bread was central to our survival, and it was central to our celebration. While bread graced every meal, and the numerous snack times between, "special" breads announced festivity. Sweet buns awaited the Christmas Eve or the Easter Vigil mass. Their appearance indicated the time of fasting and abstinence had ended.

Even though bread was abundant, it was sacred. Never could we waste. Dried crusts were turned into bread pudding for ordinary days, and chicken or turkey dressing for feast days. Uneaten scraps fed the dog and many cats, or were soaked and softened in milk for baby ducks and goslings. We recognized that our daily bread was a gracious gift. We partook of it freely, yet we understood bread graced our celebration tables and quieted our gurgling tummies only because of the love and the toil of each member in our family, and because of the graciousness of our God.

Bread is made of flour. Flour is made of grain. Our livelihood depended on the grain crops. We valued the soil, the rain and the sun. These, in the right mixtures, were necessary for a bountiful harvest. We honored the labor of planting, harvesting and milling. We appreciated the kneading and the shaping of large batches of dough. As a family, in the work of producing our daily bread, while some tasks were done by machine, others were too precious. These were mastered by love and human skill.

Jesus must have had similar reflections when he prayed, "Give us this day our daily bread." He must have thought, as well, that good bread also needs salt, and it needs leaven. Salt is a preservative. The prayer for daily bread asks, as well, that we be preserved, that we be kept safe and protected. Jesus loved allegory. He would have contemplated on the leaven, for leaven causes the dough to rise. He would have us ask that like the effect of leaven on the dough, we too be given what we need to rise to our full-blown potential. Jesus would have recalled the little known passage in The Book of Numbers[1] which speaks of the way in which the Israelites were to carry forth the Ark of the Covenant. While oxen and carts could be used to carry the tent and most of the sacred trappings, the Holy of Holies was to be carried on the backs of men.

Jesus would have known of the labor required to make our daily bread. He reminded us that when we ask we receive, but planting seeds for the future also requires effort on our part. Fertility in life is brought to us through our active efforts. Jesus knew that when we make the effort, and when we ask with gratitude, we receive in abundance.

Jesus would have known of the gratitude in the hearts and on the lips of those who till and plant and mill and bake. He would have known of their respect for the soil, and the sun and the rain. In our farming home, each meal began with a blessing, "Bless us Lord, and these thy gifts which we are about to receive." And each meal ended with thanksgiving, "We give you thanks Almighty God for all the benefits we have received."

From my parents I learned gratitude. From them I also learned mindfulness. As a child I was taught to pause in my daily work to recall the many blessings I had received. While there were times when I neglected this assignment, its value has come home to reside.

Each noon we were drawn from the midst of our labors to be mindful of the abundance in our lives. As the bell in the church tower chimed, we paused to recite the Angelus. Of all the memorabilia in my mother's home, connecting me to the roots I treasure, I valued most the prints of the Angelus and the Gleaners.

While during my dark nights I could find little to be grateful for, the turning point tiptoed upon the heels of my intentional practice of relearning mindful gratitude. Whispering "thank you," as the spring sun streamed across my kitchen table was rewarded with warm golden glows of courage.

Pleading for help in my desperate situation, with the faith that somehow this could happen, and trusting just enough to hope for what I myself could not accomplish, was the spark of gratitude which thrust me over the rugged peak of the mountain of grief. The arduous and treacherous climb through the ragging storm had all but ended as gratitude bore me to the summit.

The world was different at the peak. The sun really did rise. It did shine, even on those enveloped in cloud. While the trek down was not without trial, it was less formidable for the travel was by day, and I could clearly recognize the guidance of those providing direction.

Theologians often speak of grace and break the concept into "grace given" and "grace received." They would probably speak of my experience in terms of grace. Yet I, personally, have never found a fitting definition for "grace." After considerable study and reflection, I am unable to separate grace from the energy of the Creator. To me, "grace given" means our soul's innate awareness of our connection to the Creator, and because of this knowing we long to rejoin in total Oneness that from which we are formed and to which we belong.

I believe that "grace received' is our own volition to move in the direction of seeking this Oneness. We have free will. We must make the first step, but with even a hint of movement on our part comes an infusion of the Spirit, of the Energy (the Wind, the Breath) of the Creator. The further we advance in this movement, the more open we become to receiving more fully of the Creative Life Force, and the greater our ability to give, to co-create, in turn.

Movement forward is choice. Choice must be the first step in healing. The treacherous rapids within the waters of grief, from whatever the cause, be it from the loss of a loved one to death, separation or divorce, or from the loss of self, suffered following violence or abuse, can completely submerge us. While the current may carry us far adrift, at some point we must choose to sink or swim. We have no other choices. It is easiest to sink, for in descending into the ever-increasing frigidity of the ever-deepening waters, pain becomes frozen. But buffered from pain we are buffered from living.

If we swim we must be prepared to thrash about out of control, doing all we can to keep our head above the ever-increasing turbulence. We must come to the point when, just prior to giving up, to drowning, we call for help. That instance seems only available at the moment we realize our desperation, at the moment we recognize how little control we really have. Yet somehow, and most incredibly, it is only in the total submission of our control to the hands of the Almighty that control returns to our lives.

Attempting to control every aspect of our lives, and often the lives of those around us, forms a vise-grip squeeze upon the tip of the funnel which brings energy from the abundant universe into our being. Our chakras are like spinning funnels, guiding the energy from the universe down into our being. These vortices guide the energy flow of what we need into our lives. All we must do is realize that we are not separate and apart from the universe, that we cannot maintain on our own, and that all in the universe is available to us when we connect, in gratefulness, to the Creative Presence. When we open ourselves in gratitude to receive the energies of love and light, we open ourselves to the tremendous abundance of the universe.

When I first studied about and then began to feel the chakras, the energy vortices on myself and on those to whom I was guiding energy, I was reminded of the cornucopia. The chakras felt and appeared in my mind's eye like a cornucopia, the Horn of Plenty. The feast of Thanksgiving has always held significant meaning for me. So during the years when I felt disconnected from the universe, the celebrations around Thanksgiving were most painful. The Horn of Plenty carried numerous reminders of what I had once had and of what I no longer seemed able to connect with. The dullness and inactivity over my energy centers confirmed the blockages of energy flow.

As a child I learned that the Iroquois women wove the cornucopia baskets as a reminder to be grateful for the good things given to assist us in the physical reality. The Horn of Plenty, filled with vegetables, symbolizes the abundance that manifests itself in the physical reality from the abundance of the universe. Corn sustained the life of the Iroquois. Abundant corn was reason for celebration. They celebrated in gratitude the corn received, as my farming family celebrated the abundance of wheat.

We most often credit the origin of the feast of Thanksgiving to the Pilgrims. Yet it was the Iroquois who tried to teach, through the Horn of Plenty, that thanksgiving is something we must do on a continual basis. The Iroquois tried to impress upon the colonists the importance of giving thanks, even before receiving, knowing that it is gratefulness which makes the abundance manifest. Through the Horn of Plenty the Iroquois attempted to inform the newcomers they need not hold to their ideas of scarcity. The immigrants, coming from countries which had for centuries been ruled by the greedy, were unable to conceive of such notions and chose instead to catalogue these ideas as superstition. The sacred teachings of the Iroquois taught that we receive in accordance to what we give. They encouraged those newly arrived on Turtle Island to return in gratitude, to the Earth Mother, a portion of what they had taken, thereby keeping the flow of abundance moving through the cornucopia.[2]

My oldest daughter is a teacher. A few years into her professional career she was asked to give the Thanksgiving celebration homily to the students and staff at her school. On an evening walk we discussed what would be important to include in such a message. She wanted to make her words "meaningful" and the expression of gratitude "real." We reflected on the abundance we had received in the past year, and we pondered the blessings for which we were grateful.

Her grandfather had been blinded following accidental radiation of his optic chiasm. We were grateful for our sight. My cousin now lived in a nursing home because she was unable to bear her own weight due to multiple sclerosis. We were grateful for our legs, and for our independence. My friend and colleague, whom my daughter knew and admired, had lost her hearing as a result of auditory nerve damage caused by allergic swelling. Hearing impairment had forced her not only to resign her chosen and much-loved career, but caused her to face enormous change in every aspect of life. We were grateful for our hearing.

While my daughter did not focus on any of these issues, her talk reminded the students of their many opportunities. Several students in her classroom had come from third-world and war-torn countries. They shared their appreciation of the abundance in their new surroundings, and as a group they offered prayers of gratefulness.

A number of years ago, I accepted a teaching assignment in Peru. It was a difficult contract to fulfill. The supports and resources for instructing were few. Such situations teach gratefulness, not only for what we have, but for the gift of learning and the gift of life itself. Later, I shared these experiences with a group of middle-class Canadian adults who, while still in their fifties and early sixties, were choosing retirement. I encouraged them to think seriously of what the rest of life would bring. I informed them the life expectancy in Peru continues to be only thirty-five years of age. I asked that they consider, in comparison, upon their retirement they would still have a full lifetime. How would they spend a lifetime?

As the discussion of this middle-aged group moved to the topic of gratitude, a most dramatic story of gratefulness was shared. A woman told of reading how the behavior of an alcoholic husband was completely turned around by the power of gratitude.[3] The woman, of whom the story was told, had attended a series of talks on manifesting abundance. She became convinced her lack of gratitude had contributed to the hold alcohol had on her partner. Upon conferring with her four adult children, it was decided to begin a journey of gratitude by celebrating the good things they had received. It was concluded that even for all of his faults, their father had contributed positively in each of their lives. To begin the celebration, the mother invited the children to a Friday evening meal. Each arrived, but her husband did not. He celebrated, instead, in the local bar, and did not appear until long after the last child had returned to her own home. Yet the wife persisted. On the Saturday evening, again the children gathered to "share their gratefulness for daddy." Once again their father chose to remain away. Yet a third time, on the Sunday evening, again in the absence of their father, the children and their mother gave thanks for the gift of their father and husband, and for the blessings bestowed upon them because he had been a part of their lives.

On the Sunday evening, as the husband stumbled home, he heard singing. Opening the door, hoping to join a drinking party, he literally fell into the midst of a meeting of Alcoholics Anonymous (AA). He never drank again.

While it most often takes much more than three days of gratitude to reform an alcoholic, the story is a powerful tribute to gratitude. And if it

is possible for one human being to change life circumstances by gratitude, the same is possible for each of us. AA taught the husband how to
be grateful for the gift of life, and how to control alcoholism by placing
trust in the healing power of his God.

The twelve-step program teaches that we can be released from the
powerful hold of addiction when we admit our inability to manage our
lives and give over control of our destiny to God. But we sometimes con-
fuse giving over control of our lives to God with giving control of our
lives to another. I believe that sometimes tragedy happens to show that
we must rely on God, not on others, to co-captain our ship. We, trusting
in the guiding hand of the Creator, must master our own destiny. Often
when we grieve and feel adrift, we grab unto the first person or company willing to throw us a life jacket. Yet our first action in healing soul
pain, and in moving our life forward, is to remember where the control
really belongs. Only then, can we gently slide into the captain's chair.
When our trust is placed in the right source, we can steadily gather
speed and gain the confidence needed to man our own vessel for we
know that our course has been mapped, and that we are protected and
guided as we journey.

Materialistic and mechanical values are not consistent with the
notion that we are not in charge, that we actually have little control. Nor
does our culture teach that in returning, in gratitude, a portion of what
we receive, we actually gain. Driven by a mentality that demands
advancement, as rapid and as far as possible on the ladders of success, a
fierce control of resources is exerted, often extending even to the
enslavement of others.

When we have not yet learned that sharing and gratitude create the
extraordinary, we do not realize the truth seen by Albert Einstein. There
are only two ways to live life. One is as though nothing is a miracle. The
other is as though everything is a miracle.[4] Until we learn, as the wife of
the alcoholic did, that when we replace control with gratefulness miracles can happen. When we do not apply this wisdom, the supply dwin-
dles, for greed and a need to control closes the universal valve blocking
the flow of abundance.

If we continually live with an open and grateful heart, miracles are
an ordinary part of life. Abe Arkoff in *The Illuminated Life*,[5] emphasized
that our list of gratitudes should equal our years of living. I frequently
share his comments. During one course I teach, called "Living to
Potential", a seventy-eight-year-old gentleman returned the following
class day with his list of seventy-eight gratitudes. His gratitudes

included: "I woke this morning very thankful for having had a good night's sleep. I was thankful the sun was shining. Elsie and I do so much better on sunny days. I am thankful that if I had to live my life over, I would not change too much. I am thankful for Elsie, my wife of fifty-one years. I am thankful that both of us have health. I am thankful for our four healthy and loving children. I am thankful for my six grandsons."

I assign the exercise often. I have learned that being grateful not only brings the things into our life that we need, but when we reflect on the many blessings that are an often unrecognized part of our life, we receive a powerful surge of hope.

Each time I listen to, or read someone's list of gratitudes, I marvel. I have yet to see a list that does not include gratitude for the warmth of the sun. In some traditions the sun is a symbol for God, and the sun's rays viewed as a metaphor of the goodness which flow from the Creator. Regardless of our culture, we seem instinctively aware of our need for the warming glow of the sun-god in our lives. I recall the numerous times when, from the pit of despair, a song based upon the promises made by Yahweh, with those in Exodus, drifted into my consciousness. "He will raise you up on eagle's wings. Bear you on the breath of dawn. Make you to shine like the sun and hold you in the palm of His hands."[6]

We long for the warmth and closeness promised. The Talmud[7] reminds us that if the only prayer we ever said was one of gratitude it would suffice. When we are grateful, the warmth of the creative energy again begins to flow, thawing our inner-most caverns and reconnecting us to the Great Oneness.

When we approach our lives with trust, Divine Union happens and our minds become fertile ground for our own enrichment. The ancient story of the flute-playing Kokopelli tells that the God growth within primes our cycle of fertility. The fertile seeds flourish into music which can only be sung from our unique souls. The Kokopelli myth is told and retold in numerous and various ways throughout the southwestern United States, Mexico and South America. The Aztecs told that a virgin of their clan was impregnated by Kokopelli and bore a male child who became a great spiritual leader. With the gentleness of his mother and the fire of his father, the sacred child assisted the people in finding their way back to the stars.

The legend reminds us that every living creature is magical because each is a star, a spark of the Divine Fire. It is only when we turn our will to be in union with the Divine Will that our most beautiful music can be produced and shared. Fertility in life can be ours when we choose to actively join in Divine Union for the purpose of discovering, developing and sharing the music within. Kokopelli, through the magic of his song, taught that if we want the seeds we sow to fall on fertile ground we must change our consciousness and use our talents in a productive way.

This powerful message provides us with a twofold path, the path of increasing consciousness and the path of productivity. Gratefulness, mindfulness and meditation move us in this direction. Visualization and imagery are invaluable meditative techniques for moving our lives forward in a productive way.

While the words imagery and visualization are often used interchangeably, they are not exactly the same concept. Both techniques are based upon the knowing that all reality is created first in the world of thought, in the world of spirit. We do not change behavior and then think about it. We change first our thoughts and the behavior steadily follows. Both techniques are also based on the knowing that our brain responds to visual images. In both imagery and visualization we move into a meditative state and give the brain the pictures we want it to believe.

In visualization, we attempt to foresee the outcome exactly the way we want it to be. By engaging each of our senses: sight, hearing, taste, touch, even smell, in an active process we are more able to steadily guide our lives in that direction. For example, if we are preparing for an upcoming interview, we can enhance our chances of success by creating in our mind's eye the entire interview, the way we want it to unfold. By paying attention to the sensory stimuli we further strengthen our chances. If we are able to imagine the smells, the sights (i.e.: seeing all the people conducting the interview as friendly and smiling), and if we can hear the words beforehand, telling us that we are the candidate of choice, we increase our possibilities for success.

In imagery, we rely not on the exact image but, instead, apply symbols to represent what we desire. Imagery has been shown to be an effective tool for physical, emotional and spiritual healing. In *Love, Medicine and Miracles*[8] Bernie Siegel reports the power of the mind in using imagery symbols to cure even inoperable brain tumors.

The soul responds to the symbols of the collective. These are symbols which it has known since ancient times. These same symbols appear in our dreams. Imagery is often used in combination with sacred ritual for like symbols, ritual is also well known to the soul. Used in combination, the results can be even more dramatic.

A colleague shared how imagery and ritual had eased the soul pain of a young mother who had delivered a stillborn infant. Each night the mother was plagued by troublesome dreams in which she saw her child in need of cleansing and turning. A guided imagery was conducted using the symbol of water, both for cleansing of the physical body and of the soul, as well as to symbolize the stream flowing between this life and the next. The mother symbolically cleansed and nurtured her infant. She then gently placed the babe in the arms of a waiting angel. The imagery and sacred acts of ritual freed the mother from her torturous dreams.

I practice and teach meditative techniques, including visualization, imagery and sacred ritual. I use them alone, in combinations, and in combination with breathing exercises and energy-transfer techniques. I use them when there is a need to release guilt and regret. I use them when there is a need for forgiveness, when there is a need to let go of the past and move life forward, regardless of the reason.

I believe one of the most difficult things to do in healing is to free oneself from the past. Yet until we do so, until we let go of all that is holding us there, we cannot really make progress.

My conscious efforts to heal were dramatically and positively affected by the writings of Louise Hay. I have given numerous copies of her book *You Can Heal Your Life*[9] to those I work with. From her, I learned the healing power of ritual. From her, I learned to affirm myself. During those intense dark times, shrouded in the navy velvet of depression, I copied from her book twelve affirmations which applied to my life and to my need for healing. Determined, I forced myself early from bed each morning and made my way to the stillness of the room which I now call my sacred space. Since in my depressive state I was unable to memorize, I read each affirming statement over and over, until every cell was filled to overflowing with the new information it needed in order to replace the old that had for so long been so tightly lodged within. Months later I was able to recite them as I walked outdoors.

One of the most difficult things to come to terms with was that I had not been able to say goodbye to my son. I dreamed.

My son appeared, looking much as he had at about five years of age. He paused in our present home's entrance to examine, in detail, the clay carvings he had created as a child. As if to reinforce some important message for me, and to validate some reality for himself, he questioned me several times, "I made these when I was your little boy?"

I knew I had been shown that my son had learned lessons from me when he was in my care. Now he had other lessons to learn, past learning that he needed to build upon. I was instantaneously aware that I was holding him from what was now important for him to be doing. I needed to set him free. He had things to do and my grief was not only holding me back, it was interfering with his ability to move toward what he was to accomplish next.

I was afraid to let go, terrified that in the letting go I would be dishonoring our relationship. Yet I knew, holding so tightly to the bonds of the past, I could not move my life forward. I knew continuing to focus on the pain of the past was consuming the energy I needed for developing other ways for using my abilities.

Mustering courage, of which I had little, I began. I chose a hill, one I had passed, weeping nearly every morning on my walks. It was early spring. The first rays were only beginning to design pink fluffy cherubs on the clouds. I reached for the sky. Holding open my palms I affirmed as I had learned from Louise Hay's book,[10] "I release the past with love." I visualized pain and sorrow flowing from my heart and streaming out of my palms, falling to the earth like black grains of coal. When I could no longer see any darkness streaming from me, I visualized gold light flowing from the hands of the Creator and into my crown. I watched as the light streamed downward, filling my entire body. I affirmed "As I release the past, the new and fresh and vital enter."

That night I dreamed. My son appeared. He approached. His arms surrounded me. I felt his warmth, his young vibrant life. I moaned, "If only I could have said goodbye." He said, "Mother, there is no need to say goodbye."

Taking a breath, which came from a depth I did not know existed within me, I wailed, "I set you free." My words surrounded him with a whirling rainbow. The rainbow swirled upward. I knew I must complete the affirmation, "As I set you free I set myself free." My son dissolved into an incredible light. The same light penetrated and surrounded me.

Transformation!

Walking the next morning, I talked with my child. I asked that even though he had things to do that I knew nothing of, nor in which I could be involved, would it be possible for him to hold my hand for a few moments during my early morning walks. My hand warmed to his touch. "Awareness" surrounded me. I did not have to say goodbye. He was not really gone from me. By setting him free, I could be closer than when I hung on so tightly.

I was reminded of a poster from somewhere in my past, with prose by Fritz Perls. "If you love someone set them free. If they come back, they're yours. If they don't, they never were."

And so for months . . . and on into years, for a few moments each morning as I trek the fields, my son holds one hand and my dad the other. I often sense that they are turning a rope, inviting me to skip, to again be childlike. I ask my son to share his sense of humor. From my dad I request his gift of courage.

Letting go of the past with love set me free and opened me to being able to receive the gifts of the new beginnings. I receive in gratitude. I am grateful for the tremendous abundance that has entered into my life since I first echoed thank you for the sun's healing light.

I am grateful for my daily bread, aware of all that bread symbolizes, and knowing that I do not live on bread alone.[11]

Forgiveness is the catalyst for movement forward.

Martin Luther King

Forgiveness

Recently I was contacted by a mother who had just been informed that her father had sexually violated her daughter during childhood. For years the mother had witnessed her daughter's emotional and spiritual pain. She never knew the source of her pain, or the root of her daughter's suicidal thoughts and frequent attempts. Recognizing the truth, and comprehending the long and arduous process of healing her daughter must face, tortured the guilt-ridden mother. Smoldering anger and intense feelings of hatred threatened her physical, emotional and spiritual life.

Anger, hatred, guilt and regret are the emotional manifestations of the spiritual need for forgiveness. Guilt and regret stem from a need for self-forgiveness. Guilt is an expression of things done we wish we had not done. Regret is an expression of things not done we know we could have. Self-hatred is rooted in the need to forgive oneself. Projected hatred is rooted in the need to forgive another. Anger, the emotional expression of hatred, can manifest when there is a need for self-forgiveness, as well

171

as when there is a need to forgive another. Anger, both at self or at the other, is expressed to the degree that feelings of hatred are harbored.

Self-anger may be turned inward in an effort to disguise it in more socially acceptable ways. The physical body is not fooled. Illness and chronic conditions, rooted in self-hatred, continue to be nourished by the food of anger, guilt and regret. Self-hatred can be expressed in negative self-talk (soul talk). Anger and hatred, constantly infused into every cell of the body, digest the vital energy necessary for healthy growth and maintenance.

Self-anger can also be expressed outwardly, manifesting in numerous self-abusive ways. Wrist slashing and drug overdose are not the only forms of self-punishment. Self-mutilating behaviors, such as picking holes in the skin, pulling out hair or eye lashes, not exercising the body, not feeding it nutritious foods, smoking cigarettes, overusing alcohol and medication, using street drugs, and being involved in life-threatening and dangerous activities, can all indicate a desire to punish or even destroy a self that feels unworthy.

Anger, rooted in hatred toward another, can also be expressed in both overt and covert ways. We may outwardly demonstrate anger toward another through hostile and abusive words or behaviors. Or we may attempt to disguise our hatred by shrouding it in sarcasm, criticism, manipulation, or by blocking the other's goals.

When we are unable to forgive another, we are unable to forgive ourselves. When we are unable to forgive ourselves, we are unable to truly love ourselves. When we are unable to see our own worth, it is difficult to see the worth in others. When we are unable to identify the good within us, we are unable to give it away. A need for forgiveness is at the root of life's most difficult to heal circumstances.

If we examine the life story of the mother, her father and daughter in a framework of living one lifetime, letting go of the anger and hatred attached to their inability to forgive their father and grandfather would be an extremely difficult task. If, however, we step back and view the situation within the larger perspective of the continuation of life, and lifetimes, we see this scenario, and all of life's traumas in a different light.

Speaking of her regression experience, one woman stated she had glimpsed levels of creation far above anything she could imagine. She was shown that everything has meaning on a higher level. Suffering is not random; it is merely part of an eternal plan more complex and awe-inspiring than we are capable of imagining.

In *Only Love is Real*,[1] Brian Weiss shares thoughts on forgiveness mouthed from men and women who had been regressed to other life-times in order to review the important lessons of the life just completed, and to examine how that life's lesson was affecting the present lifetime. One subject reported that while God forgives, forgiveness is also a personal responsibility. True forgiveness is about forgiving and being forgive by God and by others. "We have all done those things for which we condemn others. If we want to be forgiven, we must forgive them. . . . Psychoanalysis does not repair the damage. You still have to go beyond understanding and make changes, improve the world, repair relationships, forgive others and accept their forgiveness."[2]

Drawing conclusions from information collected from regressed subjects on the topic of forgiveness, I believe it is important to acknowledge that we each have to change religions, races, and nationalities. We experience lifetimes of extreme wealth and of abject poverty, of sickness and of health. We are given opportunities to learn from all sides in order to understand and to grow.

Reviewing the data gathered from my own clients, and that collected from thousands of regressed subjects by various researchers and therapists, it is impossible to draw other conclusions. The findings reported in both the professional and lay literature concur. We are thrown into lifetimes to meet the same people, and to struggle with the unmet challenges of previous lifetimes until the soul learns the required lessons.

A woman shared that her early childhood memories were shrouded by her mother's battle with fears, dreads, anxieties and feelings of inadequacy and, finally, death by suicide. During a meditation, and again in a dream, she witnessed her mother reborn and already in her teen years. She viewed the teenaged girl's attempts at taking her own life, due to perceived insurmountable inadequacies.

The woman's mother had not been able to move beyond the mental difficulties in the life they had shared. Her mother had not been able to meet the challenges which had been set for her soul's progress and was now facing, in yet another life situation, challenges similar to what she had faced before.

We discussed the notion of accumulated karma, of viewing life's challenges as lessons to be learned, and of passing the tests as soul development for movement into Oneness. We spoke of the need to forgive and to be forgiven. We discussed the possibility of lightening her mother's karma by extending to her thoughts of love and compassion. I guided an imagery in which I invited her to release her mother from the fetters holding her in bondage. I ask her to use a violet flame of love to dissolve the cord of anger and hurt connecting her to her mother's cord of guilt and regret. I guided her to extend love and compassion. I asked that she break open the shackles imprisoning her mother by granting forgiveness for the traumatizing pain that had been inflicted upon her by her mother's illness and death. I guided the smoothing of the energy field that now surrounded her rebirthed soul. I spoke to her of wiping away the erratic energy and of smoothing and bringing balance to the energy field. I asked her to surround the soul of her mother in a protective blanket of crystal clear light.

When we expand our thinking to include not only one lifetime, but the continuation of the soul, we recognize not only our ability, but also our responsibility to assist the souls of our loved ones on their spiritual journey. When we are able to fathom the incredible difference that extending love can make, we will understand, as well, our tremendous responsibility to our soul's group, and to the soul of the collective. When we are able to see the soul outside the parameters of one lifetime, we acknowledge our personal responsibility in all that happens to us.

While we do not like to admit that we have had a hand in creating the situations which now face us, and that we have actually designed our own tests in this life, the understanding of this important lesson is paramount to our soul's development. The thousands of case studies, reported from a variety of mythical, traditional and research sources, all reveal we face the same people, the same situations, until we learn the lessons required by our soul.

We are reminded in numerous ways what it is the soul needs to accomplish in order to move into Oneness with the Divine Flame. The tests set for our soul, and by our soul, are always based upon two major lessons. The soul must learn to love, and the soul must acquire knowledge of truth. Both lessons are intertwined and interdependent. With knowledge comes love. With love comes knowledge.

Forgiveness of self is required for self-love and compassion. Forgiveness of another is required for love and compassion toward the other. With knowledge comes compassion; with compassion forgiveness is possible.

But what exactly is forgiveness? I have sour memories of sermons on forgiveness. Sermons, of the same type, have been shared by numerous women who have lived in abusive situations as children and/or in their adult relationships. These same pain-filled sermons have been shared by men submerged in guilt and regret.

The concepts of forgiving, forgetting and condoning are not the same; yet they are often used interchangeably. This creates tremendous confusion in the already clouded thinking of those struggling with deep hurt. When the concepts of forgiveness, condoning and forgetting are not clearly separated, forgiveness becomes almost impossible; the formidable task creates considerable unnecessary suffering.

Abuse or hurtful behaviors of any kind must never be condoned. Such behaviors are inflicted by an enslaved soul, and such behaviors enslave the soul of another.

Psychological and educational studies have demonstrated that violence begets violence. Parents who abuse are failing themselves, their children, and all of human kind. Even though the child might have a karmic lesson related to learning how to deal with violence, the parent has been given the responsible role of teaching the child to learn loving ways in relationships. Parents who abuse are not only hindering their child's soul development, but they are also failing their own karmic tests. With every violent thought and action they are accumulating enormous negative karma; they are contributing to the critical mass of violence in the universal consciousness. We must never condone such behaviors; we must do all in our power to stop the ever-escalating violent activity in our world. Soul development is at stake. World peace hangs in the balance.

While we never condone violence of any sort, before we can be free from the strangling hold on our soul, of the hatred infused by the hurt, we must find ways to forgive ourselves of any responsibility on our part, and to release in forgiveness those who have harmed us.

In forgiveness we must come to the place where we are able to separate the person, the enslaved human soul, from the behavior. Separating the person from his or her behavior is not only a technique to learn and apply in forgiveness, it is also the most effective way to guide our children in right conduct. As parents, we must acknowledge the human spirit housed within the little being placed in our charge. When a child misbehaves, it is not only much wiser and more accurate, it is also more effective, to remind the child they are very loved but the behavior they are involved in cannot, and will not, be tolerated. It is shattering to a child's soul to hear they are bad, or to be struck. They are attempting to learn lessons. They need help from those they have selected to be their human guides. When we fail them we do considerable harm. When we do not pass our own lessons as teacher and guide, we accumulate considerable negative karma that will have to be balanced, either in this life or in future incarnations.

Perhaps, in this lifetime, but surely in another, or even in many others, an abusive person will face, from all sides, the situation in which they have inflicted pain upon another. They will bear the suffering and they will have to learn to forgive. Karmic tests will be set. They will be thrown into circumstances where the tests will be for them to find solutions other than violence.

While in the beginning of healing, forgiving the people who have hurt us (or forgiving ourselves) while condemning the behavior, sounds absurd, it really is the only way. Separation of the soul from the behavior of the human being in this present lifetime really is the only way in which true forgiveness can be accomplished. When we learn to separate the person from the behavior, and when we are able to see another in terms of his or her immortal soul, we acquire an awareness from which total forgiveness can be accomplished. When we view our own lives in terms of lessons to be learned and tests to be passed, in order to advance our soul's growth, self forgiveness becomes a reality. When we ponder the circumstances surrounding our hurts, when we enlarge our view, when we incorporate notions of soul growth over time, we recognize our responsibility. When we accept our role, our responsibility for what has transpired, true forgiveness happens.

A colleague shared an incredible story of forgiveness in terms of life's lessons. During meditation, a familiar, yet distant, voice called repeatedly. With each call, her name became more audible. When assured of her full attention, the voice inquired, "Who has wounded thee?" She whispered, "My mother, my father, my brother." The voice demanded, "Are you willing to forgive?" Beseechingly, she cried, "I truly want to forgive." The voice echoed, "Then behold your teachers!" Each in turn, her mother, father and brother appeared before her, radiating in their spirit essence. Only as they approached did she notice their shackles. Each embraced her; each thanked her for the freedom she had given. In the exchange of love and forgiveness, their shackles fell, clanging loudly as they landed. The voice interrupted the reunion, "You may now release your own." She had not noticed the chains wrapping her. They dropped. They dissolved; light sprang from the spot where they had been. The light moved, drawing her attention to a far-distant golden door. A path wound in that direction. The voice guided. "Your travels will now be lighter; journey to the threshold."

Forgiveness is an exercise in compassion. Forgiveness is an exercise in freedom. Forgiveness frees our souls and sets free the souls of the others. Anger, hatred, guilt and regret bind us to the past, keeping our souls, and the souls of the others enslaved. Forgiveness is an act of the will. Forgiveness stems from a choice we must make, a choice to release ourselves from the grip that the hurt has on us, and from the grip we have on the souls of others.

Over the centuries, seers and spiritual teachers have described the process for forgiveness. In *Guilt is the Teacher, Love is the Lesson*,[3] Joan Borysenko outlined a six-step path. The steps are:

1. Take responsibility for what you did.
2. Confess the nature of your wrongs to God, yourself, and another human being.
3. Look for your good points.
4. Be willing to make amends where possible, as long as you can do this without harm to yourself or other people.
5. Look to God for help.
6. Inquire about what you learned.

While she lists six important steps, each is a part of the first. Each demands that we examine our responsibility in the wrongdoing.

Forgiveness, both of ourselves and of others, requires that we take responsibility for our every action. Forgiveness demands that we acknowledge our responsibility to every other soul. To take responsibility means that we examine, in the most soul-searching ways, what we have done to contribute to the behavior. It means that we view the circumstances, that we examine the situation in the way the soul will examine it when we pass before the karmic judges. Our souls will review our behavior in terms of how well we have passed the karmic lessons of this lifetime, as based upon the lessons we have set for the progress of our souls in terms of our overall soul development, and the overall soul growth of humanity. Our soul progress will be judged based upon how well we have loved ourselves and the other, and on how we have shown compassion for our self and others.

During a guided imagery, one woman witnessed herself standing before her guides. She was frozen into a pillar of ice by her own unresolved guilt, by her own self-defined need for forgiveness. She was directed in ways to show more love and compassion to herself.

Dr. Whitton shares a further example to show how our unwillingness to forgive others also interferes with our soul's development. In this case, the subject found herself examining a lifetime in which she had been taken captive by a man whose tribesmen had plundered her village and killed her kin. She lived many years in the home of the enemy, never giving of herself, never forgiving, never loving in any way, and finally dying at her own hand. In reviewing the lessons of that life she recognized that she could have chosen differently. Despite the circumstances she was being asked to love those who had done her wrong. Had she chosen forgiveness, there was much good she could have accomplished, both in that lifetime and in regard to her soul's growth and the soul growth of humanity. She witnessed ways in which she could have helped the small children in the enemy camp. They had nothing to do with the actions that had caused her so much pain. Helping them would have changed her own circumstances and karmic lot, their life circumstances and karmic lot, and would have moved the entire collective forward.[4]

We are frequently reminded it is not the event but our perception, and subsequent response to the event, that creates joy or sorrow in our life. To quote Shakespeare, "Nothing is either good or bad, but thinking makes it so."[5] It is not so much what happens, even though we may have lived through an excruciatingly painful event, but it is our response to that event that will pull us either backward into bitterness or forward into peace, not only in this lifetime but in future incarnations as well. It is our willingness to compassionately forgive ourselves and those who have wounded us that determines the degree to which our souls will evolve.

In *The Illuminated Life*,[6] Abe Arkoff gives a clear example of how it is often not the event but our perception of the event that determines how we respond. A counselor was assisting brothers who had been raised by an alcoholic father. One brother drank excessively, the other hardly touched alcohol. Curious as to their perception of why this might be so, the psychologist asked of the alcoholic, "You have told me that you drank excessively for most of your adult life. Can you tell me why this might be so?" The response was quick, "Oh, that is easy. You see my father was an alcoholic. You might say that I learned at his knees to drink." Of the brother who hardly touched alcohol the psychologist asked, "You have told me that you hardly ever drink alcohol. Can you tell me why this might be so?" Once again the response was quick in coming, "Oh, that is easy. You see my father was an alcoholic. You might say that I learned at his knees that alcohol can be a poison."

We all have had bad things happen. We each must decide how we will use the experience. This is why forgiving is not the same as forgetting. We remember what we have been through. Each experience marks us uniquely. Each experience, and our response to the experience, is engraved upon every cell in our body, becomes our consciousness, and is inscribed into our Akashic Record, the record of our soul's progress.

Often, when difficult events happen in childhood, we believe that our life course has been determined by our circumstances. The circumstances have been the tests. How we meet the challenges, how we pass the tests, depends upon us. We are responsible for the choices we make. Claiming responsibility for our own lives and for our choices are the first steps in moving our lives forward. Claiming responsibility is the first step in forgiving ourselves or others. Acknowledging any blame that we own, and making amends for any part that we have played in the wrongdoing is required for forgiveness to happen.

Claiming responsibility is not easy. We would rather hide behind guilt. Somehow it seems easier to face the world with guilt than to admit to our responsibility. Hidden beneath guilt often lurks the true feeling – shame. Facing shame pushes us closer to ownership, to responsibility. What did we not do that we should have done? What did we do that we ought not to have done?

As long as I felt guilt over my son's death, self-forgiveness did not happen. And without self-forgiveness, healing was impossible. I had to face the shame. I had to acknowledge my responsibility. I was very ashamed. I had been given a child to nurture and to protect until adulthood. I had not acted in a responsible way. I had allowed my child to be in a situation that was dangerous. I had not honored my role as a parent. I had to own the responsibility.

Admitting the true emotion, the emotion of shame, and clearly voicing my lack of responsible action allowed me to ask my son's forgiveness. Admitting the true emotion, the emotion of shame, and clearly voicing my lack of responsible action allowed me to ask forgiveness from my God. Both already knew the truth anyway. Only I was blinded. I was the one who had to unearth the shame and to claim fully the responsibly for my lack of action.

Allowing the shame to be a part of what had shaped me, but yet not allowing it to hinder my life was necessary before I could fully accept the requested forgiveness. Dissolving the painful feelings associated with the emotion was also an important and necessary part.

The Buddhists teach that training ourselves in the art of mindful-breathing is crucial for knowing how to manage and release emotions. I began mindful-breathing.

In mindful-breathing we do not try to suppress the emotion or express it. In mindful-breathing we bring the energy of mindfulness to the emotion. We allow the mindful-energy to surround and nurture and hold the emotion. The practice reminded me of a technique I had learned for pain management. Years previous I had taught laboring mothers to breathe into the contraction. When I nursed palliative patients I had taught them not to avoid the pain but to breathe into it. These mindful-breathing exercises had made a considerable and positive difference to the pain experienced.

Thich Nhat Hanh[7] compares the holding of an emotion in a mindful-way to a mother holding her infant when it cries. In mindful-breathing we hold our emotion and our pain in a caring, nurturing loving way and allow it to come to peace within the arms of love and compassion.

Mindful-breathing is effective. I practice and teach mindful-breathing whenever there is need to control and release physical or emotional pain. The energy from mindful-breathing not only calms, but after a time it moves our attention deeply to the source. The insight that comes allows us to see the truth about the situation, allowing us to examine the root of the emotion, the pain. The insight which follows can lead us to the place where forgiveness can happen.

While mindful-breathing practices are believed to be based upon Eastern thought, I gained similar understanding of the management of emotions from a gifted teacher. While it took a long time for me to gain the awareness, I finally recognized the numerous similarities between the sacred practices used by peoples from various parts of the world. Some believe this is because the continents were once joined. Or is it because we all come from the Source – from Great Oneness? Is it because, each of us is in and a part of All?

According to the teachings of the Sacred Wheel, the lessons of forgiveness are learned in the North. Our journey to the North of the Sacred Wheel is in search of Wisdom. Wisdom is acquired through listening, through forgiveness, and through living in balance. These three roads must be traversed many times. Each time we are tempered by the fire of experience. Like the warrior who begins his training and often feels overwhelmed by the sheer difficulties of running and of going without food, those who journey to the North, the place of wisdom, the place of the elder, must be prepared to persevere. Nothing is gained without a price.[8]

The shell, the pipe and the tomahawk are often used as symbols of the North. The shell teaches that listening to the voice of the Creator in all of creation leads to wisdom. The tomahawk represents peace, but the peacemaker must know when to bury the hatchet and forgive, and when to defend the truth.[9]

The wise know their responsibility in the proper use of truth and forgiveness. Harmful deeds cannot be condoned, but they must be forgiven. Without the proper use of truth and forgiveness there can be no justice. Without justice there can be no peace or security in the affairs of the world. The lesson of balance teaches that all things fit together, the road walked during our physical life and the road of spirit, our male side and our female side. Balance, when applied to the interconnectedness of all human beings, becomes justice.

I began to understand responsibility in a much bigger ways. I added a prayer requesting forgiveness for all the times I had not loved as I should have. I begged, "God of Love, take my imperfect love. Transform it into Your Perfect Love and fill with Your Perfect Love all whom I should have loved better."

Under heaven all can see beauty as beauty only because there is ugliness. All can know good as good only because there is evil.

Lao Tsu – *Tao Te Ching*

Temptation, Sin and Evil

Prior to my son's death I had given little thought to the notion of evil. I had generally assumed that since I did not break the Commandments, evil was a remote enemy that did not touch my existence. Similarity, I had never thought much about the concept of sin. Yet, somehow in grief, each time the word appeared in dialogue, prayer or worship, it drew my full attention, submerging me in waves of stormy emotion.

The more attentive I became, the more I recognized the many ways in which the prayers I had recited, probably a million times, and with probably a million others, carried strong messages reinforcing our unworthiness as human beings. Anger flowed from deep internal conflict. I had become aware of giving lip service to something I did not believe about myself, my self-worth and my relationship to my Creator. But more importantly, at that time in my life the sin overtones threatened my beliefs about my son's worth in the eyes of the Father-Mother God and, therefore, his life after death.

I did not believe I was a sinner, nor did I believe I had lived a sin-filled life. I did not believe my son was a sinner or that he had lived a sin-filled life. Yet I knew that both he and I had done deeds that were within my religion's definition of sin.

I recalled as a youngster making a list of sins so I would have them ready for confession, which happened every Saturday night. Some of my friends had to make up sins to have something worthwhile to confess. I never had to. I always had the fights with my brother to report on. And I knew my son and his sisters had been engaged in similar childhood struggles. Had these "sins" made him unworthy in the sight of God?

I had been taught that sin was opposite to God. How could an unworthy sinner hope to rejoin a sinless God? Yet how could a child of God, someone who had come from God, and was of God, be sinful? The inconsistencies burned.

It was shattering to question whether the numerous references to sin in the prayer and sermons of my childhood were yet another control tactic. I could no longer believe or defend the ideas of sin I had learned. I could no longer mouth the words of the numerous prayers that did less than support the sacredness of my spiritual heritage, or that of my son's.

I needed to know the truth about this concept. While there were references to sin in the Bible, I was surprised at how few, and most of these seemed to use the word interchangeably with the word evil. Were evil and sin the same thing?

Jesus had not used the word sin. He had used the word evil. He had asked that we pray: "Lead us not into temptation, but deliver us from evil." In *The Dictionary of the Bible*[1] John McKenzie states that "the word (sin) is more common in 1 John than in the Synoptic Gospels and it more commonly signifies not the single act but the state or condition induced by the evil act." I pondered. McKenzie saw sin as a single act and evil as a condition. Did that mean accumulation of sin led to an evil condition? Was evil always the opposite of good? Life had taught me the two were not necessarily dichotomous.

In *The Prophet*,[2] the elders of the city asked the Prophet to speak about good and evil.

He replied, "Of good in you I can speak, but not of the evil. For what is evil but good tortured by its own hunger and thirst?" He adds, "You are good in countless ways and you are not evil when you are not good. You are only loitering and sluggard."

We are reminded that when we are loitering and sluggish we are not evil, but nor are we as "good" as we are capable of being. Doing less than is our best keeps us from knowing our greatest "good" for it retards movement in that direction. The Prophet noted, "Pity that the stag cannot teach swiftness to the turtles."

Was Jesus, as Gibran, reminding us that while it is easier to do only what gets us by, such a choice is the slow road to Godliness. Jesus was saying, do not be tempted by the little sins of doing less than what you are capable of. Little sins rip away at our shield of goodness. The shield of godliness keeps evil from penetrating. Jesus would have comprehended what the ancients knew and what is still practiced in numerous cultures around the world. We do need to shield from evil, for evil does exist in the physical world and in the world of the spirit. One of the best shields is to be always moving in the direction of goodness, the path to Oneness. For we are then surrounded in the armor of love.

The Ten Commandments have guided Jews and Christians in what not to do to achieve goodness. Jesus came to teach what to do. Jesus taught love. The Buddha, like Jesus, taught what to do. The Buddha taught right action.[3]

In *Only Love is Real*,[4] Brian Weiss tells of a lesson about right action that a subject received while glimpsing a past life. "Action becomes right action when it becomes action along the way, along the path toward God. . . . Action that fosters justice and mercy and love and wisdom, and the attributes we call godly or spiritual is inevitably right action."

The Five Wonderful Precepts of Buddhism that teach of right action are: reverence for life, generosity, responsible sexual behavior, speaking and listening deeply, and ingesting only wholesome substances. Following these precepts leads to goodness in ourselves, in our family and in our society.

In *Living Buddha Living Christ*[5] Thich Nhat Hanh rephrases the Precepts of Buddhism to address the problems of our times. He describes that the "precepts inter-are." When we practice one fully, we practice them all. Each is interwoven into the next.

Ripping at the fabric of our society and our world are behaviors which desecrate the precepts of right action. Ripping away at our social fabric is the destruction of life, exploitation, social injustice, lying, stealing and oppression. Sexual activity involving violence and abuse against children, and against those disempowered from choice by lies and greed, rip at our fabric. Greed, in the overuse of food, drink and the resources provided through the abundant universe, rips at our fabric. Such actions defile and desecrate the sacred order in the universe.

Desecration of the sacred order is evil. This, I believe, is what Jesus referred to when he used the words, "deliver us from evil." Jesus was aware of the misuse of power, and of how power is often used to control in order to get greed needs met. Jesus was aware of how the misuse of power can give instant gratification. He was also aware of the karmic debt build when one does so. Jesus encouraged us to pray for the strength to resist this temptation. Jesus knew the temptation for instant gratification. He also knew that it can lead to evil. Jesus was aware that we must be armored against evil for evil, robs the soul of Divine Light.

Our soul is like a microcosm – a universe, made of many parts. Each soul part is alive because of the Divine Spark within it. Each part glows with the Eternal Flame. Each part has unique characteristics, unique gifts. At our creation, our soul was overflowing with Divine Presence. As a torch lit from the Divine Flame, we were endowed with heritage gifts.

Evil dims the Divine Light in our soul parts and robs the heritage gifts enshrined there. Evil can invade from our own actions, our own karma, the actions or the karma of others. When the light in a soul part dims, confusion sets in.

Jesus knew that we needed to protect ourselves from evil. The ancients were much closer to the world of spirit. They appear to have had a better understanding than most of us of the forces of good and the forces of evil. They had well-developed practices of shielding and guarding. These practices have been previously described in the chapter titled Soul's Armor. We need to reinstitute these practices. We need to protect ourselves and our loved ones from the escalation of evil which is invading our universe.

Jesus knew we would need help in protecting from evil and with being delivered from evil. Jesus came to offer salvation. Salvation comes from the Latin word "salvo" meaning to "save," "to heal," "to make whole." I believe salvation means to rid of spiritual intrusions and to reclaim each lost soul part. Jesus frequently cast out evil spirits, and through his touch made the person whole. He knew we would be in need of help in ridding ourselves of evil intrusions, in being made whole and in reclaiming our lost soul parts. He knew that, only in our completeness, in our total goodness, could we rejoin in Oneness with the Flame from which we came.

Ancient traditions recognized spiritual intrusions and soul loss. Shamans respond to the needs of the soul. In the Early Christian tradition, spiritual intrusions were recognized. Ritual was performed to protect from evil, to exorcize, and to reclaim spiritual essence for the soul.

While the concepts of good and evil, spiritual intrusions and soul loss are not used in common parlance, nevertheless, the need for soul-healing rituals are very real.

I have experienced soul loss and soul retrieval. I know how incomplete I was during those empty years. I know how differently I felt immediately following the return of soul parts, once following a personal healing ritual, once through the mediation of a Shaman. I work with those who have soul-shattering experiences. I witness the positive changes in their lives following the extraction of spiritual intrusions and the return of lost soul parts.

I once believed that soul loss and spiritual intrusion were a result of experiences faced in this lifetime. But I now know that souls do not necessarily come into a lifetime totally whole and complete. Children have phobias and fears, skin conditions, allergies, birthmarks and even physical conditions resulting from the traumas of past lives.[6,7] Therapists performing past-life regression find that traumatic memories arise more frequently than peaceful memories. Spiritual intrusions and soul-shattering experiences are carried over into the next lifetime because the karma carried with that experience still requires balancing.

In the Catholic religion parents are told to baptize their infants quickly, for should they die the infant soul would be suspended in limbo. In *Spirit Song*,[8] Shaman Mary Summer Rain, shares information from her spiritual guides on the relationship between limbo and non-baptized souls. " Specific sect beliefs have no bearing on the reality . . . here." Furthermore, the souls of dead infants "are not infant souls but are really eons old."

Yet, I sometimes "hold the space," creating a safe environment for the physical body while the spirit of a Shaman journeys. Retrieval of a lost soul part, or parts is frequently required to complete the healing of the person for whom the Shaman journeys. While lost soul parts linger in various fear-based locations, on occasion the Shaman is required to jour-ney to the "Valley of the Dead" to reclaim a zombie-like soul part. The first time I heard the description of this setting, I was astounded that the images shared were identical to the image I had conjured of the Plain of Asphodel in Hades, which I had read about in Homer's *Iliad*.[9]

While many associate Hades synonymously with hell, Hades was actually described as a spiritual realm consisting of three plains. Elysian Fields was the place of reward for those who had greatly pleased the gods. The Plain of Asphodel was dismal. There night and day merged into eter-nal twilight. There stayed those who could not convince the judges their life merited the rewards of Elysian Fields. Tartarus, the place of eternal damnation, would be most similar to the Christian notion of hell.

While some might conceive of the Plain of Asphodel, or the Valley of The Dead, to be the place described in Christianity as purgatory, Mary Summer Rain[10] shares that her guide revealed that purgatory is not in the world of spirit, but is of the physical realm. The living-hell situations we find ourselves and others in are purgatory opportunities, purging opportunities, given to the soul to balance karma.

While I believe I was originally given an inaccurate message about limbo, and about what happens after death, my work with traditional healers has convinced me there is such an afterlife state as limbo. I believe it to be the place where a soul or soul parts exist that are barely able to keep alight the Divine Spark.

I also believe there is an important reason why the practice of baptism was initially introduced, and remains important in Christian practice. Baptism is a sacrament. The spirit of God is invited to descend during a sacrament. The practice of baptism is a ritual instituted to balance "original sin." Is it possible that during baptism soul parts lingering in a limbo state are drawn into the soul through the infusion of spirit?

We like to think of original sin as the sin of Adam. We like not to own blame, not to bear our own responsibility. Yet Adam is a symbolic representation of each of us. We each have committed our own original and subsequent sins. We each have committed original and subsequent acts for which karma descended. The way home, the path to Oneness, is through soul healing, through the balancing of karma and through the infusion of the energy of the Great Spirit, the Holy Spirit, the Breath of Life, the Breath of God, or by whatever other name we choose to describe the essence of the Creator which fills us and moves us forward.

Soul healing is essential for a broken soul is incomplete. The more complete we are, the more capable we are of drawing in Divine Energy, and the more capable we are of sending it forth from us in the form of good deeds, good works.

While Shamanic practices and sacramental ritual provide soul healing, other rituals and practices also restore and heal the soul. We can reclaim lost soul parts for ourselves through the practices of meditation, sacred imagery and visualization, and through prayer. I believe, however, that for prayer to be truly healing it must come from the soul of the seeker. A dialogue with the Creator, in a voice which cries from the depth of one's brokenness, rather than from the reiteration by rote memory of the words formed within the soul of another, is the catalyst for soul healing.

Healing practices have been used since ancient times to restore souls and to heal soul pain. When I was in South America I was introduced to a symbol I have come to recognize as the Whirling Rainbow. It is a symbol for achieving unity and wholeness. I often apply the Whirling Rainbow in a ritual by surrounding, in a whirling vortex of rainbow colors, any area of concern, or any request. After surrounding the request within a vortex of whirling rainbow colors, I encase the rainbow vortex in a second vortex of whirling colors. Colors in the second rainbow vortex resonate above the frequencies of the earth plane rainbow. The first color in the second vortex begins just above the frequency of violet.

Violet in the earth plane rainbow has the highest frequency of the rainbow colors. The frequency of violet resonates most closely with the frequency of the spiritual plane. Violet is the point of transition to the next octave of light.

There are many stories of healing and self-transformation that describe violet to be the transcendental color between the physical and spiritual worlds. In *Violet Flame to Heal Body, Mind and Soul*,[11] Elizabeth Clare Prophet interprets these ancient practices of self transformation. "The Violet Flame changes negative energy into positive energy, darkness into light, fate into opportunity. . . . The violet flame is able to transmute or mitigate our negative karma." . . . The Violet Flame works by changing vibrations. In physics, vibration is the speed of oscillation – the speed at which something moves back and forth. On the atomic level, vibrations can be understood to be the speed at which electrons orbit around the nucleus of the atom. The Violet flame works by changing vibrations on this level." Negativity equals density. More spiritually developed persons have less density within each atom. Because of this their electrons whirl faster and faster, thus raising the vibrations.

According to the teachings surrounding the use of the Violet Flame, we can raise our own vibrations to a more spiritual level by infusing into our being vibrations of violet. Infusions of violet transmute negative energy held within the atoms of our being by transforming it into light.

The Bible teaches that it is a good and holy thing to pray for the dead.[12] Freeing, those who have left the physical realm from the bonds of karma that bind them to us is among the worthiest of prayers. The Violet Flame is a powerful meditation for burning away karmic bonds and works as well to release us from karma with someone who is living as well as with someone who has died.

During meditation I visualize a Sacred Fire before me. I image the flames turning from red-orange to violet. When they are glowing vibrantly violet, I invite the flames to move toward me, to engulf me, to fill every cell with violet, and to then flow into and completely fill my aura. When my aura is filled with violet flame, I visualize the person I believe I might have negative karmic bonds with. I instruct the flame to burn away any karmic bonds which bind me to the other, and the other to me. I visualize the flame moving from the Sacred Fire to engulf and infiltrate the being now standing before me, and to burn away any karmic ties. I then draw the flames back into myself, then into the Sacred Fire just in front of me, and invite the other to move from me, free from any bondage to me or with me. Next, I visualize two souls, full and complete, neither needing to own nor to bind, both free to move into the light of Oneness.

I have been taught similar meditations for increasing the Sacred Fire within. I like to visualize the light, warmth and goodness from Grandfather Sun joining and blending, at the center of my being, with the fire energy from the Earth. In this powerful meditation for achieving wholeness, the vibrant love energy flowing from the flaming core of the Earth Mother is brought up through the soles of my feet and into my Centre. Here, the nurturing fire from the Earth Mother joins in Sacred Union with the life-giving fire breathed into the Centre from Grandfather Sun. Once the fire from above, from below and from the self meld, it can be breathed into every cell of the body and moved into the aura to act as protective armor. No evil can penetrate this powerful shield of Divine Fire.

Sacred practices such as just described, that draw on the Divine Force within the elements, have been used around the world, and since ancient times, to heal and to shield from harm and from evil.[13, 14]

Many of these practices employ the use of symbols to add power to the protection and healing efforts. Such practices and their symbols are generally provided throughout the earth during troubled times and in miraculous ways. The practice of Reiki and the giving of the Reiki symbols is one such example.

Reiki, which originated in the Eastern world, provides symbols and practices for reclaiming wholeness. The second-degree symbols of Reiki, that can be reviewed in such books as Diane Stein's, *Essential Reiki*,[15] are powerful for shielding from evil and harm, and for offering healing for wounds sustained in this life as well as those which have originated in a previous life.

During a Reiki healing, the Power Symbol is used to open the condition to the flow of Divine Energy. *Hon Sha Ze Sho Nen*, the symbol for distance healing can be used to send healing energy into the past, including past lifetimes, as well as into the future. The energy associated with the *Sei He Ki* symbol brings mental and emotional balance. Reiki energy can heal the wounds of past karma and the karma collected within this lifetime. Reiki energy draws forth Divine Energy to be used in self-healing and for the healing of the body, mind and soul of another, as well as for the healing of the universe.

The Reiki symbols were given anew to the earth at the beginning of the 19th century. These symbols were to help draw in a more spiritual energy in order to accelerate the spiritual vibrations on our planet. Since then, new and more powerful symbols have been given. These include the Syrian energy symbols, one of which is a symbol for unconditional and universal love. This series of symbols is being channeled to the Earth's people from beings of a higher spiritual dimension. While they have not yet appeared in written form, they are being transmitted rapidly from one healing practitioner to another. There is a strong desire by spiritual beings from the higher dimensions to assist the Earth and her people to become more spiritual. The ultimate goal is to assist us in healing ourselves and our planet, thereby protecting the Earth from destruction.

It is also valuable to recognize that spiritual forces are not only assisting the Earth's people to becoming more spiritual, they are actually imprinting the Earth herself with sacred symbols. Crop circles are now to be found in many parts of the globe. Crop circles are impregnated with symbols. Many of the symbols are recognized as ancient sacred symbols, once used for healing and for protection. Others of the symbols are not recognizable, likely because information about them and their use has long ago been lost.

The spirit world is assisting our healing and protective efforts in numerous and various ways. We are being invited to partner with the spiritual realms in drawing into our world a more spiritual energy for the healing of our planet and of the Earth's people. The need is great.

Let us not be led into the temptation of believing we do not require such help. While we have a grave responsibility for creating good in our world, evil does exist. We have faced it before. Some battles we have won; some we have not. Trailing us is the karma acquired from the battles lost. We have been given numerous teachings and have been provided practices for freeing ourselves from further revolutions upon the karmic wheel. The kingdom awaits our decision.

I have no other master than the beeches and the oaks.

Bernard of Clairvaux

The Kingdom, Power and Glory

I have worshiped in great churches, temples and mosques around the world. I have stood on the hallowed ground of sacred sites and shrines. I have studied the doctrines and the dogmas. Yet none affirm as do the natural spires. Unconfined by the walls of man, the Cathedral of the Universe speaks of the power and glory of the Great Architect. The sermons of the mountains have been etched into my soul. The sacred message whispered by the pine and the willow, and re-echoed in the cry of the gull and the moan of the wind, resonates within my being.

As the Earth revealed herself as a living being, the rocks and trees, and indeed all within the natural world, have become awesome and holy. But most importantly, the magnificent order without has led to the discovery of the splendor within.

How could I have ever seen so many realities as dichotomous? How could I have viewed God and man, heaven and earth, sacred and secular, good and evil, living and dying at opposite ends of a continuum? Why had it taken so long to understand, as Ralph Waldo Emerson had, that "God is man in ruins,"[1] and that our ultimate aspiration is to mend the fractured human soul? Why had I not recognized sooner that the kingdom is not a place we are going to, but rather an experience we carry within?

Why had it taken me so long to discover what was really valuable in life? I believe that my son knew, at a subconscious level, that his life was short. He knew he would be leaving early in order that soul-growth lessons could be learned. In numerous ways throughout his young life, as well as since his death, he has guided me to view reality differently. While I would give anything to have learned, in less painful ways, the lessons his death taught me, I am aware that my son has been my greatest teacher.

In *Only Love is Real*,[2] Brian Weiss writes that over and over his hypnotized patients tell that death is not an accident. They emphasize that when children die, we are given opportunities to learn important lessons. "They are teachers to us, teaching us about values, priorities, and most of all, about love."

From my son I have learned about love. From my son I have learned about priorities. I have learned that when we live solely for the gain of this world we lose our roots and flutter in the tree tops. My son loved the natural world. I wish I had joined him more at the fishing hole and under the stars. There was much I could have learned. Had I been awake I could have discovered, so much earlier, the sacred lessons available along the path.

For some time now I have studied stones. I am becoming versed in their language. They share their history in picture form and in energy vibration. Recently, I found lying at the side of my well-worn path a most unusual rock. I cannot explain why I had not noticed it before. I can only assume I was not yet ready for the lessons it could offer.

There was no mistake. The imprint facing me was clearly that of a buffalo. Etched in white, against a clay-colored background, the impression was clear. I gladly accepted, in exchange for sweet sage, the gifts and the lesson contained there. The image invited an exploration of the prophecies of the return of the White Buffalo.

One teaching found in various spiritual traditions is that we are living in the time just prior to the dawning of the Fifth World of Peace. Thousands of Rainbow Warriors of both genders have rebirthed in order to bring about this reality. They are remembering the Sacred Knowledge learned before. The truths now being rekindled will be used for the benefit of all the Earth's children.

The prophecy warns that, before the return of the buffalo, fire from the sky will drop into the Earth's oceans. Purification will result. The ancient knowledge being remembered by the Rainbow Warriors, of how to grow food, how to heal, and how to connect to nature, will be needed by those who survive the time of enormous change.

We have not reverenced the glory and power of the Creator and Creation. We have over-used and over-burdened the Earth Mother. The prophecy warns the time is near. We must act responsibly. We can protect the future by responding now. A prophecy can be changed, and prophecies can be shifted, but we must act. We must pay attention to what is really important in life. There are many Rainbow Warriors waiting to make manifest the Fifth World of Peace.

Each warrior knows where the kingdom lies. Each knows of the power and glory of the Creator manifested in all of creations. Each knows the importance of finding first the Divine Spark within, for it is only when we truly identify the glow within that is it visible without. Each Rainbow Warrior, regardless of color or creed knows:

> If there is light in the soul, there will be beauty in the person.
> If there is beauty in the person, there will be harmony in the house.
> If there is harmony in the house, there will be order in the nation.
> If there is order in the nation, there will be peace in the world.
> Chinese Proverb

Each Rainbow Warrior knows the journey to find the light within is the most sacred of journeys. And so I leave you residing in the power and the glory that permeate the universal soul.
The End.

Chapter References

Chapter 1: In Search of Spirit (8-15).

1. Sams, J. (1990). *Sacred Path Cards*. New York: Harper Collins.
2. Levine, C. (1996). Take time to care for the soul. Religion Section, *Edmonton Journal*, Jan.13. Edmonton, AB. Canada.
3. Frost, R. The secret sits. In, S. J. Kennedy (ed.), (1986). *Introduction to Poetry* (6th. ed.). New York: Little, Brown & Co.
4. Canfield, J. In, J. Canfield & M. Hansen, M. (eds.), (1993). The golden Buddha. *Chicken Soup for the Soul*. Deerfield Beach, Florida: Health Communications Inc.
5. Ibid. Canfield.
6. *The Bible*, Job 19:7-10.
7. Hopkins, G. M. That nature is a heraclitean fire, and of the comfort of resurrection. In, Society of Jesus (1967). *Selected Poems* by Gerald Manley Hopkins. London: Oxford University Press.
8. *The Bible*, Jonah 2:11.
9. Frank, A. (1992). *At the Will of the Body*. Boston: Houghton Mifflin.
10. Shapiro, Rabbi R.M. (1993). *Wisdom of the Jewish Sages: A Modern Reading of Pirke Avot*. New York: Bell Tower.
11. Lao Tsu, Tao Te Ching, Translation, Gia-Fu Feng & J. English (1997). New York: Random House. (Based on Chapter 33).
12. *The Bible*, Genesis 28: 10-14.
13. Uhlein, G. (1983). *Meditation With Hildegard of Bingen*. Santa Fe: Bear & Co.

Chapter 2: The Power That Gives and Maintains Life (16-25).

1. Schwartz, W. The robin's song. *Comfort Ye My People*. Self Published. Shellbrook, Sask., Canada.
2. Carmack, B. J. (1991). The role of companion animals for persons with AIDS/HIV. *Wholistic Nursing Practice*, 5(2), 24-31.
3. Simington, J. (1995). The power of expressive touch. *Humane Medicine*, 11(4), 162-165.

4. Perkins, S. (As told to Bill Holten). Saddle therapy. In, J. Canfield, M. Hansen, M. Becker, & C. Kline.(Eds.), (1998). *Chicken Soup for the Pet Lover's Soul*. Deerfield Beach, Florida: Health Communications Inc.
5. Gurney, D. The Lord God planted a garden. In, H. Fellman (ed.), (1936). *Best Loved Poems of the American People*. New York: Double Day & Co.
6. Bourgault, L. (1997). *Secrets of Crystal Healing*. New York: Foulsham.
7. Miles, C. A. In the garden. In, M. Leiper and H.W. Simon (1953). *Great Song Thesaurus*. New York: Simon & Schuster.

Chapter 3: Soul Growth (26-37).

1. Einstein, A. *The World As I See It*. Translation, A. Harris (1956, 1984): New York: Carol Publishing Group.
2. Shakespeare, W. *Hamlet*, III, i, 41.
3. *The Bible*, Matthew 9: 5.
4. *The Bible*, Luke 8: 43-47.
5. MacNutt, F. (1974). *Healing*. Notre Dame, Indiana: Ave Maria Press.
6. *The Bible*, Mark 16:17-18.
7. *The Bible*, 11 Corinthians 12:11b-12.
8. Fanslow, C. (1983). Therapeutic touch a healing modality throughout life. *Topics in Clinical Nursing*, 5(2), 72-79.
9. Dyer, W. (1992). *Real Magic*. New York: Harper Collins.
10. Landry, C. (1985). Companions on the Journey (song). Phoenix, Az.: North American Liturgical Resources.
11. *The Proverbs* 17:13, 22.
12. O'Conner, E. (1972). *Search for Silence*. Waco, Texas: Word Books.
13. Chopra, D. (1993). *Ageless Body Timeless Mind*. New York: Harmony Books.
14. De Chardin, P. T. (1984) *On Love and Happiness*. San Francisco: Harper & Row.

Chapter 4: Soul Armor (38-46).

1. Daniel, A., Wyllie, T., Ramer, A. (1992). *Ask Your Angels*. New York: Ballantine Books.
2. Johnson, P. G. (1997). *God and World Religions: Basic Beliefs and Themes*. Shippensburg, PA.: Ragged Edge Press.
3. *The Bible*, Genesis 19:12; 22:11; 28:12-16; 32:25-30.
4. Hinnells, J. R. (1984). *The Facts on File: Dictionary of Religions*. New York: Facts On File Inc.

5. *The Bible*, Luke 1,2; Matthew 1:20, 24.
6. Jung, C. G. *Psychology and Religion: West and East*. Translation, R.F.C. Hull. (1959). Princeton: Princeton University Press.
7. Jung, C. G. *Psyche and Symbol*. De Laszlo, V. S.(ed.), (1991). Translation, R.F. C. Hull. Princeton: Princeton University Press.
8. Kelsey, M. (1992). *Dreamquest: Native American Myth and the Recovery of Soul*. Rockport, Mass.: Element.
9. Ibid Kelsey.

Chapter 5: Soul Energy (47-53).
1. *The Bible*, Matthew 25:14-30.

Chapter 6: A Road Map of Soul's Growth (54-62).
1. *The Bible*, Isaiah 35:1-10.
2. Kilpatrick, D. G. & Resnick, H. S. (1993). Posttraumatic stress disorder associated with exposure to criminal victimization in clinical and community populations. In, J. R. Davidson (ed.), *Posttraumatic Stress Disorder: DSM-1V and Beyond*. Washington, DC.: American Psychiatric Press.
3 Allen, J. G. (1995). *Coping With Trauma*. Washington, DC.: American Psychiatric Press.
4. Center for Prevention of Sexual and Domestic Violence (1995). Seattle.
5. Sakheim, D. (1992). *Out of the Darkness: Exploring Ritual Abuse*. New York: Macmillan.
6. Rose, D. S. (1993). Sexual assault, domestic violence and incest. In, D. E. Stewart (ed.), *Psychological Aspects of Women's Health Care*. Washington, DC.: American Psychiatric Press
7. Terr, L. (1991). Childhood traumas: An outline and overview, *American Journal of Psychiatry*, 148, 10-20.
8. Herman, J. (1997). *Trauma and Recovery*. New York: Basic Books.
9. Gelinas, D. J. (1993). Relational patterns in incestuous families, malevolent variations, and specific interventions with the adult survivor. In, P.l. Pattison (ed.), *Treatment of Adult Survivors of Incest*. Washington, DC. American Psychiatric Press.
10. Campbell, C. (1989). *Meditations With John of the Cross*. Sante Fe: Bear & Co.
11. Campbell, C. (1985). *Meditations With Teresa of Avila*. Sante Fe: Bear & Co.
12. *The Bible*, Isaiah 40.

13. Roethke, T. In a dark time. In, A. Poulin (1980). *Contemporary American Poetry*. (3rd. ed). New York: Houghton Mifflin.

14. Cugno, A. (1982). *St. John of the Cross: the Life and Thought of A Christian Mystic*. London: Burns & Oats.

15. Boryshenko, J. (1993). *Fire in the Soul*. New York: Warner.

Chapter 7: Soul Loss (63-71).

1. Borysenko, J. (1993). *Fire in the Soul*. New York: Warner.

2. Wilkinson, T. (1996). *Persephone Returns: Victims, Heroes and the Journey from the Underworld*. Berkley, CA.: Pagemill Press.

3. Cowan, T. (1998). *Fire in the Head: Shamanism and the Celtic Spirit*. San Francisco: Harper.

4. Driver, T. (1991). *The Magic of Ritual: Our Need for Liberating Rites That Transform Our Lives and Communities*. San Francisco: Harper.

5. Ibid Cowan.

6. Hanh, Thich Nhat (1995). *Living Buddha, Living Christ*. New York: Riverhead Books.

7. *The Bible*, Psalm: 19:1-7.

8. Kharitidi, O. (1996). *Entering the Circle: Ancient Secrets of Siberian Wisdom Discovered by a Russian Psychiatrist*. San Francisco: Harper.

9. Harner, M. (1980). *The Way of the Shaman*. New York: Harper Collins.

10. Ingerman, S. (1994). *Welcome Home*. New York: Harper Collins.

11. Ibid. Kharitidi.

Chapter 8: Awakening (72-77).

1. Martin, K. & Elder, S. (1993). Pathways through grief: A model of the process. In, J. Morgan (Ed.). *Personal Care In An Impersonal World*. Amityville, NY.: Baywood.

2. Stoll, R. The essence of spirituality. In, V. B. Carson (ed.), (1989). *Spiritual Dimensions of Nursing Practice*. Philadelphia: W.B. Saunders.

3. Hungelmann, J., Kenkel-Rossi, E., Klassen, L., Stollenwerk, R. (1985). Spiritual well-being in older adults: harmonious interconnectedness. *Journal of Religion and Health*, 24 (2), 147-153.

4. Frost, R. (1920). The Road Not Taken. *Poems by Robert Frost*, Mountain Interval (website).

Chapter 9: The Many Faces of God (78-85).

1. *The Bible*, Jonah 3-4.
2. *The Bible*, John 11: 1-44.
3. *The Bible*, Luke 24:1-12.
4. Pagels, E. Introduction. In, Thich Nhat Hanh (1995). *Living Buddha, Living Christ*. New York: Riverhead Books.
5. The Bible, Luke 11:1-5.
6. Mitchell, W. O. (1947). *Who Has Seen the Wind?* Toronto: Macmillan Paperback reprinted 1998.
7. Winters, Sister M. T. (1965). Spirit of God. In, *Joy is like the Rain*. (Audio cassette). Philadelphia: Medical Mission Sisters.
8. Sarett, L. God is at the anvil. In, C. Miles Hill (ed.), (1954). *World's Greatest Religious Poetry*. New York: Macmillan.
9. Sams, J. (1990). *Sacred Path Cards*. New York: Harper Collins.
10. James, W. (1958). *Varieties of Religious Experiences*. New York: New American Library.
11. Arkhoff, A. (1995). *The Illuminated Life*. Toronto: Allyn & Bacon.
12. Cousins, N. (1989). *Head First: The Biology of Hope*. New York: Dutton.
13. Schwartz, W. The daisies tell. *Comfort Ye My People*. Self Published. Shellbrook, Sask., Canada.

Chapter 10: The Forms of God (86-97).

1. Waldherr, K. (1996). *The Book of Goddesses*. Hillsboro, OR.: Beyond Words Publishing.
2. *The Bible*, Matthew 3:17.
3. *The Bible*, Mark 9:1-8.
4. *The Bible*, John 14:12.
5. *The Bible*, Luke 3:22.
6. *The Bible*, John 8:31-38.
7. *The Bible*, Hosea 2.
8. Dyer, W. (1992). *Real Magic*. New York: Harper Collins.
9. Jung, C. G. *The Essential Jung*. Selected and Introduced by A. Storr (1983). Princeton: Princeton University Press.
10. Chetwynd, T. (1993). *Dictionary of Symbols*. Hammersmith, London: Aquarian Press.
11. Boushahla, J. & Reidel-Geubtner, V. (1983). *The Dream Dictionary*. New York: Berkley Books.
12. Jung, C. G. Seminar on Dream Analysis Given in 1928-1930. W. McGuire (ed.), (1984). *Bollingen Series XCIV*. Princeton: Princeton University Press.

13. Martin, B. (1966). *If God Does Not Die*. Richmond: John Knox Press.
14. *The Bible*, Matthew 7:7, Luke 11:9.
15. *The Bible*, Isaiah 40:4.
16. *The Bible*, John 8:1-11; John 4:4-42.
17. Lalani, N. In Sharon Adams (1996).The female face of God. Religion Section, *Edmonton Journal*, May 18. Edmonton, Canada.
18. Reilly, P. L. (1996). *A God Who Looks Like Me: Discovering a Woman-Affirming Spirituality*. New York: Ballantine.

Chapter 11: Heaven (98-109).

1. *The Bible*, John 12:24.
2. Hanh, Thich Nhat (1985). *A Guide to Walking Meditation*. New York: Fellowship Publications.
3. *The Bible*, Ecclesiastes 3:15.
4. *The Bible*, Genesis 9:12-17.
5. Boisvert, Sr. Brendalee. (1986). Indwelling. In, *Destiny* (Audiotape). Antiganish, NS. Canada: Bethany.
6. Bohm, D. (1980). *Wholeness and the Implicit Order*. London: Routledge & Kegan Paul.
7. Talbot, M. (1991). *The Holographic Universe*. New York: Harper Perennial.
8. Einstein, A. *The World As I See It*, Translation, A. Harris (1956, 1984): New York: Carol Publishing Group.
9. Kubler-Ross, E. (1983). *On Children and Death*. New York: Macmillan.
10. Moody, R.A. (1988). *The Light Beyond*. New York: Bantam.
11. Morse, M. (1992). *Transformed by the Light*. New York: Villard.
12. Ring, K. (1984). *Heading for Omega: In Search of the Meaning of the Near-Death Experience*. New York: Morrow.
13. Ring, K. (1980). *Life at Death- A Scientific Investigation of the Near-Death Experience*. New York: Morrow.
14. Schipperges, H.; Translation, J. A. Broadwin, (1997). *Hildegard of Bingen: Healing and the Nature of the Cosmos*. Princeton, NJ.: M. Wiener.
15. Jung, C, G. (1953- 1973). The archetypes and the collective unconscious (Vol 9. Part 1). Translation, H. Read, M. Fordan & G. Adler. *The Collected Works of C.G. Jung*. Princeton: Princeton University Press.
16. Jung, C. G. (1963). *Mysterium Coniunctionis* (Vol. 14). Translation, R.F.C. Hull. Princeton: Princeton University Press.

Chapter 12: Hallowed Be Thy Name (110-121).

1. Franz, I. Holy God We Praise Thy Name. (Song). Translation, A. Walworth (1820). Princeton: Summy Birchard Music.
2. *The Bible*, Psalm 27:1, 4, 7-8.
3. Schierse Leonard, L. (1995). *Creation's Heartbeat: Following the Reindeer Spirit*. New York: Bantam.
4. Ibid. Schierse.
5. Irenaeus, Saint, Bishop of Lyon. *The Scandal of the Incarnation: Irenaeus Against the Heresies*. (1990). Selected by H. U. von Balthasar; translation, J. Saward. San Francisco: Ignatius Press.
6. Hanh, Thich Nhat, (1995). *Living Buddha, Living Christ*. New York: Riverhead.
7. Sams, J. (1990). *Sacred Path Cards*. New York: Harper Collins.
8. Blake, W. (1780). The marriage of heaven and hell. *The Norton Anthology of English Literature* (3rd. ed.) Vol.II. M.H. Abrams (ed.). New York: W.W.Norton & Co.
9. Borysenko, J. (1993). *Fire in the Soul*. New York: Warner.
10. Nelson, A. (1994). *The Learning Wheel*. Tuscon, AZ: Zephyr Press.
11. Walker, B.J. (1990). *Women's Book of Symbols and Sacred Objects*. San Francisco: Harper.
12. Constable, G. (1986). *Mexico*. Chicago: Time-Life Books.
13. Ibid Nelson.
14. Sopa, L., Jackson, R. & Newman, J. (1985). *The Wheel of Time: The Kalachakra in Context*. Ithaca, N.Y.: Snow Lion Publications.
15. His Holiness Tenzin Gyatso (the fourteenth Dalai Lama), Tsong-ka-pa, & Hopkins, J. (1977). *Tantra in Tibet*. Ithaca, N.Y.: Snow Lion Publications.
16. Drewal, H. J. Pemberton, J. (1989). *Yoruba: Nine Centuries of African Art and Thought*. NY.: Harry N. Abrams.
17. Ibid. Nelson.

Chapter 13: Thy Kingdom Come (122-131).

1. Pagels, E. (1981). *The Gnostic Gospels.* New York: Vintage Books.
2. Dart, J. (1976). *The Laughing Savior.* New York: Harper and Row.
3. Pagels, E. Introduction. In, Thich Nhat Hanh (1995). *Living Buddha, Living Christ.* New York: Riverhead Books.
4. Oxtoby, W. G. (ed.), (1996). *World Religions: Eastern Traditions.* Toronto: Oxford University Press
5. R. Smith, Under the editorship of C.T. Cayce (1989). *Edgar Cayce: You Can Remember Past Lives.* New York: Warner Books.
6. Larsen, R. (ed.),(1988). *Emanuel Swedenborg: A Continuing Vision.* New York: Swedenborg Foundation.
7. Stevenson, I. (1974). *Twenty Cases Suggestive of Reincarnation.* Charlottesville: University Press of Virginia.
8. Stevenson, I. (1987). *Children Who Remember Previous Lives.* Charlottesville: University Press of Virginia.
9. Stevenson, I. (1975-1983). *Cases of the Reincarnation Type* (Vols.1-4). Charlottesville: University Press of Virginia.
10. Stevenson, I. (1993). Birthmarks and birth defects corresponding to wounds on deceased persons. *Journal of Scientific Exploration,* 7(4), 403-410.
11. Weiss, B. (1988). *Many Lives, Many Masters.* New York: Fireside Books.
12. Weiss, B. (1992). *Through Time Into Healing.* New York: Simon & Schuster.
13. Woolger, R. J. (1988). *Other Lives, Other Selves: A Jungian Psychologist Discovers Past Lives.* New York: Bantam Books.
14. Wambach, H. (1979). *Reliving Past Lives: The Evidence Under Hypnosis.* New York: Bantam Books.
15. Fiore, E. (1978). *You Have Been Here Before.* New York: Ballantine Books.
16. Ibid. Wambach.
17. Cannon, A.(1953). *The Power Within.* New York: Dutton.
18. Ibid Fiore.
19. Bowman, C. (1997). *Children's Past Lives: How Past Life Memories Affect Your Child.* New York: Bantam Books.
20. Whitton, J. & Fisher, J. (1986). *Life Between Life.* New York: Warner Books.
21. *Tibetan Book of the Dead,* Translation W.Y. Evans-Wentz.(1960). London: Oxford University Press.
22. Marsh, R. (1994). *We Are Not Alone.* Minneapolis: Eckankar.
23. Ibid. Tibetan Book.

24. Van Praagh, J. (2000), *Reaching to Heaven*. New York: Signet.
25. Ibid. Whitton.
26. Great Master Yung Chia of the Tang Dynasty. Translation, Dharma Realm. *Song of Enlightenment* (1983). Talmage, CA: Buddhist University International Institute for the Translation of Buddhist Texts.
27. *The Bible*, Matthew 5:3.
28. Ibid. Oxtoby.
29. Bopp, J., Bopp, M., Brown, L., Lane, P. (1984). *The Sacred Tree*. Lethbridge, AB. Canada: Four Winds Development Press.

Chapter 14: Thy Will Be Done (132-145)

1. Chopra, D. (1993). *Ageless Body, Timeless Mind*. New York: Harmony House.
2. Bowman, C. (1997). *Children's Past Lives: How Past Life Memories Affect Your Child*. New York: Bantam Books
3. Ibid. Bowman.
4. Whitton, J., & Fisher, J. (1986). *Life Between Life*. New York: Warner Books.
5. Netherton, M. & Schifferin, N. (1978). *Past Lives Therapy*. New York: William Marrow.
6. Cornwell, B. (1995). *Sharp's Regiment*. Hammersmith, London: Harper Collins.
7. Ibid. Whitton.
8. Trine, R. W. (1897, revised 1925). *In Tune With The Infinite*. Toronto: Musson Book Co.
9. Hanh, Thich Nhat, (1995). *Living Buddha, Living Christ*. New York: Riverhead.
10. Ibid. Bowman.
11. Rogers, M. (1980). Nursing: A science of Unitary Man. In, I. W. Clements & F. B. Roberts (eds.), *Conceptual Models of Nursing Practice* (2nd ed.). New York: Appleton-Century-Crofts.
12. Keyes, K. (1985). *The Hundredth Monkey*. Coos Bay, OR: Vision Books.
13. Dyer, W. (1989). *You'll See It When You Believe It*. New York: Avon Books.

Chapter 15: On Earth As In Heaven (146-158).

1. *The Bible*, Matthew 16:19; 18:18.
2. *The Bible*, John 8:32.
3. Gallup, G. & Proctor, W. (1982). *Adventures In Immortality*. New York: McGraw Hill.
4. Christie-Murray, D. (1981). *Reincarnation: Ancient Beliefs and Modern Evidence*. Devon: Newton Abbot.
5. Cranston, S. (1998). *Reincarnation: The Phoenix Fire Mystery*. Pasadena: Theosophical University Press.
6. *The Bible*, Exodus 21:23-25.
7. *The Bible*, Matthew 26:52.
8. *The Bible*, Genesis 9:6.
9. Marsh, R. (1994). *We Are Not Alone*. Minneapolis: Eckankar.
10. *The Bible*, Galatians 6:5.
11. *The Bible*, Matthew 11:30
12. Prophet, Elizabeth Clare (1991). *Karma, Reincarnation and Christianity*. (Audiotape of Lecture). New Orleans Airport Hilton, Louisiana. Royal Teton Ranch, Park County, Montana. Box A, Livingston, MT.
13. *The Bible*, Matthew 12:36-37.
14. Schmidt, C. (ed), (1978). *Pistis Sophia*. Translation, V. Macdermat. London, E.J. Brill.
15. Ibid. Cranston.
16. *The Bible*, Exodus 21;24, Leviticus 24:20, Deuteronomy 19;21.
17. *The Bible*, Obadiah 15.
18. Ibid. Prophet.
19. *The Bible*, Genesis 22.
20. *The Bible*, 1 Kings 3:9.
21. *The Bible*, Matthew 5:17-18.
22. Hanh, Thich Nhat, (1995). *Living Buddha, Living Christ*. New York: Riverhead.
23. Ibid. Prophet.
24. *The Bible*, Matthew 7:2, Mark 4:24, Luke 6:38.
25. *The Bible*, John 8:32.
26. *The Bible*, Matthew 11:29.
27. *The Bible*, Matthew 19:19, 22:37-39, Mark 12:28-31.
28. *The Bible*, Deuteronomy, 6:5, 11:1, 13, 22,19:9, 30:6.
29. *The Bible*, John 10:10.
30. *The Bible*, John 9:1.
31. Ibid. Whitton.
32. Ibid. Marsh.

Chapter 16: Our Daily Bread (159-170).

1. *The Bible*, Numbers 7:1-9.
2. Sams, J. (1990). *Sacred Path Cards*. New York: Harper Collins.
3. Dyer, W. (1992). *Real Magic*. New York: Harper Collins.
4. Einstein, A. *The World As I See It*, Translation, A. Harris (1956, 1984): New York: Carol Publishing Group.
5. Arkhoff, A. (1995). *The Illuminated Life*. Toronto: Allyn & Bacon.
6. Joncas, M. (1979). *On Eagle's Wings*. Phoenix AZ: North American Liturgical Resources.
7. Shapiro, Rabbi R.M. (1993). *Wisdom of the Jewish Sages: A Modern Reading of Pirke Avot*. New York: Bell Tower.
8. Siegel, B. (1986). *Love, Medicine and Miracles*. New York: Harper & Row.
9. Hay, L. (1984). *You Can Heal Your Life*. Carson, CA: Hay House.
10. Ibid. Hay.
11. *The Bible*, Matthew 4:4.

Chapter 17: Forgiveness (171-181).

1. Weiss, B. L. (1996). *Only Love is Real:* New York: Warner Books.
2. Ibid. Weiss.
3. Borysenko, J. (1990). *Guilt is the Teacher, Love is the Lesson*. New York: Warner Books.
4. Whitton, J., & Fisher, J. (1986). *Life Between Life*. New York: Warner Books.
5. Shakespeare, W. *Hamlet*, II, ii, 253.
6. Arkhoff, A. (1995). *The Illuminated Life*. Toronto: Allyn & Bacon.
7. Hanh, Thich Nhat, (1976). *The Miracle of Mindfulness! A Manual of Meditation*. Boston: Beacon Press.
8. Bopp, J., Bopp, M., Brown, L., Lane, P. (1984). *The Sacred Tree*. Lethbridge, AB. Canada: Four Winds Development Press.
9. Sams, J. (1990). *Sacred Path Cards*. New York: Harper Collins.

Chapter 18: Temptation, Sin and Evil (182-190).

1. McKenzie, J. (1965). *The Dictionary of The Bible*. Milwaukee, WI: Bruce.
2. Gibran, K. (1996). *The Prophet*. New York: Knopf.
3. Hanh, Thich Nhat, (1995). *Living Buddha, Living Christ*. New York: Riverhead.
4. Weiss, B. L. (1996). *Only Love is Real*: New York: Warner Books.
5. Ibid. Hanh.
6. Bowman, C. (1997). *Children's Past Lives: How Past Life Memories Affect Your Child*. New York: Bantam Books.
7. Stevenson, I. (1993). Birthmarks and birth defects corresponding to wounds on deceased persons. *Journal of Scientific Exploration*, 7(4), 403-410.
8. Summer Rain, M. (1993). *Spirit Song*. Hampton Road.
9. Homer, *Iliad of Odeysses*. Translation, S. Lombardo (1997). Indianapolis: Hackett.
10. Ibid. Summer Rain.
11. Prophet, E. C. (1989). *Violet Flame to Heal Body, Mind and Soul*. Summit University Press: Corwin Springs, MT.
12. *The Bible*, 2 Maccabees 12: 44-55.
13. Wolfe, A. (1993). *In the Shadow of the Shaman*. Llewellyn Books: St. Paul, Minn.
14. Andrews, L. (1990). *Teachings Around the Sacred Wheel*. Harper: San Francisco, Calif.
15. Stein, D. (1997). *Essential Reiki: A Complete Guide to an Ancient Healing Art*. Freedom, CA: The Crossing Press.

Chapter 19: The Kingdom, Power and Glory (191-193).

1. Emerson, R. W. Self Reliance. In C. Bode (ed.), (1981). *The Portable Emerson*. New York: Viking.
2. Weiss, B. L. (1996). *Only Love is Real*. New York: Warner Books.

Send *JOURNEY TO THE SACRED* to a friend

Journey to the Sacred: Mending a Fractured Soul is $21.95 per book plus $4.00 (total order) for shipping and handling.

___ Number of copies _____ x $21.95 = $ _____

Shipping and handling _____ = $ __4.00__

Subtotal _____ = $ _____

In Canada add 7% GST OR 15% HST where applicable _____ = $ _____

Total enclosed _____ = $ _____

    U.S. and international orders, payable in U.S. funds/Price is subject to change.

NAME: _____

STREET: _____

CITY: _____ PROV./STATE: _____

COUNTRY: _____l_____ POSTAL CODE/ZIP: _____

TELEPHONE: _____ FAX: _____

Please make cheque or money order payable to: **TAKING FLIGHT BOOKS**
17823 – 93 Street
    FAX: 780-472-0885   **Edmonton, Alberta**
    www.takingflightbooks.com   **Canada   T5Z 2H8**

For fund raising or volume purchases, contact **Taking Flight Books** for volume rates.
Please allow 2-3 weeks for delivery.

Send *JOURNEY TO THE SACRED* to a friend

Journey to the Sacred: Mending a Fractured Soul is $21.95 per book plus $4.00 (total order) for shipping and handling.

___ Number of copies _____ x $21.95 = $ _____

Shipping and handling _____ = $ __4.00__

Subtotal _____ = $ _____

In Canada add 7% GST OR 15% HST where applicable _____ = $ _____

Total enclosed _____ = $ _____

    U.S. and international orders, payable in U.S. funds/Price is subject to change.

NAME: _____

STREET: _____

CITY: _____ PROV./STATE: _____

COUNTRY: _____ POSTAL CODE/ZIP: _____

TELEPHONE: _____ FAX: _____

Please make cheque or money order payable to: **TAKING FLIGHT BOOKS**
17823 – 93 Street
    FAX: 780-472-0885   **Edmonton, Alberta**
    www.takingflightbooks.com   **Canada   T5Z 2H8**

For fund raising or volume purchases, contact **Taking Flight Books** for volume rates.
Please allow 2-3 weeks for delivery.